Cawthorne 1790-1990

"I never realised that there was history, close at hand, beside my very own home. I did not realise that the old grave that stood among the brambles at the foot of our farm was history."
Stephen Leacock

Cawthorne
1790-1990

A SOUTH YORKSHIRE VILLAGE REMEMBERS ITS PAST

BARRY JACKSON

This book is dedicated to my wife, whose desire to return to the village of her ancestors brought me to Cawthorne, to my daughter who was brought up and educated there, and to my doctors who made the completion of its writing possible.

Copyright ©Barry Jackson 1991
All rights reserved.

ISBN 0 9518786 0 3 (Hardback)
ISBN 0 9518786 1 1 (Paperback)

Published by
Cawthorne Victoria Jubilee Museum
Taylor Hill, Cawthorne, South Yorkshire

Design and Production: Ron Swift

Set in Baskerville by
Armitage Typo/Graphics, Huddersfield, West Yorkshire

Printed and bound by
Amadeus Press, Huddersfield, West Yorkshire

Contents

- vi   Acknowledgements
- ix   Preface
- 1   **The Cawthorne of John C. Nattes and Abel Hold**   1807-1866
- 32   **The Cawthorne of Rev. Charles T. Pratt**   1866-1915
- 157   **Cawthorne in Two World Wars**   1914-18 and 1939-45
- 190   Sketch Map pre 1930
- 191   **The Years of Change** 1945-1990
- 220   Ordnance Survey Map 1850
- 222   Index

Acknowledgements

I am deeply indebted to Martin Charlesworth for permission to use his father's Yorkshire dialect poems and his diary, and to the Trustees of the Cawthorne Victoria Jubilee Museum for use of all manner of pictorial and documentary material including old volumes of the Parish Magazine.

Mr. Maurice Hepworth of the Barnsley Library Local Studies Section has been unstinting in his efforts to supply census material, extracts from old issues of the "Barnsley Chronicle" and "The Record", plus scrapbook jottings made by such past Barnsley antiquarians as Burland and Wilkinson.

The present owner of the Cannon Hall Estate, Mr. Simon Fraser has very kindly given permission for me to use material from the Spencer Stanhope papers, which are currently housed at Sheffield Library and the Cartwright Museum at Bradford, while his agent Mr. John A. G. Lees has patiently answered my questions concerning the Estate records.

Concerning the village school, I am grateful to the Headmaster, Mr. J. Sawyer for material from the school log-books, and to Mrs. Anne Earnshaw (nee Fish) for use of her unpublished B.Ed. thesis on Cawthorne School from 1870.

I am grateful to the Vicar and Churchwardens for the material such as the Churchwardens' accounts, vestry books etc. which were once housed in the Parish Chest but are now deposited at the Wakefield Diocesan Records Office, Newstead Road, Wakefield and to the family of the late Noel Moxon for use of his note-books.

All necessary steps have been taken to secure permission from copyright holders when quoting from published works. This has not been easy since some of the original publishers have now gone out of business or been absorbed into other firms. I am grateful, however, to those whom I have managed to track down who have readily given permission.

Illustrations

The John Nattes drawings belong to Cannon Hall Museum and the Cawthorne Victoria Jubilee Museum, and I am grateful to Mr. Brian Murray, the Curator of the former, and to the Chairman and trustees of the latter for permission to use them. (Initials C. H. and C. V. J. identify them).

The portraits of John Spencer and Walter Spencer Stanhope are reproduced by kind permission of their owner, Mr. Simon Fraser.

I have made every effort to name the original photographers, but this has not been possible in every case. When Noel Moxon salvaged Rowland Wilkinson's glass-plate negatives from his garage many were too contaminated with oil etc. to save. I have endeavoured to reproduce as many of them as possible from the many negatives which Esther Moxon, Noel's widow, passed on to me. For the rest, I have re-photographed originals loaned to me by too many villagers to name individually, but all of whom I thank sincerely. Chief among them I must name Rowland Wilkinson's daughter, Connie, now Mrs. Jim Moxon, whose information about people and places on the photographs has been invaluable. It added tremendously to the thrill of producing these prints to hear from someone, who, as a girl, had spent many times in the darkness of Chantry House cellar helping her father develop the original plates and printing from them.

The photographers are identified by initials as follows:-

R. W. – *Rowland Wilkinson*
H – *Houghton*
B. C. – *"Barnsley Chronicle" (by courtesy of the Editor, Don Booker)**
B. H. – *Bamforth of Holmfirth*
W. G. – *Warner Gothard*
N. F. M. – *Noel Moxon*
D. B. – *David Broadhead*
G. B. J. – *the author*
J. E. G. – *Jane Greaves*
W. P. – *Wilfred Parkinson*
M. C. G. – *Mark Greaves*
S. S. – *Samuel Swift*
J. J. – *Joan Jackson*
D. – *Denton of Barnsley*

*He also gave permission to reproduce written extracts.

I am very grateful to the Barnsley Canal Group for providing me with one of the photographs of the Barnby Basin Warehouse and Jolly Sailor.

Mr Michael E. Ware, Curator of the National Motor Museum at Beaulieu kindly identified motor cars for me from Rowland Wilkinson's photographs, while Mr. Terence Pepper of the National Portrait Gallery helped me with the portrait photograph of Roddam Stanhope.

My thanks go to Mr David Broadhead, who has made available to me aerial photographs which he took of the village and Wilfred Parkinson for those which he took down the Tivydale Pit.

I must thank Stan Bulmer (Senior) for photographic advice and Norman Bailey for photographic assistance.

My former schoolmate, G. Richard Northern kindly read the proofs, but any mistakes remain my responsibility.

Oral History

Villagers who have contributed their memories by tape recorded or written reminiscences and which are quoted directly in the text are numbered below. Their contributions may be located by their number:-

7 Noel Moxon (1903-79) Electrician, organist, bell-ringer, parish councillor, photographer, churchwarden, cricketer, Museum Secretary and village historian: Noel was, at one time or another, all of these. His was typical of the spirit of service to the community which village life seems to foster. The Moxons along with the Fish family and the Shirt family are probably the three oldest families in Cawthorne. Richard Moxon was the Parish Clerk of the 1790s mentioned in "The Cawthorne Musicians".

8 Miss Mildred Holroyd (1903-87) was born and died in Cawthorne, but spent a good deal of her working life away in Health Administration. The written accounts which she did for me (preferring writing to taping because of a slight speech impediment) show a keen observation of and warm affection for village life before 1920. She was Museum Treasurer and sang in the Church choir and the Choral Society.

9 Mrs. May Caswell (1892-1989) born Mary Louisa Lisle, was the granddaughter of John Blacker and worked as a pupil-teacher under Mr. Arthur Senior at the village school. Although a lifelong Methodist, she regarded All Saints' as her village church and said she was happiest when she could see its tower.

10 Miss Alice Moxon (1898-1979), born and educated in Cawthorne, lived her whole life there, serving as a Parish Councillor and an official of the Methodist Church. A school teacher, she was for many years Headmistress of the Darton Secondary Girls' School.

11 George Swift (1903-90) was the last of a long line of George Swifts of Cawthorne who have combined the roles of builders and churchwardens going back to the 18th Century. He was still an active Church Council member and the Church Electoral Roll officer at the time of his death. He was a former Parish Councillor.

12 Mrs. Margaret Wood (1900-91) was the widow of Kenneth H. Wood, former conductor of the village band. She was the daughter and grand daughter of Cawthorne farmers and the elder sister of Mildred Holroyd.

13 Laurie Morley (1902-78). Miner, church choir member and curator of the village museum.

14 Robert Bagshaw is the son of Sam Bagshaw. He worked in local mines, often in wet conditions, which has left him crippled with arthritis.

15 James A. (Jim) Moxon (b.1899) is the elder brother of Noel Moxon. He began his working life in the family butchering business, but later moved into Local Government. He has a formidable record of service to the village as Clerk to the Parish Council and as Treasurer to the Church. Although retired from these posts, he still works every month for the Church, defying his arthritis by stapling together over 350 Parish Magazines at the age of 92! He is probably Cawthorne's last surviving World War One Veteran.

16 Douglas Stables is the present Secretary of the Cawthorne Museum Society and Captain of the Church bell-ringers. He is a mine of information on "Old Cawthorne" and does many slide lectures on the subject to organisations in South Yorkshire.

17 Mrs. Isabel Rusby, who once worked at Cannon Hall, recalled Mrs. Stanhope's generosity to the family of her late husband, Herman (who was a long-serving church choir member and bell-ringer).

18 Wilfred Clarkson (1897-1980) gave me one of the most delightful of my taped interviews, delivered in a voice which twinkled with humour. By contrast with the rumbustious tales which he told of his childhood at Cawthorne Basin and his school days, he was a most gentlemanly and cultured man. He and his friends ran a gramophone circle in their own homes and he was responsible for fostering the author's love of opera and lieder. He fought in France during the First World War.

19 A friend and former teaching colleague, Michael Fitton, kindly supplied details of his ancestors, the Puddephatts.

Rev. Charles Tiplady Pratt.

22 Philip O. Walker is the retired senior partner of Bury and Walker, an old established firm of solicitors in Barnsley. He was one of the officers (and subsequently Commanding Officer) of the Cawthorne Home Guard, whose exploits he still, at the age of 88, recalls with a keen sense of humour – the loudest chuckle perhaps coming as he recalls that, at the end of the war, one prominent lady resident approached him with thanks for "keeping Cawthorne safe"!

I hope that I have not missed out anyone who merits special thanks, but I must conclude by acknowledging my debt to four groups of people. Firstly there are my typists Mesdames Una Newton and Maureen Parkin, Miss Marjorie Hopton, and my daughter Jane Greaves, plus my son-in-law, Mark Greaves and mother-in-law, Ada Kenworthy (grand-daughter of John Fretwell), who have given a variety of clerical assistance. Secondly, I must thank my wife and daughter for enduring so long what must have seemed to them a stubborn preoccupation with the past, plus all the documentary and photographic "clutter" which this has entailed. Thirdly, I must record an enormous debt of gratitude to Ron Swift, without whose help publication would not have been possible. After his father George's funeral, and in accordance with what he thought would have been George's wishes, he offered to take over responsibility for the design and lay-out of the book, and for all negotiations with printers. The weight which he thus removed from my shoulders is incalculable.

Lastly, Christine and Frank Draper of the Post Office and Trudi and Keith Hutchinson of the Village Stores have been extremely patient and helpful as collectors of subscription slips, money etc.

Bibliography

The books from which direct quotations have been given are numbered below and may be located in the text by the number allocated to each book:-

1 "Annals of a Yorkshire House" (2 volumes) by Mrs. A. M. W. Stirling (niece of Sir Walter Spencer Stanhope): published by Bodley Head 1911.

2 Elie Halevy: "History of the English People in the Nineteenth Century", Volume one: published in 1961 by Ernest Benn.

3 Rev C. T. Pratt: "History of Cawthorne": Published privately in 1882.

4 "Life's Little Day" by Mrs. A. M. W. Stirling: published 1924 by Thornton Butterworth.

5 Leslie Baily: "B.B.C. Scrapbooks Vol. 1 (1896-1914)": published 1966 by George Allen & Unwin Ltd.

6 Richard Hilary's description of the role of the fighter-pilot comes from the "B.B.C. Scrapbook for 1940".

20 R. J. White: "Waterloo to Peterloo": published by Heinemann. "R. J." was the author's Director of Studies at Cambridge; a generous, humane, humorous man, brought up in Derbyshire and possessing a deep knowledge of Northern 19th Century Social History. I would like to feel that, had he been alive, he would have approved of this foray into a subject of which he was so fond and so expert. It was heartening, having written my book, to re-read his work and find him backing up the idea of the independent-minded cobbler.

21 Charles Sorley – born Aberdeen 1895 and educated at Marlborough. He was killed at the age of 20 serving as a captain in the Suffolk Regiment at the Battle of Loos. The extract is from an untitled poem.

Other books which have been consulted and could be of use to anyone wishing to know more about the Stanhopes of Horsforth and the Spencer Stanhopes of Cannon Hall are:-

A. W. M. Stirling's "Letter-bag of Lady Elizabeth Spencer Stanhope", and "A Painter of Dreams" which deals with Roddam Stanhope, J. F. Herring and the De Morgans (William and Evelyn).

Hugh Owen's privately published book "Four Northern Families – Stanhope, Atkinson, Haddon and Shaw" (1985).

The following give information concerning the Silkstone Railway or Waggon Road:

C. H. Hewison – The Silkstone Railway.

W. N. Slatcher – The Barnsley Canal: Its First Twenty Years.

John Goodchild – a paper on the Silkstone Railway delivered to the Newcomen Society.

Preface

When I tell people that I live in Cawthorne, the reaction which I get is usually, "What a lovely place to live". However, the village to which they are referring is the Cawthorne of houses which are high-priced in terms of Barnsley-area housing, but which attract buyers from all parts of the British Isles; a 'picture-postcard' village which is the current holder of South Yorkshire's "best kept village" title. This middle-class village is a product of the last thirty years, before which Cawthorne was a very different place, and it is with this earlier village that my book is concerned.

I became interested in the history of the village shortly after moving to live there in 1968, and this interest was further stimulated as a result of joining the Cawthorne Museum Society (of which my wife's great grandfather was one of the founders) and there seeing and hearing the late Noel Moxon's slide lectures on 'Old Cawthorne'. In 1976 my practical involvement began, when I did an exhibition of written and photographic material of "Cawthorne in 1871" and, with Noel Moxon's encouragement, my collection of information has continued to grow ever since. A tremendous store of written information exists about the village, but it is in fragmented and scattered form. To find it one has to consult the Spencer Stanhope archives lodged at the Sheffield Library, the Wakefield Diocesan Archives, which contain Vestry books and old Churchwarden's accounts, the bound volumes of the Parish Magazines 1870-1915 preserved in the Village museum, the books written by Mrs. Stirling (niece of Sir Walter Spencer Stanhope) and Rev. Charles T. Pratt, along with extracts from local papers, especially the "Barnsley Chronicle". It is a synthesis of this material which I hope to present in this book, but to it I have added, for the period 1900-1988, the reminiscences of old Cawthorne residents, which was captured by my tape-recorder from 1973 onwards.

To these written images of Cawthorne life, I have added a large number of pictures. The village has been well-served by artists, chief among whom have been John Claude Nattes, drawing master to the Spencer Stanhope children during the period of the Napoleonic Wars, and Abel Hold, exhibitor at the Royal Academy, who lived and worked in Cawthorne from 1852 to his death in 1896. With the advent of photography, the attractions of the village and its people grew, and Cawthorne people should be grateful that, in the late 1930's, Noel Moxon's interests in photography and the village's past converged. As a result, he collected together a large number of glass-plate negatives photographed between 1870 and the 1920's by such well-known local photographers as Bamforth of Holmfirth and Warner Gothard; plus the fascinating records of village life taken by the village postmaster, Rowland Wilkinson; and, between 1897 and 1907, by a man whom we only know as Mr Houghton, a chemist from the Huddersfield area, whose family donated his slides and negatives to Noel Moxon. (It is indicative of Noel's priorities that the entry in his diary for V.E Day 1945 was "Went with Rev. Hugh Meanley to fetch the Houghton slides etc!") All these negatives of Cawthorne life, plus those added by Noel Moxon from the late 1930's until his death in 1979, were passed to me by his widow, and will eventually be stored in the Cawthorne Victoria Jubilee Museum; which institution will be, I hope, the financial beneficiary from this book, compiled as a long "labour of love", and offered by me to the "Old Cawthorners" as my "thank you" for welcoming me to their village. I hope that it will help "comers-in" such as myself to understand how the village in which they have chosen to live has developed its present character. It is a portrait of some two-hundred years in the life of a South Yorkshire community, which, though not as complete as I would have liked it to be, is as complete and accurate as existing evidence, memories and time will allow.

June 1990

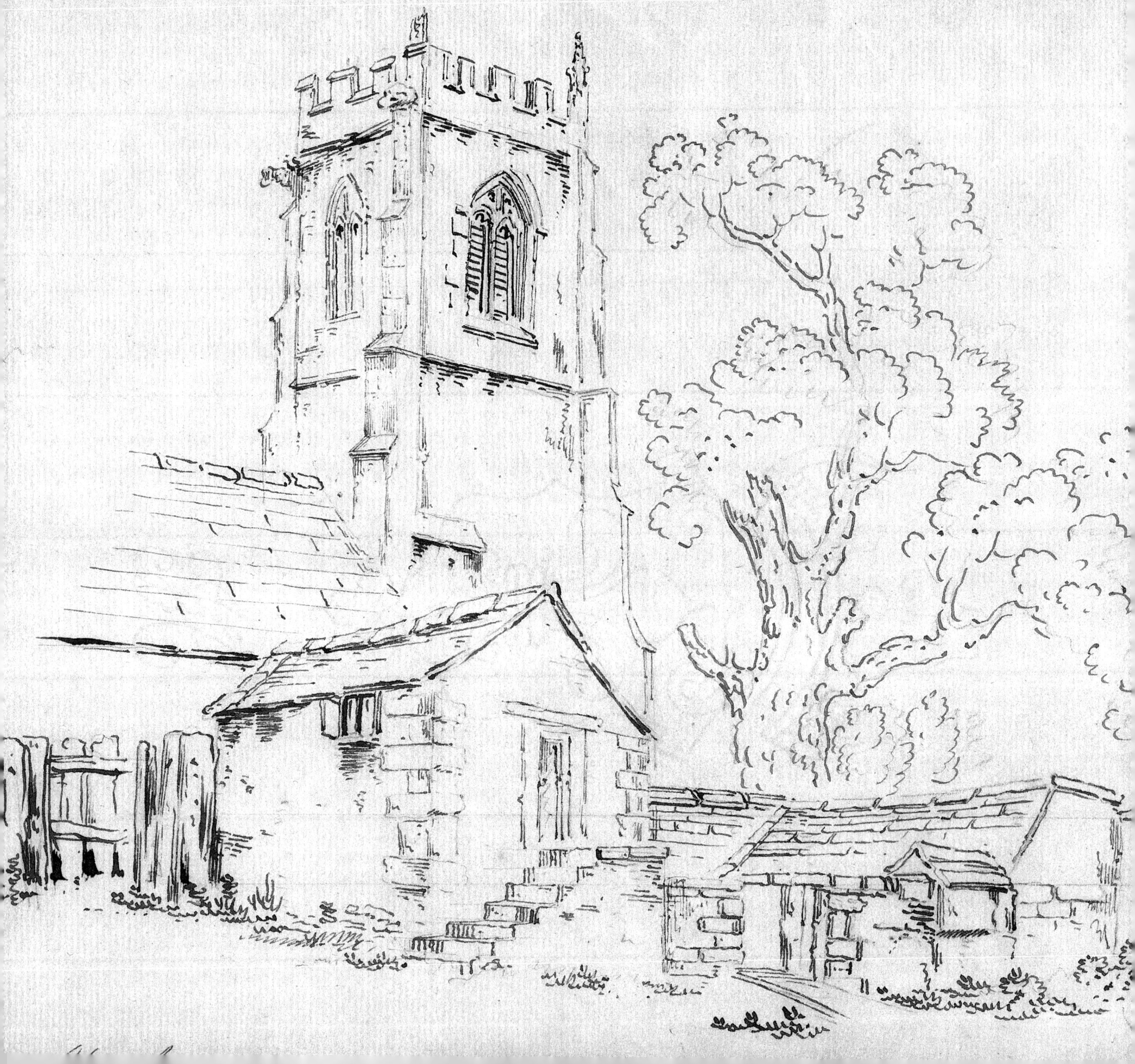

The Cawthorne of
John C. Nattes and Abel Hold

1807-1866

"the central government did nothing to secure the public safety, provided no schools, made no roads, gave no relief to the poor. With the solitary exception of the postal service, the State performed no function of immediate benefit to the tax-payer. In the eyes of the public the State appeared only as the power that enlisted men and levied taxes."
Halévy

Living their lives in remote villages, forgotten hamlets, and sleepy country towns, the people of the old England lived at a tempo which matched the slow, grave beauty of the land. They could tell the time by the sun, moon and stars, and their calendar was regulated by the great Feast Days of the Christian religion and the principal events of the farming year, plough-time, lambing-time and harvest-home. News of the great world came to them slowly and by devious channels.
R. J. White

CAWTHORNE 1790-1990

SOME of the earliest recorded images of Cawthorne are the drawings made by a somewhat volatile Irishman, John Claude Nattes in a sketch-book entitled "Views from Nature by J. C. Nattes from August 11th to the 26th 1809. Cannon Hall and Wentworth Castle, Yorkshire". They are thought to be the product of an intensive period of drawing undertaken while working as drawing master at Cannon Hall, and are now the possessions of Cannon Hall Museum and Cawthorne Victoria Jubilee Museum, the sketch-book having been broken up circa 1960 and its pages sold separately. The whole collection known to us comprises some seventy drawings of locations as far apart as Cawthorne, Penistone, Silkstone, Thurlstone, Denby, Bretton Hall and Heath Hall near Wakefield, and show such a diverse and detailed observation of architecture, industry and social history that one cannot but wonder whether, taking into account poor roads and the slowness of transport, it was physically possible to fulfil such a schedule in the space of fifteen days. Indeed the date "1807", which is to be found on some of the drawings in the Victoria Jubilee Museum coupled with a letter from Charles Spencer Stanhope, which speaks of two of the female members of the family "learning to paint for these last two years, and make (I think) but slow progress", leads one to wonder if, perhaps, Nattes' connection with Cannon Hall was longer than the two weeks specified on his sketchbook? However long it was, the drawings produced during this time give a fascinating picture of Cawthorne during the Napoleonic wars; the Cawthorne of Walter, first of the Spencer Stanhopes of Cannon Hall, who had inherited the house and much of the village from his uncle, John Spencer, in 1775.

By 1807, Cannon Hall was beginning to look (externally at least) very much as it does today, but the household had undergone the considerable change from bachelor establishment to family home. However, the changes were not merely those brought by the presence of a wife and children, but reflected the contrast between the "Old Squire" and his nephew: John Spencer, except for his bachelor status, could well have emerged from a Henry Fielding novel, as the following descriptions of his exploits show:

> The old iron industry, whereby the ancestors of John Spencer had accumulated wealth, was not yet extinct; while the coal-pits in the

John Spencer, the old Squire of Cawthorne.

vicinity afforded an increasing source of employment. But the work was intermittent, and the hours of idleness must often have hung heavy on the hands of the villagers but for the constant interest and excitement afforded by the doings of the restless Squire. He kept the lonely village gay with the merry horn of his huntsmen and the baying of his hounds, the coming of his friends from town, the clattering of his racehorses as his grooms exercised these along the winding village road, or the rattling of his coachwheels down the steep entrance into his park. On Sundays he rode to church on a fine bay mare, during the hunting season occasionally arriving in pink, booted and spurred as though for the chase; and tramped loudly up the aisle to the old family pew, casting keen glances around to note the names of any who dared to remain absent from Divine Worship. In the afternoon of the Sabbath it was an open secret that he often planned a cock-fight in his park, at which the privileged among his tenantry were permitted to attend, and at which it is hinted that the parson himself occasionally put in an appearance as if by chance. For Parson Phipps, Vicar of Cawthorne, Silkstone and Penistone, was no Puritan: He lived at Banks, a fine old house, with a spacious hall and magnificent staircase of inlaid oak, whence he gladly rode two miles to Cannon Hall for his frequent glass and rubber with the Squire of an evening.

But John Spencer, who, with the brain of a scholar and the habits of a toper, presented the anomaly afforded by the men of his generation, was likewise, as his sisters had recognised, a man of cultivated taste and sound judgment. If the letters which have survived prove that he was a bold rider, a hard drinker, and violent of temper and speech to those who opposed him, so, too, they prove that he was open-handed and warm-hearted, courtly in his manners to his equals, fatherly to his dependents, affectionate and liberal to his relatives who adored him. A scholar of no mean order, he amassed a valuable library; and in the interest afforded by his books, his friends or the superintendence of his estate, he found ample satisfaction and contentment. He cared nothing for the great world and never meddled with affairs of State, though these obviously occupied a considerable place in his thoughts, and his views thereon, if liberal, were unalterable...

Mr Edmunds went to Cannon Hall, where Squire Spencer had asked his friends of the field back to dine. Sixty bottles of port were drunk, averaging three a man, yet Sir John Kaye arose, and in a somewhat confused speech, complained that his glass had not "been filled fair." His expostulation, however, was brought to an untimely end by the fact that his legs gave way under him, and he fell flat upon the floor. Mr Spencer thereupon gravely rang the bell, and in the most courteous manner directed two servants who entered to carry off the fallen orator. One by one the guests succumbed in like manner, and one by one were they respectfully removed by the waiting attendants, to be deposited upon a couch or bed till they felt capable of returning to their respective homes. When all had been thus disposed of, the Squire, whose head seemed stronger than his neighbours', or who was perhaps mindful of his early experience at Winchester, rang the bell finally and directed the servants to extinguish the lights, when ended this festive evening, so typical of the times.

John Spencer was driving home one evening with the parson after a carousal in the neighbourhood, at which both had indulged freely in the pleasures of the table. As the old coach rumbled heavily along the lonely Yorkshire roads, to the Squire's confused brain there came the alarming sound of a horse's hoofs accompanying the vehicle. The more he listened, the more convinced he became that the hoofs were following, not preceding, the vehicle. At last he turned to his companion. "Parson," quoth he, "do you hear that fellow pursuing us?" "I do!" responded the parson, with bated breath. "'Tis a highwayman," pronounced John Spencer with conviction. "But I fear no man. Stop the coach, parson, and I will give the fellow a lesson he shall carry with him to his dying day!"

Port, taken freely, disposes a man to be valiant, and John Spencer, despite the remonstrances of his servants, clambered out of the door, and stumbled round to the back of the coach. There, sure enough, in the dark he encountered a man, a stout fellow, who set upon him furiously. The two fought and pummelled each other, striking out manfully in spite of the fact that neither could see his antagonist, until finally the postilions, who had come to the rescue, succeeded in dragging off John Spencer, with the assurance that his enemy had fled.

Bleeding, but triumphant, the Squire clambered back into his coach, and there met the parson, equally dishevelled, crawling in by the opposite door. "How now, parson?" panted the exhausted Squire. "Were you, too, in it with that terrible scoundrel?"

"I could not leave you to be killed!" panted the parson bravely; and the two heroes, grasping hands, compared notes of their bold exploit till they arrived at Cannon Hall, where they celebrated their victory in yet another bottle of port.

It was not till the next day that John Spencer learnt from his postilions that he and the parson, having left the coach by opposite doors, had met in the dark behind it, and fought each other in mistake for the highwayman, who existed only in the imagination of each![11]

Unlike his more parochially-minded uncle, Walter Spencer Stanhope was very much involved with "the Great World and affairs of State," which old Squire Spencer had rejected. Educated at Bradford Grammar School, followed by University College, Oxford and Law Studies at the Middle Temple, he was already Member of Parliament for Carlisle (the first of four constituencies which he represented) when in 1775 he inherited his Cawthorne estates and changed his name from Stanhope to Spencer Stanhope. He was a close supporter of the Younger Pitt and a friend of the great Yorkshire anti-slavery campaigner, William Wilberforce, who was a frequent visitor to Cannon Hall. His estates, plus the income from the Spencer iron furnaces and coal-mines, rendered him financially "comfortable," while his marriage in 1783 to Mary Winifred Pulleine, an only child, gave him the future prospect of considerable wealth and property in North Yorkshire and Northumberland. The marriage and the family life produced by the couple's fifteen children were both extremely happy.

The effect of all this made Cannon Hall and the village of Cawthorne much less harsh, cruel places than they had been in the days of John Spencer. Walter Spencer Stanhope had demonstrated his humanitarian instincts pre-1775 by having all his Horsforth tenants subjected to the revolutionary medical practice of vaccination, but these instincts acquired a new, more deeply religious basis as a result of his friendship with Wilberforce and his support for the abolition of slavery. Indeed the great reformer used to write to Cannon Hall for information concerning "the situation of our labouring poor – a matter of the first importance in political economy." In 1787 Walter began the practice of delivering a sermon on Sunday evenings to the whole assembled household, while his further devotion to the religious well-being of others was remembered and very seriously recounted by his daughter Frances, long after his death (although those hearing the tale must have found it extremely difficult to remain as straight-faced as the story-teller). It appeared that a lady guest at Cannon Hall inadvertently locked herself in her toilet and the only way to free her was to send a servant twelve miles to fetch a locksmith, during which time the unfortunate captive would have missed Sunday morning service. "But my father was a singularly kind-hearted man, he did what nothing else would have induced him to do – he absented himself from church and read her a sermon through the keyhole!"

Similarly, he disapproved of many of the pastimes which gave pleasure to the working man at the expense of great cruelty to animals. In his diary is an entry for July 23rd, 1794 which reads: "Took up a man as a Rogue and Vagabond for travelling with a bull to bait in Cawthorne. Before 11 o'clock the man consented to shoot him, and I bid the Constable to release him." Such an action shows not only great idealism, since bull-baiting was not made illegal until 1835, but great courage in single-handedly depriving a mob of miners of their sport and thus outlawing a barbarous practice in Cawthorne forty years before it was outlawed nationally. This is not to imply that Walter Spencer Stanhope was "soft." In many ways he lived as vigorous a life as had his uncle, and it was as well that he was a fearless and first-rate driver of coach and horses, because he often had to drive himself home from dinners when his coachman had returned from the servants' hall too drunk to stand up. To even consider his (as he often did) driving a coach-and-four at break-neck speed down Cliffe Hill (which was then the main coach road to Cannon Hall) is enough to bring a shudder of fright to one who simply walks this track, but Stanhope was no stranger to the rigours of late 18th and early 19th Century road

Walter Spencer Stanhope as a young man.   *A portrait by Hoppner*

travel, having been dumped in the mud of London's Parliament Street, when the axle of his coach broke as he was returning from a dinner and ball at Gloucester House; and on another occasion encountering a snowdrift on the top of Pule Hill and having to leave his coach wedged there for several days.

As a young man Walter Spencer-Stanhope attended the wedding at Versailles of the ill-fated Louis XVI and Marie Antoinette. Of the latter, he wrote home to John Spencer, "Sometime or other, I prophesy, she will have great influence in this country." Little could he have imagined how disastrous that influence would be or that he would be involved in the possible defence of England, following the declaration of war upon the Revolutionary regime in France and against Napoleon. It is difficult now, following two World Wars, and living in an age of such easy mass communication, to appreciate the tension felt in 1805, when a French invasion threat had not yet been averted by Nelson's victory at Trafalgar, and the only means of relaying news that such a threat was a reality would be by horse-borne letter or by lighted beacons (which were sometimes wrongly illuminated as a result of seeing a heather-fire on distant

The Volunteers Vase or Urn presented to Walter Spencer Stanhope after the false alarm over Napoleon's invasion 1805.

Cawthorne Volunteers.

Music arranged by George Frudd.

Edited by John Hutchinson, Barnsley.

As sung by Mr. Joseph Clegg, the celebrated Tivy Dale Tenor.

Come, listen to my ditty, lads, And open wide your ears, While I relate a song to you Of Cawthorne volunteers. 'Twas in the time of Bonaparte, When war was all the go, Our volunteers they shoulder'd arms, And march'd to meet the foe. To me fol di la ra la di O, Me fol di la ra la, Me fol di la ra la di O, Me fol di la ra la.

There was Andrew Dyson's mother, she did now't but fret and cry;
Likewise old Betty Jessop's eyes, she could'nt keep them dry;
She says, surely good neighbours, it never can be so,
For if it is, I'll pack my clothes and go with our Joe.—Chorus.

Old Tommy Shirt in Cawthorne Lanes, it is his whole discourse;
Saying my lads they shall never go, unless that they be forced;
They've taken my brother's youngest son, and now they want the elder,
Sager Tom's gone out of the lanes—Ben Healy and David Gelder.
Chorus.

In comes old Matty Gibson, and she is all in a frown;
She says, there's now't but tumults, going up and down this town;
For if they take my lad away, I shall never rest in bed,
For I'd rather ten times over, they would take old Tom or Ned.
Chorus.

In comes old Matty Scott, and she's as happy as a queen;
She says, they wont take our Abraham, for he has such great 'een;
And as for our old Jim, he has been in 'twar before;
And our George will not be ready for this dozen years or more.
Chorus.

In comes old Dame Hattersley, and she's all in a huff,
For she walks up and down the town, and takes a pinch of snuff;
She says that her son Dicky's wife, does now't but fret and talk,
For she says, she would march with them, but she is too fat to walk.
Chorus.

As they did march on Barmby Lane, 'tis true what I relate,
Old Mally Fish stepped into 'tranks, and says, this day will decide his fate!
If Colonel Stanhope will say the word, and grant me leave to go,
I will boldly tuck up my sleeves, and fight with our Jack and Joe.
Chorus.

Last lad that Matty Gibson sent, was Ned with diamond eyes,
All 't sergeants on the racecourse could'nt learn him 'texercise;
They'd never have made him a soldier, if they'd kept him 20 year—
So with a hatchet, sword, and hairy cap, they made him pioneer.
Chorus.

And so, now to conclude, and finish up my song,
I hope there's none in 'tcompany, will think I've penned it wrong;
There was such to do 'i Cawthorne town, when they went out to feight,
Had not the war concluded, they'd have put them all to reight.
Chorus.

ALL RIGHTS RESERVED.

Printed and Sold by Alfred Whitham, New Street, Barnsley.

moorland). Such was the nervous state of South Yorkshire when Walter Spencer Stanhope was involved in 1805 in the turning out of the Staincross Volunteers, an event chronicled by Mrs. Stirling as follows:

> In 1805, when England was living in terror of an invasion from Napoleon, Stanhope was commanding a company of 600 Yorkshiremen known as the Staincross Volunteers. On the occasion of some fresh colours being presented to the regiment, he made a soul-stirring speech to his men, which not only thrilled his hearers, but evoked an almost unparalleled outburst of applause throughout England. One sentence in it was long quoted – "The Chief Consul of France tells us we are a nation of shop-keepers. Let us, shop-keepers, then melt our weights and scales, and return him the compliment in bullets." It is said that the tone in which Stanhope uttered the word bullets moved those who heard him in a manner of which it is impossible to convey any impression. So great a sensation did his oratory cause, that an extract from it as follows was printed on posters or broadsides, and distributed or posted up in the streets of London and throughout the length and breadth of England.
>
> "My father's speech," relates John Stanhope, "was in

The wedding photograph of Joseph Clegg, described on the sheet music of "The Cawthorne Musicians" and "The Cawthorne Volunteers" as "the celebrated Tivydale tenor".

English Mastiffs,

WE, by this Address, publicly and solemnly, before God and our Country, pledge our Fortunes, Persons, and Lives, in the Defence of our Sovereign and all the Blessings of our glorious Constitution.

There is not a Man that hears me, I am persuaded, who is not prompt and eager to redeem that pledge. There is not, there cannot be a Man here, who would leave undefended our good, tried, and brave *OLD KING* in the Hour of Danger.

No, Sir! we need now no Warning voice; no string of Eloquence; no Thoughts that beat, and Words that burn, are necessary to raise a Host of hardy Men, when the King, the Parliament, and the Country are in Distress. CALL OUT TO YORKSHIREMEN, "*COME FORTH TO BATTLE!*"—our Answer will be, One and All—"WE ARE READY! —*Where is the Enemy!—Lead on!*"—Sir; that Enemy is not far off; a very numerous, well-appointed, ably-commanded Army, to whom is promised the Plunder of England, are now hovering round, and Part of them in daily Sight of the promised Land. They view it, like as many famished Wolves, Cruel as Death, and Hungry as the Grave, panting for an Opportunity, at any Risk, to come into our Sheep-Fold;—*but*, and if they should, is it not our Business, our first Duty, to have such a Guard of old faithful ENGLISH MASTIFFS, of the old Breed, as shall make them quickly repent their temerity.

The CHIEF CONSUL of France tells us, that we are but a Nation of Shopkeepers: let us, Shopkeepers, then melt our Weights and our Scales, and return him the Compliment in Bullets. SIR; we may have a firm Reliance on the Exertions of as gallant a Fleet as ever sailed; but the Fleet cannot perform Impossibilities; it cannot be in two Places at once; it cannot conquer the Winds and subdue the Storms. Though our old TARS can do much, they cannot do every Thing; and it would be unsafe and dastardly to lie skulking behind them. With the Blessing of GOD, and a good Cause, we can do Wonders; but, if we depend upon our Naval Prowess only we have much to fear. NO, SIR: England will never be perfectly safe, until she can defend herself as well by *Land* as by *Sea;* until she can defy the haughty Foe: if there was *even a Bridge* between CALAIS and DOVER, and that Bridge in Possession of the Enemy, still she can say, in the Language of a good *English Boxing Match*, "A FAIR FIELD AND NO FAVOUR!"

Printed for J. GINGER, 169 Piccadilly,
Price SIXPENCE per Dozen for Distribution,
WHERE MAY BE HAD ALL THE PATRIOTIC PAPERS PUBLISHED, PROPERLY ASSORTED.

W. MARCHANT, PRINTER, 3, GREVILLE-STREET, HATTON-GARDEN.

Cliffe Hill as it is today – and Walter Spencer Stanhope drove a coach and four at breakneck speed down here.

everybody's mouth and was the general subject of conversation in London. He became the lion of the day, the extract was printed on a placard and met our eyes everywhere upon the walls in London.'' On the next occasion when Mrs Stanhope went to Court, the Princess Elizabeth stepped out of the royal circle on purpose to tell her how delighted the King and the Royal Family had been at such a fine burst of oratory from ''a true English Gentleman.''

The effect on the volunteers themselves was soon apparent. At that date beacons were in readiness, inland as well as along the coast, to give the alarm in case of news arriving that the French were attempting to land. Late in the evening of August 14th, Stanhope received a letter from Mr Dixon, the clergyman at Woolley and one of the magistrates of the Division, informing him that the beacon at Pontefract was lighted, and that he was giving orders for lighting the one standing upon Woolley Edge, a wild, bleak height which dominates the surrounding country for many miles. Instructions had previously been given by the General of the district that upon lighting of this beacon the regiment was to march to Pontefract immediately, and Stanhope realised that not a moment was to be lost. With methodical dispatch he sent off his servants to muster the regiment from every locality where the beacon could not cast its warning light. The members of his corps were scattered far and wide through the outlying hamlets to which his messengers galloped. They were, for the most part, poor colliers or farmers, previously little used to discipline, while between them and their destination lay, in most instances, rough country to traverse through the darkness and wildness of a stormy night. Yet in an incredibly short space of time, from far and near, they had assembled; till out of six hundred only nine were absent, one being Stanhope's own son, John, who was away in Wales, two being ill, and the others from home when the summons came. Before daylight dawned – although many of them were already footsore and weary with having tramped a long distance on the preceding night – they commenced their march to Pontefract in orderly fashion, with their Captain at their head, and they had already got to Hemsworth, a distance of about twelve miles, when they were overtaken by a messenger bearing the following note:-

To Colonel Stanhope.
Dear Sir,

I have sent a Servant to the Beacon at Pomfret this Morning as I could learn nothing here, and find that the Pomfret Beacon was *not* lighted and that the Woolly People were deceived by the burning of a Brick Kiln placed near the Beacon. You are sure I am truly sorry to have occasioned you all the Trouble you have had.

I remain, dear Sir,
Very truly yours

Jer. Dixon
Thursday Morng, August 15th 1805.

The gallant troops, however, although summoned on a false alarm, received an ovation at Hemsworth, the populace collected to cheer them, the taverns offered them hospitality, the farmers feted them and proffered the loan of their wagons for the return journey, while all the way home from their bloodless campaign the countryside turned out to present them with refreshment, till, as Stanhope's son relates, ''It was an exceedingly hot day, and the farmers and others regaled the returning troops so hospitable, that, in the evening, as wagon after wagon poured into the stableyard at Cannon Hall, its freight of men were seen to be not quite in marching order!" [1]

The whole exploit became the subject of a local song, whilst the commemorative urn presented to Stanhope as Commanding Officer remained at Cannon Hall until comparatively recent times (but was fortunately photographed before its removal).

In 1807, Cawthorne was a village of some 1,100 inhabitants, most of whom were employed by the Spencer Stanhopes or by such colliery-owners as the Thorps and the Wilsons. It was a place where its inhabitants worked long hours at jobs which were labour-intensive and where the strong, manual element had not yet been eased by the advent of the machine. As the Nattes drawings show, even the production of timber for building purposes was a laborious task for two sawyers pulling a hand-saw so large that it had to be used in a saw-pit. Transportation was, for some, horse-drawn, and, for most of the population, by their own two feet, even when carrying heavy packs or baskets of produce. A water-powered sawmill (the Jowett sawmill, which continued its work until comparatively recent times) provided the timber requirements for the Estate and flour was provided by the Killamarsh windmill (near to the present farm of the same name) and Low Mill (on the road to Kexborough). The alcoholic needs of the village were provided by the malt-kilns of the West family, whose bee-hive tops can be seen on the Nattes drawings of the centre of the village, and which gave a name to the present-day Malt Kiln Row. Most of the coal-mines in the village were bell-pits or drift-mines, but the colliery at Norcroft, where nine men out of eleven descending the shaft on May 23rd, 1821 were killed when the chain broke, was a much bigger establishment, which went deeper for its coal. Its operating life, however, was not a long one, because in 1826 its pit spoil-heap was removed to allow the road to Silkstone to be widened, the colliery, presumably having closed.

At this time, the Church of All Saints enjoyed the position of architectural dominance in the village which it has today, but this, and its spiritual role, were not the only ways in which the Church influenced the community. The Spencer Stanhopes owned the village and exerted their influence by virtue of holding a variety of local offices, but the village was subject to

The author photographed on an ancient but newly renovated clapper bridge, overlooking the ford through which Walter Spencer Stanhope would have driven.

the system of local government which was current in England at that time and which centred upon the Church. This system was described by Elie Halévy in the first volume of his "History of the English People in the Nineteenth Century" as follows:

> But it is more surprising that the government of the parishes themselves – those small units of local government into which the whole of England is divided – was also government by public meeting. The parish was administered by five officials, who together constituted the parochial executive – the churchwardens, the constable, the surveyor of highways, and the overseer of the poor and by an assembly, the vestry meeting, a meeting of all those interested in the administration of the parish. This assembly exercised a control over the actions and the expenditure of the executive, and in certain cases nominated these officials, or at least took part in their nomination. The vestry, which owed its name to the fact that it met regularly in the vestry of the parish church, naturally played a very important part in the choice of the churchwardens. These were partly secular, partly ecclesiastical officers, responsible both to the ordinary of the diocese and to the parochial meeting. While it was their duty to keep the church accounts, they also took part in the local police, and in the administration of the poor law. The vestry also drew up the list

Two Swift family photographs of members of the family obtaining water from one of the communal taps installed in the village around 1890.

One of the Blacker family drawing water from a well

of substantial persons from which the magistrates selected the surveyors of highways.

In the vast majority of rural or semi-rural parishes the line of cleavage between those who paid the local rates – the farmers and shopkeepers – and the agricultural labourers who did not pay them, was sufficiently distinct to make it easy to exclude the latter from the vestry meeting. In these circumstances the parochial assembly was composed of a small number of persons, who where usually, as tenants, dependent on the class from which the magistrates were taken. [2]

This system depended heavily upon part-time service and goodwill, resting, as it did, upon the idea that shared social responsibility was expected of all good citizens. (N.B. Some of the more onerous duties, such as those of Overseer of the Poor were often given a small financial reward.) The records of the working of the vestry system, which are known as vestry books, provide an interesting sidelight upon aspects of Cawthorne life during the first half of the 19th Century.

The repair of the highways was a constant problem. The Eighteenth Century had brought a large increase in road transport and Turnpike Trusts had been set up as a way of providing money to maintain certain roads. Such a road ran through Cawthorne, but in 1826 we still find in the vestry books that "The Surveyors of the Highway are ordered to set the unemployed to work at breaking stones"; and in September of that same year, a Committee was set up to look at the provision of work for "the unemployed poor" on the Highways, as a result of which it was decided to widen the road at Norcroft and Woolstocks Lane. At the same meeting, it was decided that no more "liquor" should be supplied for the Vestry meetings! In January 1829 a poor rate of 1s. in the pound was levied and from it yarn was bought "for the purpose of employing widows and others in knitting." A man and his wife were to be "allowed 2s. a week (20p)" and she was to be put on the knitting list. By 1832 concern was so great concerning the danger of cholera that a

THE CAWTHORNE OF JOHN C. NATTES AND ABEL HOLD (1807-1866)

Board of Health was set up. The same sort of concern must still have been felt in 1864 when a Vestry Meeting was called to consider "the best means of improving the public supply of water to The Township of Cawthorne." The final outcome of this and the setting up of the fountain in Church Street was reported in the "Barnsley Chronicle."

> **OCCURRENCES**
>
> *1867*
>
> 1867—Nov. 5—The completion of new waterworks and opening of a new fountain was celebrated at Cawthorne, by a "public Tea," when about 300 persons, including the family from Cannon Hall, and Banks Hall, assembled in Tivydale School. The trays were superintended by cottagers' wives. After tea an address presented on the occasion was as follows:—"To the several members of the Stanhope family.—We, the inhabitants of Cawthorne, in public meeting assembled, and in commemoration of the completion of the water works in Cawthorne, desire to offer the subjoined address: We specially wish to tender our sincere thanks to Walter Spencer Stanhope, Esq., of Cannon Hall, for his praiseworthy efforts in bringing the supply of water, in the first instance, to the village. We desire him to convey our sincere thanks to W. B. Beaumont, Esq., for allowing the supply of water to be conveyed from his estate, and that he will further express our gratitude to such members of the Stanhope family as may have assisted in this good work, but who, from their peculiarly unostentatious spirit, may not have appeared prominently in it, particularly to the Misses Spencer Stanhope, of Banks Hall, for the last, but not least, share they have taken in rendering the fountain an ornamental as well as an useful work. We feel deeply indebted to the whole united family for their benevolent actions on all occasions. To the esteemed Lady Elizabeth Spencer Stanhope whose numerous acts of kindness during a long period of years have endeared her and her aged and affectionate partner, John Spencer Stanhope, Esq., to the hearts of all. In conclusion, we trust that the same unity, harmony, and goodwill may always prevail, as it has hitherto done, between the Stanhope family and the inhabitants of Cawthorne, and that the present surviving branches may enjoy health and happiness for many years to come, heightened by the consolation of looking back on the past and knowing that they have faithfully discharged their duty in the high sphere of life into which it has pleased God to call them; and when it shall please him to summon them from amongst us may they enjoy eternal rest and bliss, as the reward of their labours. It is the earnest prayer of the inhabitants of Cawthorne.—5th Nov., 1867."

The Fountain – a village water supply provided by the Spencer Stanhopes in 1867. In the background is the Fountain House, which in 1871 was William Moxon's Post Office.

II

The church in which these Vestry Meetings took place differed considerably from the present church, which has been repaired and extended in 1826 and further extended in the 1870's. It once had, moreover, two features, a gallery and a "three-decker" pulpit, which remind us of two very important elements in Church services of that time, the Church musicians and the Parish Clerk. It is not certain when Cawthorne Church acquired a pipe-organ, but in 1841 a parish document for December 6th says, "Resolved that John Cook be paid two guineas for singing and playing the organ up to this date, and Wm. Hinchliffe have one guinea for blowing the organ, to be paid by the Churchwardens annually at Christmas." What we do know is that in the late Eighteenth Century days of Parson Phipps a small orchestra and a band of singers inhabited the gallery above the West Door. These were the "Cawthorne Musicians," a group of players and singers reminiscent of those described by Thomas Hardy and George Eliot or seen in the "Village Choir" painted by Webster; a band whose independence and determination to dictate tempi and choice of hymns brought them into conflict with the Vicar. As the words of an old song about them say, "How they went on!"; they "went on" to such an extent that, as the song reminds us, "Mr Phipps would let them sing no more." In December 1838, their successors signed an agreement with the Minister and Congregation in which, among other things, "the singers are to endeavour as much as possible to select the easiest and most simple tunes, in order that the Congregation may join in the singing." This was, however, not the last example of friction between the Vicar and those providing ancillary musical services at the Church, as this entry from the bell-book shows:

"November 8th 1921. Mr Woolley reported that he could reach no satisfactory agreement with the younger ringers, but that the older ringers would resume under the following conditions:-
1) No drinking, gambling or swearing in the belfry.
2) An agreement to ring twice on Sundays for half an hour at £14 a year with two extra ringings on Christmas Day at 30s and one extra ringing on Easter Day at 15s.
3) Substitutes to be trained.
4) Failure to ring entails forfeiture of 3s per service."

That the end-product made up for the friction is shown by the following extract from the Parish Meeting of June 1906: "We desire to place it on record in these pages that our bells have been thoroughly over-hauled and rehung at the expense of Sir Walter Spencer Stanhope K. C. B. The work was arranged before we were aware of this generous intention. Even those in the parish who never respond to their call to God's House of Prayer take some pleasure in hearing the church bells on a Sunday. It has been remarked to us more than once: 'One feels quite lost of a Sunday without the bells!'"

It is now difficult to appreciate what part the Parish Clerk played in the late 18th and early 19th Century Church of England. He would be the verger, probably read a lesson, announced the hymns, gave out the notices, said the psalms with the vicar, and often conducted the choir and/or the orchestra. If the parish did not have a resident vicar, the clerk would look after the Parish Registers, receive banns of marriage, and arrange christenings, weddings and funerals. In some parishes he combined with his own duties those of sexton, tending the churchyard, digging graves and looking after burials. It is not surprising that from among the ranks of men who carried out such a multiplicity of tasks in Cawthorne, there should have been some who have stood out as "characters", about whom stories have been passed from generation to generation. Richard Moxon, who followed the trade of a weaver, was Parish Clerk from 1762 and died aged 84 in 1800. He was the Parish Clerk mentioned in the song "The Cawthorne Musicians", receiving £2 as his annual salary, £1 extra for washing the Vicar's surplices and a further 10s (50p) for washing the church windows and supplying bread for the Communion Service. This latter seems to have occupied a very minor place in the Sacrament, because in one year's account a definite imbalance is shown by the charge of 10s (50p) for bread as opposed to £4 for fifteen gallons of wine. A man who could justifiably make Figaro's claim that "I am the factotum of all the town" was John Livesley, who farmed six acres of land (operating from what we now call "Golden Cross Cottage") but who, at different times between 1801 and 1833 served as Parish Clerk, Churchwarden, Inspector of the Worsted Manufactory for the Poor, Member of the Vestry, and the salaried post of Assistant Overseer of the Poor. Parish records tell us a little about some of the remuneration which he could

The gallery, removed from the West end of Cawthorne Church circa 1875, which was the home of the Cawthorne Musicians.

The old East window which was removed when the Church was extended in the 1870's.

Cawthorne Musicians.

Music arranged by George Frudd.

As sung by Mr. Joseph Clegg, the celebrated Tivy Dale Tenor.

Edited by John Hutchinson, Barnsley.

Come, listen a-while, and I'll sing you a song, About Cawthorne musicians and how they went on;

Jude Hinchliffe play'd t'fiddle, Billy Clegg he play'd t'bass, Jonathan Hinchliffe play'd t'o-boe, and pull'd a faal face, Ra

CHORUS.

fol di dol la di ra, fol di dol la di, Ra fol di dol la di ra, fol di dol la.

In comes Dicky Taylor, and thus does begin—
If you want some bass singing I'll soon put some in;
Na! Na! says old Jossey, that never will do!
I pray thee be quiet—Na! do, Dicky, do!—Chorus.

In comes Joseph Ibbotson, and he looks very mute,
Some times he plays t'fiddle, and sometimes plays t'flute;
But he's a bad hand at either, his music's so thin!
Stand by, says Johnny Allott, and let Billy English come in.—Chorus.

Will Allott, in music he takes great delight;
Ned Greenwood he sings, while he ruttles in t'throit;
John Harrison sings a hearty good Bass;
And Joe Jubb he sings Tenor, while he goes red in t'face.—Chorus

Will Hutchinson sings sweetly, his voice is so soft;
Jim Wigglesworth he shouts, you can hear him in t'loft;
George Webster comes in, and thus does begin—
Up Jumps Joe Bates, and sticks his face in.—Chorus.

A company of young men did then enter in,
With these old Musicians to learn to sing.
There wor' Jonathan and Jim, they made a great din,
And George Schofield he gaped, but you could'nt hear him.—Chorus.

Tommy Rhodes was one of them, I very well know;
And Tom Holling he squeaks, just like a young crow;
George Chappell, gets up, and he crookles his face,
If you ask him what he sings, he'll soon tell you "Bass".—Chorus.

This company of Musicians, they soon did give o'er.
Because Mr. Phillipp's would'nt let them sing more;
They were heartily grieved, if you had but them seen;
Up jumps Jude Hinchliffe, and says, where's my te deum.—Chorus.

The Sexton he chimes, when he thinks it is time;
The Parson comes in and he puts on his gown,
He opens his book and he rabbles away,
He scarce give the Clerk time "Amen" for to say.—Chorus.

ALL RIGHTS RESERVED.

Printed and Sold by Alfred Whitham, New Street, Barnsley.

13

have received; "There is due to the Parish Clerk (who is appointed by the Minister) for every Christening 6d, for every proclamation in the Churchyard 2d. There is also due to him from every family keeping a separate fire 2d." The last Parish Clerk was Joseph Milnes, who served from 1853 to his death in 1868, when the new curate, Charles Pratt, abolished the office. The three-decker pulpit, in which successive Clerks had proudly occupied the bottom deck, was removed before 1820. The present pulpit came with the renovation of the church in the 1870's carried out by the brothers Walter and Roddam Spencer Stanhope in honour of their late parents, John and Lady Elizabeth. The building, which was reopened for full worship in 1880, was extended and redecorated in Pre-Raphaelite style to the designs of Bodley and Garner. Out also went the gallery (the choir now becoming a robed choir at the front of the church) and the private enclosed Spencer Stanhope pew (which had its own stove), Colonel Stanhope now opting to sit in view of the rest of the congregation.

Two real characters, however, were holders of the office of sexton, Ben Taylor (from 1839 until his death, aged 67, in 1879) and William ("Bill") Ward, who succeeded him in 1879 and retired aged 81 in 1921. They were recalled by the late Noel Moxon as follows. "Ben Taylor was rather vindictive and when he had buried one with whom he was unfriendly, he would jump up and down on his grave shouting 'I've got you now!' During the latter part of his office, the new burial-ground was opened and, as it was hard going, Ben preferred to dig in the old ground, telling the Vicar that there was still plenty of room. However, after an interment the previous day, the Vicar was passing through the churchyard on his way to early service and he was alarmed to see some bones protruding from under a heap of clay. Apparently Ben had disturbed some of the old inhabitants to make room for newcomers, but a heavy storm during the night had helped to reveal what he was doing. Ben was succeeded by William Ward, who lived with his wife in the corner house of Malt Kiln Row. He was a carter, working for Heslops of Barnby Hall, and also drove on the Silkstone wagon road. When Malt Kiln Row was made into dwelling-houses, he did the carting. He was a good-living man and his house was used as the Church bookshop, where hymn-books, prayer-books, bibles and the like could be purchased. The sexton's work in his

The newly renovated and extended Church (late 1880's?)

"A village choir" by Thomas Webster. This painting, now in the Victoria and Albert Museum, is of a group of singers similar to the Cawthorne Musicians. It is reproduced by permission of the Victoria and Albert Museum.

day would be heavy for, in addition to numerous buckets of coal to be carried into church, there were a multitude of lamps to be trimmed, candles replaced etc., ready for the services. He also mowed the church-yard, trimmed the paths, and, during the service, sat on his chair under the tower. He would be present at weddings with his wife Bess, who always wore a large apron, which she held out to receive coins from the wedding party. Boys caught smoking in the church porch received scant courtesy – often a blow with the flat of a fire-shovel!! He retired in 1921 (having given up his grave-digging duties about 1914 to William Machen), living on until 1930 when he died aged 91." [7]

JOHN NATTES DRAWINGS OF CAWTHORNE (1807-1809)

The deer-shed at Cannon Hall   C.H.

CAWTHORNE 1790-1990

The Cannon Hall Brew-house which catered for the liquid refreshment of the Spencer Stanhopes and their guests.   C.H.

JOHN NATTES DRAWINGS OF CAWTHORNE (1807-1809)

Rear of Gamekeeper's House (Beet House).   *C.H.*

CAWTHORNE 1790-1990

The tannery at Dean Hill with soaking-pits in the foreground.   C.H.

Boiler at Dean Hill. The caption says "Rendered useless by the invention of extracting acid for tanning by steam."   C.H.

JOHN NATTES DRAWINGS OF CAWTHORNE (1807-1866)

A Saw Pit on Tivydale near the Forge. Here two men were needed with their large two-handed saw to split up timber into boards etc. Leonard Rusby, the sawyer of Tivydale, was one of the Cawthorne Volunteers.   C.H.

Mr West's house (now known as Red House) with one of his malt-kilns on the right. This picture confirms memories passed down by old people that the area in front of the house (now a walled garden) was an open space upon which fairs were once held.   C.H.

Church Street, Cawthorne. The beehive top of the malt-kilns can be seen on the left. The figure on the left is thought to be J. C. Nattes.   C.H.

JOHN NATTES DRAWINGS OF CAWTHORNE (1807-1809)

The Killamarsh windmill, which was demolilshed in the 1840's. C.H.

South Lodge (photographs of which appear later in the book). This drawing is interesting because Rev. Pratt (who never saw it) states that the Lodge was built in the early 1820's to designs drawn by Rev. C. Spencer Stanhope. What actually happened (as Estate repair-workers confirmed) was that a new facade was built on to this structure and that facade was presumably designed by Rev. Stanhope   C.V.J.

JOHN NATTES DRAWINGS OF CAWTHORNE (1807-1809)

North Lodge, looking towards High Hoyland. C.V.J.

North Lodge. It is said that the occupants lived at one side of the gates and slept at the other. C.V.J.

Jowett Saw Mill before it was extended (late 1840's) using material from the demolished Killamarsh windmill.   C.V.J.

Brook House seen from Tivydale.   C.V.J.

CAWTHORNE 1790-1990

Raw Royd. The last traces of the buildings have gone only in the last twenty years.   C.V.J.

George Roberts, who after his retirement from farm work, gave stalwart service to the Parish Council as village handyman, keeping Cawthorne tidy and well cared-for.

Wilfred Vollans and his son, Wilf.

Walter Machen.

George Swift

Four latter-day Cawthorne 'characters' engaged in the country craft of dry stone-walling and the art of the stone-mason.

27

William ("Bill") Ward, the Sexton, photographed in old age.

James Balme, a blacksmith, who, during the 1880's, was the Church choirmaster and ran a group of singers which gave concerts in the village.   R.W.

The Spencer Stanhope family were patrons of the arts and it is said that Rev. Charles Spencer Stanhope first brought J. F. Herring to public notice having learnt of his painting in the course of a conversation on the Sprotbrough to Doncaster coach, of which the artist was then the driver. Subsequent introductions set him on the road to fame. He later befriended an artist who was to bring a certain degree of fame to the village of Cawthorne. Abel Hold (1815-96) was born at Alverthorpe near Wakefield and was originally apprenticed to a firm of house painters, a trade which he followed for a few years. In his own time, however, he began to indulge his artistic talents, painting show-cloths for travelling showmen, before moving on to portraiture and landscapes. It was as an animal and game painter that he achieved his fame. Between 1849 and 1851 he lived in Church Street, Barnsley, before moving to Brook House at Cawthorne in 1852, where he spent the rest of his life. Between 1849 and 1871 he had sixteen exhibitions at the Royal Academy, one at the Royal Institution, Pall Mall, one at the Suffolk Street Galleries, plus others at Manchester, Liverpool, Birmingham and Wakefield. He never had an entry for the Royal Academy rejected and his last one in 1871 was of a "Dead Snipe".

Abel Hold's life at Cawthorne was a simple one, and in economic terms, he was never a rich man. Indeed there are stories still told of the urgent sale of new works to enable him to pay bills, and how he relied upon the patronage and support of Colonel (later Sir) Walter Spencer Stanhope. It is said that, when he required money, he sent a picture of a starving man to Charles Wemyss at the Estate Office and this never failed to produce the required result! What he did have, however, were great riches in artistic terms, ranging from river pebbles which he ground down to provide pigment, through to the leafy lanes down which he walked to observe the wild animals and birds which were his models. For Abel Hold, Cawthorne was one great natural treasury.

Brook House, early 1890's, when it was the house of the artist, Abel Hold.

In May 1873, a Barnsley Chronicle reporter visited him and produced the following report:

An Hour in the Studio at Cawthorne

Strolling in the bright May sunshine on a recent afternoon, among the beauties of Cannon Hall, enjoying the exhilarating freshness of the present spring-time we found ourselves in the rustic cottage of Mr Abel Hold, and were by and by ushered into the Artist's Sanctum – that mysterious chamber, "The Studio." To us studios are always queerly suggestive places, with their strange medley of furniture, and heterogeneous accumulation of odds and ends. One might easily fancy they had got into an antiquarian lumber room, or the closet of a theatrical property man: but then you know that here the painter's fancies take shape, you begin to have a feeling of awe, as if you were in a magician's cave, while all the grotesque odds and ends about but await the conjuror's touch to assume new forms and group themselves into poetic and artistic combinations that would astonish and delight the onlooker.

We hope we break no confidence when we hint of numerous ghosts of pictures, hovering round the apartment. Thus on a wide bench lie in every conceivable position what had been feathered denizens of the distant moorlands, or adjoining cover, intermingled with broken branches, bits of heather, etc. While these are decaying on the board, their shades seem to have taken refuge, and show in dim outline on bits of canvas around the room. There, on a canvas that partly covers the wide boards put up to keep the light from getting in, in any but an orthodox way, are the shadows of some – most likely barn yard fowls, that have evidently been waiting long, with exemplary patience, for those touches requisite to give them life and permanence. Here, in the corner, lurks in dim outline a very handsome dog fox; right behind him, on another canvas, struggles a shadowy pack in full cry after a shadowy reynard, with shadowy huntsman trying hard to come through a shadowy wood. Near by is the graphic outline of a very fine boy, having in his arms the ghostly head of a sleeping pointer. Here – there – everywhere are numerous more or less defined sketches of beasts, birds, mountain, moorland, or woodland scenery, outlines and shadows which quicken imagination and kindle hope, for after all it is from amongst the confused knick-knackery of such promiscuous sketchings that there emerges year after year from the studios of the world those embodiments of purest nature, reflections of sweetness, beauty, simplicity, and tenderness, as well as those illustrations of power and grandeur which when unveiled awakens in the onlooker somewhat of that divine joy which thrills the spirit of the artist as he watches his

Abel Hold at work in his studio.

work pass from the hazy outline of the first rough sketch until he hears it acclaimed a masterpiece.

On and about the easels in the centre of the apartment are a number of pictures, finished, or nearly so, bearing unmistakeably the stamp of Mr Hold's handiwork, and showing that at the present time he is in a fine vein of inspiration; for although none of them are what we can call ambitious pictures, they still shew forth some of the finest characteristics of his pencil. We most sincerely regret that he has not attempted larger canvases and more complicated combinations, for most assuredly, with the finish and the power displayed in those now before us, he has but to do so to secure both wealth and fame to an extent his own diffidence has hitherto kept from him.

The mallard drake and duck are elegant with beauty. The feather painting we do not hope to see surpassed by any artist living or dead. The green head of the drake glistens in the light, and his beautiful form, as he lies stark on the sward, amid most appropriate accessories, makes it an admirable specimen of the artist's best manner. Two pairs of single birds have just got their finishing touches. We presume to select two and put them in a proper light to have a better look at them. We call the one morning and the other evening. Morning presents a cock grouse proudly treading the heath with a conscious air of beauty and power – the eye instinct with life, the clear morning air bespeaking a brilliant day. Evening in the other is closing over the landscape in the gloom, while the bird having fallen beneath the sportman's rifle, has dropped anyhow in the moorland.

On a smallish canvas, just beginning to emerge from the shadowy state is a hare on, as we think, a tender slab, but he calls for no special notice just yet, and all the more so that, close at hand and ready for the frame is one of the very finest – if not the very finest of painted hares that ever took shape under Mr Hold's brush. Puss, full-sized, has just dropped at the root of a tree. He has ceased to palpitate, and yet we are not even sure of that; but there is no mistake he is yet warm. Well nourished and muscular, he does credit to the woodland he has ranged, while his clean, clear coat shows beautifully against the deep shade of the trees beyond, and your fingers feel as if they felt the soft warmth of the downy fur, which seems to be trembling in the silvan breeze; and as we pass out to the open air, and away to other scenes and associations, we linger on the threshold to congratulate Mr Hold that he still retains all his finish and power, and we fervently breathe the prayer that the hand whose delicate manipulations has produced those wonderful feathered embodiments, and that exquisite fur coat, may long be preserved to contribute to the high art of his native land.

May, 1873. ION

Abel Hold and his daughter, Florence.   W.G.

Florence Hold feeding chickens outside Brook House, 1890's.

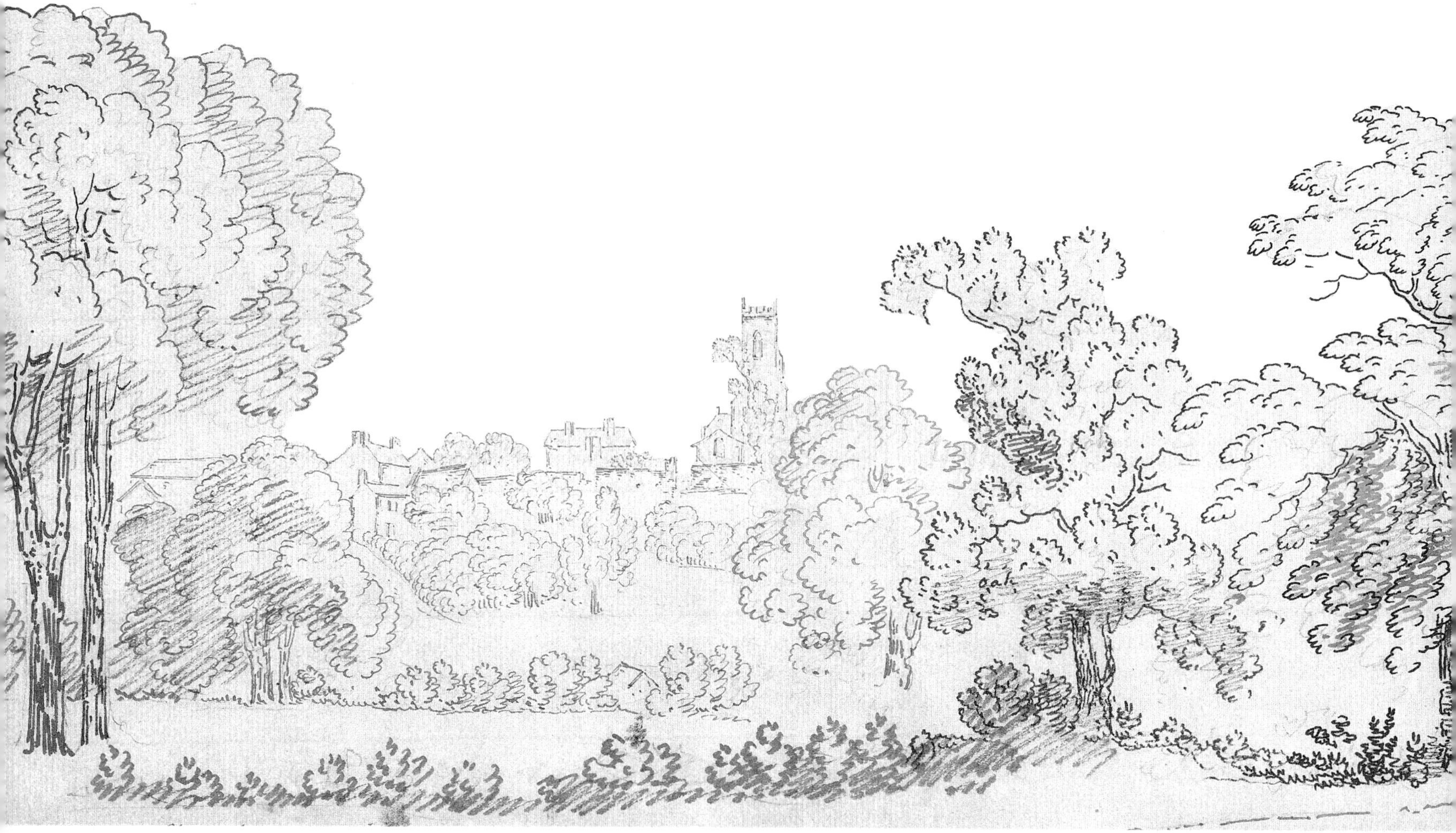

The Cawthorne of Rev. Charles T. Pratt

1866-1915

The Parson
When communication was so difficult and infrequent, he filled a place in the country life of England, that no one else could fill. He was often the patriarch of his parish, its ruler, its doctor, its lawyer, its magistrate, as well as its teacher, before whom vice trembled and rebellion dared not show itself.

Dean Church (The Oxford Movement, pp. 4-10).

And the little towns and villages, where most people lived, were full of "meditative professions", occupations which afforded time for reflection while one was engaged upon the daily task. The bookseller in a country town, the village schoolmaster, the smith at his anvil, the cobbler at his last: these men had time, if not to stand and stare, at least to think while they worked. They needed no other music for that purpose than the small sounds of their tools.

R. J. White [20]

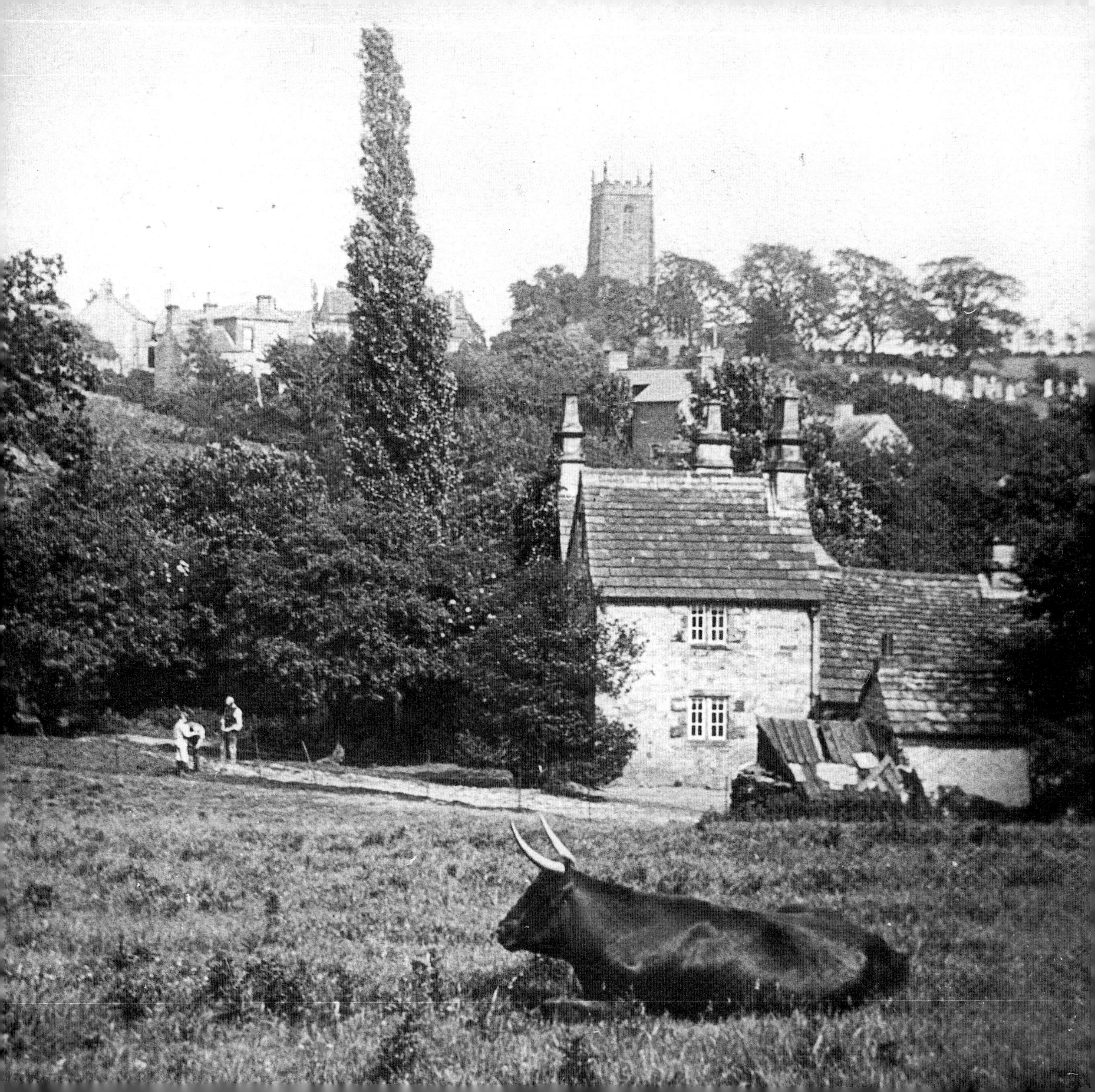

THE CAWTHORNE OF REV. CHARLES T. PRATT (1866-1915)

CAWTHORNE is fortunate in that between 1866 and 1915, it was served and influenced by a man of tremendous energy, Charles Tiplady Pratt; one whose imposing physical stature was matched by his strength of moral character, willingness to work for his fellow villagers, and the forthright way in which he spoke out against what he thought to be wrong, both in the village and in society in general. Born in Stokesley, North Yorkshire, he was educated at Queen's College, Oxford and came to South Yorkshire in 1865 when he was licensed for "the new Mission District of Hoyland swaine". In 1866 he became Curate-in-charge of Cawthorne and succeeded to the living in 1874 following the death of Rev. Charles Spencer Stanhope, who had been absentee Vicar of the parish for fifty-two years. (He had spent all his time at his other parish of Weaverham in Cheshire and employed a succession of curates to look after Cawthorne for him.)

Pratt continued as Vicar of Cawthorne until June 1915, when a stroke compelled him to retire to Cheltenham, where he died in 1921. During his long incumbency, he became a real "Father of his Parish", as a result of his desire to be involved and help with a very large variety of village activities. It is possible to build up a picture of the village when he arrived by using the 1871 Census and drawing upon the memories which old Cawthorners have/had of people named on that census, while Pratt's own "History of Cawthorne" provides a little more information. (It does not, however, go very far, having been published in 1882).

Charles Pratt's writings in his "Parish Magazine" provide commentary and comment on the period 1870-1915 and I shall use a selection of them in that capacity throughout this section of the book, while memories collected by me on tape will usually be reported in quotation marks.

Of Charles Pratt and his family the following memories remain:

"Rev. C. T. Pratt was a tall, ruddy-complexioned gentleman with white hair and long flowing beard; an autocrat who commanded respect and indeed awe in small children. Looking back, I think he was really bigoted against Methodism or other denominations, except his own Church of England. He always wore a long, black frock-coat and flat, shovel-type hat, and carried a walking stick or crook. Mrs. Pratt, whom I only saw on rare occasions, was a dainty little lady who wore black silks and a lace cap. One of his daughters, 'Miss Winnie' as she was known, was a great help and superintended much of the church activities – Sunday School, nature walks and various classes. There were two other sisters, Miss Ethel and Miss Beatrice, the former a missionary, and the latter who played the violin. A son, Mr. Ernest, became a country clergyman...

Mr. Pratt always attended Sunday School and one thing I remember and hated each week was that we had to be able to recite the Collect applicable to that Sunday. Also, in his time, we learned psalms and portions of the Scripture in order to be awarded a Bible or Prayer-Book (or both) under the Lord Wharton Trust. Mr. Pratt also often visited the Village School and gave oral Scripture examinations...

One little incident I remember vividly was when I was about five (c.1908). Coming along Tivydale from the Infants School, I met Mr. Pratt and he nipped my cheek saying 'Dear, dear, what do you think about me having one of your rosy cheeks in exchange for half my beard?' I went home very troubled wondering what I should do with half that long beard. Along with other little girls, I used to help Miss Winnie and Mrs. Stanhope decorate the Church at festive times." [8]

One feature of which many old villagers have spoken was Charles Pratt's tendency towards sibilance; in short, he tended to whistle through his teeth as he spoke. The more agitated and passionate his speech became, the more he whistled. A powerful sermon must have been quite a musical event!

The Village in 1871.

The period 1821–71 saw a steady decline in the population of the village. Its highpoint was 1,518 (561 males, 554 females) living in 242 houses. (A century later, the 1971 census showed 1,251 people inhabiting 440 houses – a comparison which illustrates not only the extent of modern-day building development, but also the cramped housing conditions which must have existed in 1871). The dominance of the Spencer Stanhopes over the village was virtually complete. A rating survey done in 1851 showed John Spencer Stanhope as owning 2,056 acres in Cawthorne with a gross estimated rental value of £3,178 and a rateable value of £1,670. A similar survey done in March 1880 showed that, out of 285 rateable properties in the village, 202 were owned by the family.

The Cannon Hall Estate provided the largest single source of employment in the village, but since in working on census returns a fair amount is left to conjecture, it is impossible to arrive at an accurate figure of the proportion of the total village population employed by the Stanhopes. At Cannon Hall there were twenty-six domestic "living-in" employees, four at Hill House, and eight at Banks Hall. These positions, however, were not filled by Cawthorne-born, such posts of trust in close proximity to the family being held by servants from other parts of the country (who would, no doubt, be less likely to pass on tit-bits of gossip to the village). Some of these had come from other estates belonging to the Stanhopes or from estates to which they were related by marriage. Estate positions filled by villagers were as follows:

Woodmen	4
Wood-labourers	6
Gardeners	4
Garden-labourers	6
Gamekeepers	2
Game-labourers	4
Lodge-keepers	1 (There were three Lodges but the occupants of two of them did other jobs).
Shepherds	1
Brickmakers	3
Home-farm-labourers	5
Estate-labourers	7
Pit-labourers	3
Carpenters	7

Cannon Hall in the time of John Spencer Stanhope.   B.

B.

In addition, it is possible to calculate from the census seventeen men of the village doing casual labouring work to supplement their incomes, plus the work provided by the Estate for stone-masons, saddlers, and blacksmiths; and last came all the agricultural labourers employed by farmers who rented their farms from the Estate.

From 1866 to 1916 the Cannon Hall Estate (and, therefore, most of the village of Cawthorne) was owned by three successive

John Spencer Stanhope (1787-1873), Abel Hold's patron throughout his time in Cawthorne.

members of the Spencer Stanhope family; John (1787–1873), Colonel (and later Sir) Walter (1827–1911) and John Montague (1860–1944). The biographical details of the family at that time are well covered, as follows, by Pratt in his "History of Cawthorne":

> The late John Spencer Stanhope, Esq., of Cannon Hall, was born on Sunday, May 27th, 1787, and educated at Westminster and Christ Church, Oxford. He was the author of a work which Hunter speaks of as "one of the most elegant works in modern literature," and by a "distinguished native and resident in this (Staincross) Wapentake." The work is called "Olympia, or Topography illustrative of the actual state of the Plain of Olympia and of the Ruins of the City of Elis." It was published by Murray in 1817, and dedicated to "the Royal Academy of Inscriptions and Belles Lettres of the Institute of France." It was republished in 1824 and 1835, and again with the addition of many engravings in 1865, under the title of "Plataea, Olympia, Elis," receiving a most favourable notice from the press, and notably from the *Saturday Review*.

> In 1810, Mr. Stanhope left England on board H. M. Ship "Vestal" to visit those parts of the Peninsula which were then independent of France, intending to proceed by way of Sicily to Greece. After many adventures in Spain, he took ship at Valencia for Majorca, "but," he says in the Preface to his Work, "after spending three days on board of this miserable vessel, I was treacherously carried into Barcelona and delivered as a prisoner into the hands of the French." At Barcelona he took fencing lessons of a master who became implicated in a discovered plot for delivering the place up to the Spaniards, and was himself suspected and thrust into a cell in the citadel and threatened with death. After being removed to the great fortress of Verdun, he was allowed to spend three months in Paris, where he made the acquaintance of many members of the Institute. Through their interest, application was made to allow him to continue on his travels on parole. The great Napoleon set him altogether at liberty without any conditions in a Passport still preserved at Cannon Hall in the Study:

> "Passeport   Police Generale de l'Empire.
> L'Etranger   Laissez passer librement Mr. John Spencer
> Signalement   Stanhope, savant Anglais, prisonnier de
> Age de 24 an.   guerre sur parole a Paris Natif de Londres
> taille d'un metre   Demeurant a (blank)
> 70 centimetres   Allant en Grece
> cheveux chataines et donnez-lui aide et protection
> front ordinaire   en case de besoin.
> yeux bleus   Le present passe-port accorde par decision
> nez ordinaire   de S. M. I. R. qui degage cet etranger de sa
> bouche moyenne   parole comme prisonnier de guerre, et lui,
> barbe brune   permet d'apres la demande de l'Institut
> etc, etc,   Imperial de France de passer en Grece qu'il
>   desire visiter pour l'interest des sciences.

> "Fait delivre a Paris le quatorze Mai, 1813.
> "(Signed by) Le Ministre de la Guerre."

> Mr. Stanhope returned to England through Germany, and afterwards went through Germany to Greece, where he made his researches amid many difficulties arising from illness and other causes. His visit was shortened by a severe attack of fever, which nearly proved fatal, and from which he did not for some years altogether recover.

> After his return home, these researches were in 1814 laid before the French Institute, and in 1817 were published in London. He was afterwards elected an Honorary Correspondent of the French Geographic Society:

> "La Societe de Geographie
> "Admet au nombre de ses membres Mr. John Spencer
> "Correspondant de l'Institut Royal de France. Paris le 20 Decembre, 1882."

> He was also elected at home a Fellow of the Royal Society and of the Society of Antiquaries. It was through his explorations that a slab of the Frieze of the Parthenon at Athens was brought to this country, being presented by him to the British Museum, and added to the Elgin Greek Sculptures.

> His only other publications were "A Catechism on Agriculture" and "A Catechism on Cattle," printed at Barnsley for the author, being plain instructions on a subject he desired to see taught in our country schools. It was through this great interest in agriculture that he made the acquaintance of his friend and future father-in-law, the

celebrated Norfolk agriculturist, Mr. Coke, afterwards created Earl of Leicester.

Mr. Stanhope died at Cannon Hall on Friday, Nov. 7th 1873, having only a few days outlived his beloved wife, Lady Elizabeth, who had died on Thursday, Oct. 31st. At an interval of a few days they were buried side by side in the family mausoleum.

In a village address, presented to the Stanhope family in 1867, it was most truly said, that Lady Elizabeth Stanhope's "numerous acts of kindness during a long period of years had endeared her and her aged and affectionate partner, John Spencer Stanhope, Esq., to the hearts of all."

The present owner of Cannon Hall, Walter Thomas William Spencer Stanhope, Esq., J.P.,D.L., was born on St. Thomas' Day (Dec. 21), 1827. He was educated at Eton and Christ Church Oxford, of which latter Foundation he was a Student. His name appears in the First Class at the Final Examination in Mathematics in 1848. He married Jan. 17th, 1856, Elizabeth Julia, eldest daughter of Sir John Jacob Buxton, Bart., of Shadwell Court, Norfolk, and his wife Elizabeth, daughter of Sir Montagu Cholmeley, of Easton Hall, Grantham. The following children have been born to them: John Montague, now of Magdalene College, Cambridge, Lieut. 4th Batt. West Yorks. Regt., born Dec. 31st, 1860; Walter, Lieut. 1st Batt. S. Yorks. Regt., born Nov. 17th, 1861; Edward Collingwood, of Trinity College, Cambridge, born March 2nd, 1863; Hugh Robert, born April 21st, 1864, died Jan. 6th, 1865; Philip Bertie, born Dec. 17th, 1868. Their daughters: Mary Gertrude, Cicely Winifrid, Margaret Isabella, Alice Mildred, and Winifrid Julia; a sixth daughter only survived her birth a few hours.

Mrs. Stanhope died at Bournemouth, Sept. 30, 1880, and was buried at Cawthorne, Oct. 6th.

For many years Mr. Stanhope has taken a most active and prominent part in magisterial and county business; he has been Captain of the 1st West Yorkshire Yeomanry Cavalry; is Colonel of the 4th Administrative Battalion of West York Rifles; a Deputy Chairman of the West Riding Quarter Sessions; Vice-Chairman of Aire and Calder Canal Co., etc., etc.

He has four times contested the South West Division of the West Riding in the Conservative interest, and was first returned as Knight of the Shire to the Commons House of Parliament, July 8th, 1872, at an uncontested election on the resignation of Lord Milton.

He was first defeated in 1865 along with Mr. Christopher Beckett Denison:

1865: Nomination, at Wakefield, July 21st; Declaration of the Poll, 24th:

Lord Milton 7,258
H. F. Beaumont 6,975
C. B. Denison 6,884
W. S. Stanhope 6,879

At this Election there were riots at Rotherham and Wath, the Cavalry being called out to quell them.

1868: Nomination, at Wakefield, Nov. 24th; the Declaration of the Poll, Nov. 26th:

Lord Milton 8,810
H. F. Beaumont 7,943
W. S. Stanhope 7,935
L. R. Starkey 7,621

1872: Unopposed Return of Mr. Stanhope, July 8th; proposed by Mr. Rowland Winn, M. P., seconded by Mr. L. R. Starkey.

Sir Walter in old age, with his son, John Montague.

1874: Declaration of Poll, February 11th:

W. S. Stanhope 9,705
L. R. Starkey 9,639
W. H. Leatham 8,265
H. F. Beaumont 8,146

1880: Declaration of the Poll, April 10th:

Hon. H. W. Fitzwilliam 11,385
W. H. Leatham 11,181
W. S. Stanhope 10,391
L. R. Starkey 10,028

Mr. Stanhope is joint Lord of the Manor of Horsforth, Silkstone, Gawber, Thornton, and Skelmanthorpe, with estates situated in the Parishes of Cawthorne, Silkstone, Penistone, Clayton West, Scissett, Thurgoland, Hoylandswaine, Gawber, Barnsley, Denby, Cumberworth, Horsforth, Calverley, Denholme, etc.

He is returned in what has been called the "Domesday Book" of 1873 as possessing 11,357 acres with a rental of £11,070.

Mr. Stanhope is Patron of the Vicarages of Cawthorne, Horsforth and Hoylandswaine. Towards the new church now being built at Horsforth, of which Mrs. Stanhope laid the Memorial Stone, he has been a very large contributor, besides giving the site, and the Church and Vicarage of Hoylandswaine were built almost entirely at the cost of the different members of the Stanhope family at Cannon Hall and Banks, Mr. and the late Mrs. Stanhope taking the most active part and interest in the work.

Mr. Stanhope's younger brother, John Roddam Spencer Stanhope, Esq., late of Hillhouse, Cawthorne, now of Villa Nuti, Florence, has for many years devoted himself to art, and been a conspicuous exhibitor in the Royal Academy, and especially ever since its establishment in the Grosvenor Gallery. He was born Jan. 21st, 1829, and married, Jan. 1859, Elizabeth, third daughter of John King, Esq., of Preston and Andover, Hants., and relict of George Frederick Dawson, Captain in the Army.

The daughters of the late Mr. and Lady Elizabeth Stanhope are Anna Maria Wilhelmina, who was married by Bishop Longley in Cawthorne Church, March 25th, 1853, to Percival Andree Pickering, Esq., Barrister-at-law, then Recorder of Pontefract, and afterwards Q. C., Attorney-General for the County Palatine of Lancaster, and Judge of the Passage Court, Liverpool; Eliza Anne, who married, June, 1858, the Rev. Richard St John Tyrwhitt, M. A., of Oxford, and died Sept. 1859; Anne Alicia; and Louisa Elizabeth, who died March 13th, 1867, aged 35.

Many of the buildings of 1871 remain, but have been extensively modernized and, in some cases, enlarged. Some old properties perished in the heady days of social reform following the Second World War when the objective was to sweep away the old order and build the "New Jerusalem", giving little thought to preservation of architectural character by property renovation. Even so the village fared much better in this respect than did many other local villages, which had their hearts torn out by the bulldozer (e.g. Monk Bretton) and one must be grateful here for collaboration in the early 1960's between the Estate and the old Penistone Rural District Council in revising old road-improvement lines, which would have demolished much of the Eastern side of Taylor Hill (including Malt Kiln Row and the Brook Houses cottages). In other parts of the village, the landscape has been altered drastically as a result of post-1945 open-cast-mining.

There seem to have been natural divisions within the village, people living in certain areas according to their occupations. The centre of the main village was inhabited chiefly by agricultural and estate-workers, while two large communities of miners were to be found at Collier Fold and Barnby Furnace. The eighteen weavers living in the village (most of them in the South Lane area) provide a reminder of the fame which Barnsley and district enjoyed for its linen and of the fact that the domestic weaving industry did not die away overnight with the advent of the factories and power-looms.

The 1870's saw the spread of a period of depression in agriculture, when the full blast of overseas competition was felt, as a result of the heavy fall in the freight rate of corn from Chicago to Liverpool. In many cases, this meant that the smaller farmers had to rely increasingly upon their secondary employment, since for many of them, farming alone had for a long time provided an insufficient living. Thus, we find the following listed in the 1871 census:-

"Walter Moxon – Butcher and Farmer of Clay Hall.

Joshua Charlesworth – Farmer and Gardener of Cawthorne Village.

Joseph Chappell – Farmer and Linen Weaver of Lane Head."

Even Joshua Kaye of Dean Hill with 90 acres to farm is listed as "Tanner and farmer".

The Toll Cottage by the village green where the Turnpike Road entered the village from Barnsley. The print is taken from a late 19th century Bamforth negative.

A dominant feature of Cawthorne was the Barnsley to Shepley Lane Head Turnpike road, which took all traffic from Barnsley to Huddersfield right through the centre of the village. The Trust which established this stretch of toll road was set up in 1825 and abolished in 1875. During its life-time it provided employment for three toll-bar keepers in the village, but must have been a somewhat costly restriction upon the activities of drovers bringing cattle and sheep to such markets as Penistone.

Farming, at this time, owed little to machines. It was labour-intensive and, in times of depression, this labour-force would look increasingly to the Estate for work and/or relief, as did the miners from the local collieries. An extract from Mrs. Stirling's ''Life's Little Day'' illustrates this:

> Both at Cannon Hall and Banks on Christmas Eve the dole was distributed to the poor, and at the latter place the butcher himself had to be in attendance to see that each joint of meat was of satisfactory weight and quality ere it was presented with kindly greeting by the Ladies themselves to each deserving recipient. During hard times the quantity was doubled or trebled. When the pits stopped work great distress prevailed in the surrounding districts, for the miner in prosperity was an improvident being, and made no provision for a rainy day. Yet he faced disaster with a stubborn courage and simple heroism which compelled admiration. One woman told me that her husband used, day after day, to go out early and walk round the country seeking work, and his breakfast of bread-and-butter was put on the table for him over-night. but it was never touched; and when, his children awoke they invariably found it divided in pieces and placed upon their pillows; their father had tramped off starving that his children might have more.

One astonishing fact, which a study of the places of birth shown on the census makes clear, is that, even at a time when travel was relatively slow and difficult, there was a considerable mobility of labour. It is mildly amusing to the writer, who was often told during the building boom of the late 1960's and early 1970's that there were too many 'comers-in' in Cawthorne, to find that, in 1871, the ancestors of those who told him so were themselves ''comers-in''. The Estate ensured mobility of labour since, when the head of the Stanhope family died, his own son often appointed a new land-agent, who in turn made his own

Dog Kennel Bar, one of Cawthorne's Toll Cottages. R.W.

time economic necessity). Cawthorne was, at this time, a village of small cottages and large families. Indeed one now wonders how such large family units fitted into such small spaces. It is easy to look at the cottages now that they have been modernised and damp-proofed and come up with a totally false impression of what housing conditions were like. Then they were cramped, damp and often smokey, with meat and oatcakes hanging from the rafters in the kitchen. Water was largely drawn from wells or centrally-placed supplies such as the Fountain – and diseases now largely eradicated were not uncommon. The health of his village flock was a constant preoccupation of Rev. Pratt as these extracts from his Parish Magazine show.

changes in the estate workforce (e.g. in 1911 Mr. Hugh Pardoe became agent and brought over from Horsforth with him several workmen whose families still live in the village). At Barnby Furnace in 1871 most of the miners who lived there were not Cawthorne-born and several came from North Wales, giving rise to speculation that, in what were the early days of the mining unions, they had perhaps been imported as "blackleg" labour to replace others involved in disputes with the colliery owners.

Old villagers often speak of sounds and smells as being especially evocative of the village as it was. Early in the morning came the sound of the miners' clogs on the dross roads as they walked to work at Barnby Furnace (or Stanhope Colliery as it was often known) or to Darton. In the daytime the sounds and smells were those of the horse and horse-drawn vehicles, while from the houses came the smells of baking and brewing (the passion for "home-brewing" being a modern revival of an old-

In August 1871 he was offering the title of a new medical book and health hints:

A most useful little book with the title 'Till the Doctor comes, may be obtained at the bookstore at Mrs. Balme's... Cleanliness, good ventilation in every room and a careful attention to the drainage – a bringing of common-sense to bear upon bad smells and stifling bedrooms with boarded-up fireplace – would save us from many an ailment".

By November 1877 he was praising the virtues of "permanganate of potash" in counter-acting scarlet-fever. "It will destroy all poisonous germs. Boiling water if really boiling will destroy them also. The floor should be mopped and the furniture dusted with cloths wrung out of this water. A packet of permanganate of potash can be had of any Druggist: a shilling packet will make about twenty gallons sufficiently strong to destroy all germs of disease."

In January 1884 he had this advice for waterproofing shoes:

"After the leather of a new sole has been worn for a day or two, let the sole be thoroughly dried at a careful distance from the fire. Then rub it over with Stockholm Tar before the fire, letting it soak well in... and then letting the soles get thoroughly hardened before being used... We have invested in a small stock of this Stockholm Tar, one half-pennyworth of which will suffice for several pairs of boots. Mrs Eliza Shaw will supply it in this quantity to those who send something to put it in".

An extract from June 1892 illustrates that the anti-smoking lobby is no new phenomenon: "Was the Chancellor of the Exchequer ever at Cawthorne? Why do we ask? Because he said in the House, 'Are young men taking earlier to smoking? I am afraid many of us in our villages see little urchins become taxpayers as regards tobacco at far too early an age'."

Cholera does not now hold any terrors for us in this country, but the horrors of the terrible cholera outbreaks of the first half of the 19th Century were very much in Charles Pratt's mind in March 1893 when he wrote the following: "A panic is surely a loud Providential call to fulfil neglected duties, whether the panic comes in sanitation or in religious, social, or political matters. Our own sanitary matters in this Parish are by no means what they ought to be from the point of either health or decency. Shall we need what we call a 'panic' before their improvement?"

Much is nowadays made of young people's complaints that they are "bored", but the same situation existed in our village in November 1896: "During these Winter months, fathers and mothers may very wisely give some thought how they can best provide some amusement for their children in their own homes... It may not be possible, perhaps, in every home to give a table to the little folks for their games, but it is surely possible to try and make the evening a pleasant, cheerful time to them, and give them a taste for innocent games and amusements and also for reading by providing some sensible Games and some Books that will interest them. It is no use telling children what they are 'not to do': they need telling what they are to do."

Lastly, in March 1899, the following suggestions were made for the general improvement of health in Cawthorne:

"It was stated by our Medical Officer of Health at a Government Inquiry held here some few years ago, that he considers that there is 'a low measure of vitality at Cawthorne, which makes it very ready in catching whatever disease there may happen to be going'... There must be some preventible causes, we feel sure, to account in a large measure for this want of rosy cheeks. We have our own very strong opinion what these causes are. Have the children the right kind of feeding, both when they are quite little ones, and also during their schooltime? Have they milk enough and oatmeal porridge? Have they good fresh air in their bedrooms? Are their bedrooms and bedclothes well ventilated in a morning? Are the girls always warmly clad enough with underclothing? It is chiefly the wrong dieting of children that makes them look so delicate. The teapot has a good deal to answer for, for the mischief it does to mothers as well as children."

Difficult travelling meant narrow horizons, Barnsley being to many of the older people of the village a different world. Their village world was a self-contained and a self-sufficient one. It had its own corn mill, and the tan-yards at Dean Hill and Cinder Hill used bark from Bark House Wood and other woods to produce leather for use by the village saddler and the shoemakers. It is perhaps surprising to children of the motor car age that a village of the size of Cawthorne could provide employment for nine shoemakers. It had its own carpenters, builders (or masons as they were usually called) and four tailors. The work of the blacksmith must have been vital to an agricultural community in the age of the horse and Cawthorne had eight blacksmiths in 1871. Shoeing, work on carts and cartwheels, the mending of agricultural implements, and the repair of metal household tools were all done at the smithy. In 1871 the Wilkinson family were the occupants of the forge in Tivydale, with Benjamin Wilkinson (Senior) as the blacksmith. Most of his sons followed in the trade and Benjamin (Junior) took over the smithy at Dakin Brook (long since closed). The tremendous variety of work done by the smith is well illustrated by an existing photograph of Benjamin Wilkinson (Junior) outside his smithy with cages made by him for Redbrook Colliery. The Wilkinsons ran the Tivydale Forge until the 1950's when the last of them, Philip Wilkinson, retired. The other main forge in the village was at Raw Green and was run in 1871 by George Wright, who features in some very atmospheric photographs.

Village "Characters" of 1871.

One of the common complaints which one hears nowadays is that "characters" are not as plentiful as they used to be. The word is used to mean someone who, by virtue of speech, service to the community, way of life, or simply departure from the common-place has become memorable in the community; a person recalled with pride, affection, and/or humour, and whose actions and sayings are always spoken of when people begin their reminiscences. It is not surprising that, in Victorian Cawthorne, long hours of hard work, none-too-generous rates of pay and spartan living conditions should produce an abundance of people who could be designated "characters". This was, after all, before "moving pictures" and television had made widely available standardised norms of behaviour for people to copy. Speech, dress and behaviour still often reflected individual character.

Sir Walter Spencer Stanhope – an excellent portrait photograph taken by Warner Gothard (probably to celebrate his knighthood). W.G.

At the highest level of village society were two whose characters had not been moulded by any of the afore-mentioned hardships, the Spencer Stanhope brothers. Colonel (later Sir) Walter Thomas William Spencer Stanhope (1827–1911) was the more serious of the two. As the elder brother, he succeeded to the family estates in 1873, to the running of which he applied himself with the same earnest diligence which he gave to all his other posts (e.g. magistrate, governor of local grammar schools, director of colliery companies and the Aire and Calder Navigation). Between 1872 and 1880 he was a Conservative M.P. under Disraeli and the spirit of social reform which led this government to transform English Society is to be seen throughout his stewardship of the Cannon Hall Estate for the rest of his life. In fact he made a point in his will of stressing that he had made no bequests, preferring instead to be benevolent throughout his lifetime. The truth of this can be seen in the provisions which he made for the village at his own expense in terms of education (land for the new school, plus regular financial assistance), village amenities (the Museum, the reading-room and the Victoria Institute) and religion (the renovation and extension of the Parish Church 1875–80 and the provision of land for the building of the Methodist Church).

For most of his life, he was a familiar figure in the village, and can be distinguished on photographs by the broad-brimmed, almost "cowboy"-style hat which he wore. He was for fifty years (1860–1910) churchwarden of the village church (of which he was also patron of the living), and was a regular lesson reader, dressed in surplice and M. A. hood.

John Roddam Spencer Stanhope (1829-1908 and usually known as "Roddam") showed his character when he chose the life of a painter in preference to that of a country gentleman. A pupil of G. F. Watts, he was equally at home in the country-house society of his family and the bohemian world of his fellow Pre-Raphaelite artists. He had a very distinctive style, renowned for his handling of colour and his specialising in subjects of a mythological or allegorical nature. Examples of his work can be found in the Library of the Oxford Union, the Chapel of Marlborough School and the Anglican Church in Florence.

His influence can be seen in the 1875-80 renovation of All Saints Church, Cawthorne, which he and his brother financed in memory of their parents, and it is his artistic tastes, as well as those of his chosen architects, Bodley and Garner, which are reflected by the finished building. In the church, he was directly responsible for the West Window ("Fides, Spes et Caritas"), which he designed, and the pulpit, which he painted. Also because of him, the church has a stained-glass window attributed to Burne-Jones, installed in the Spencer Stanhope Chapel as a memorial to Roddam's daughter, who died as a child in Florence, and two painted, Pre-Raphaelite panels done by his niece, Evelyn de Morgan, wife of the potter, William de Morgan. Roddam Stanhope had a tremendous sense of humour and, as his other niece, Mrs. Stirling, recalled in her book "A Painter of Dreams", he had an understanding with certain of his friends that, in whatever part of the world they might meet, they would greet one another in broad Yorkshire dialect. A lengthy account of the Cawthorne Harvest Thanksgiving Supper which was printed in the "Barnsley Chronicle" in September 1869 reported that "Mr. Roddam Stanhope... 'brought down the house' by narrating an imaginary conversation – we heard one good lady whisper to her companion that she did not believe a word of it – between himself and an aged male grouse on the moors." He lived at Hill House, which he remodelled into a gentleman's residence, and where part of the house (which is now sub-divided into a few dwellings) is still known as "The Studio". Asthma caused him to leave Cawthorne and the increasingly difficult climate of South Yorkshire in 1880 for a new, more healthy existence at the Villa Nuti in Florence, where he spent the rest of his life.

Perhaps it had something to do with the solitary nature of the job and the time which this gave for thought, but three of the most independent-minded villagers of Cawthorne in 1871 were shoemakers or cobblers. In the 1871 Census, John Blacker is listed as "Shoemaker, and Local Preacher (Wesleyan Reform)". In the latter capacity, he was responsible for "Blacker's Chapel", the Wesleyan Reform Chapel which occupied the premises in Malt Kiln Row, now, somewhat ironically, forming the "Top" or "Comrades" Club. Here the worship was much more congregation – centred and uninhibited than was the case in the Methodist Church in Darton Road. As his granddaughter said to me, "We were a noisy lot, but we enjoyed our religion". [9] An old villager, recorded in the late 1970's, had this to say about "Blacker's Chapel" around 1907: "That was a

Roddam Spencer Stanhope in old age (taken between 1904 and 1908). This portrait photograph was the work of Lizzie Caswall Smith, a successful portrait photographer in London's Oxford Street from c. 1895 to 1910. She occupied the Gainsborough Studio at 309, Oxford Street, where this photograph was taken, from 1904 to 1910.

Hill House, the home of Roddam Spencer Stanhope.   N.F.M.

real exciting place where people jumped up and shouted things. We liked it if we could get there, because they did odd things... My father didn't like our going about from place to place for religion, but we always used to have a tale for him. My brother used to say "Father, there is a very good man coming to the

The Church pulpit with panels painted by Rodddam Stanhope.   G.B.J.

The West window showing his Pre-Raphaelite version of "Fides, Spes et Caritas" (Faith, Hope and Charity).   G.B.J.

"The Charcoal Thieves" painted by Roddam Stanhope during his time in Italy (Reproduced by Courtesy of the De Morgan Foundation).   G.B.J.

John Blacker and some of his workforce outside his workshop.

Blacker's Chapel. He is converting people and making them better. Can we go?" My father would reply "If anything can make you better, it would be a good thing..." We really had fun. Our shoulders would heave as we tried to suppress our laughter... They once had a coloured man preaching there". [10]

As a shoemaker, John Blacker built up a village industry down in Tivydale, the size of which it is hard for many of us now to imagine. The shop had many windows, there being a window for each work bench. At its busiest, the concern employed four or five male members of the family, another man, a boy apprentice and the daughters of the family. In the back shop, the girls made the boot tops, which came into the front shop for putting onto the soles, stitching, eyelet-fixing, buttoning etc. Dominating the front shop was a large foot-operated press for stamping out leather soles. The business had a pony and cart and drew its custom from a wide radius. There were definite days of the week for collecting orders and returning the finished products to places as dispersed as Wombwell, Darfield, Jump, Elsecar, Barugh and Mapplewell. Nor were specialised orders turned away. They did a good trade in surgical boots, and fitted special soles for a Silkstone man who indulged in a bit of poaching! [9]

John Blacker's house, showing the workshop to the left. (This photograph is reproduced by the kind permission of its owner, Ian Wilson).

Part of Malt Kiln Row c.1900. The wooden porch of Blacker's Chapel can be seen in the centre of the photograph, while extreme left is the sign of the tea-room, run by Edwin Lisle, John Blacker's son-in-law.

THE CAWTHORNE OF REV. CHARLES T. PRATT (1866-1915)

Henry Alfred Puddephatt and his wife.

Richard Charlesworth in middle life.

Henry Alfred Puddephatt (1819-1803) was born at Great Yarmouth and came to Cawthorne when his father came to be the gauger or exciseman at Mr. West's Malt-kilns at the top of Taylor Hill, the family moving house from East Anglia to Cawthorne completely by barge along the canal system. In 1871, he lived in Darton Road at the end of Collier Fold and followed the trade of cobbler. However, the ram-rod straight back, the stern look and the smartness of his bearing (all of which can be seen in his photograph) bear testimony to the years which he had spent in the Metropolitan Police Force, as did his fetish for punctuality. His daily routine movements were so regular that it is said that some of the villagers set their clocks by them. The life of a cobbler suited his independent spirit and it is said that he did not repair the shoes of people he did not like, and "if anyone dared to bring him a pair of boots which were dirty, he would fling them back at them." Of his eight children, one son went to Australia, and three other sons went in 1880 to Pine Bluff, Arkansas, U.S.A., where they eventually founded a large furniture store. In 1910, in a letter to his brother in Cawthorne, one of them wrote that what he missed most about Cawthorne, and longed for, was a glass of cool, clear spring water from the Quarry Well. [19]

In 1871, Richard Charlesworth is listed as a shoemaker, but a glance at his account-books, which are preserved in the village museum, shows that he was well on the way to becoming the general dealer of the village. Older people still talk of his shop at the top of Taylor Hill with affection and speak of the sense of wonder which a visit to it could bring to the young mind. It was one of those shops reminiscent of an "Aladdin's Cave", where everything possibly needed in the village was kept in stock. In the 1862 account-book we find the following:

Fiddle strings	–	1s
Pair of new boots	–	14s
Pump leather	–	6d
3 stones of flour	–	7s
3 lbs lard	–	2s 3d
2 lbs sugar	–	1s
5½ lbs cheese	–	4s 1½d
Ham 19½ lbs	–	19s 6d

He could arrange for the delivery of a load of coal at a cost of 1s 11½d! Richard Charlesworth subsequently took over as postmaster and an example of the service which he ran can be seen from the following jotting from Rev. Pratt's Parish Magazine:

47

Our Post Office

On April 1st, a change is made in our Postal arrangements. They are now as follows: Mail cart arrives 7.20 am; Letterbox closes at 5.55 pm; Parcels received up to 5.30 pm. Telegraph open 8 am to 8 pm; on Sundays, from 8 to 10 am. Post Office Orders and Postal Orders from 9 am to 6 pm; on Saturdays till 8. It is convenient that letters be posted before 5.45 pm, and Postal Orders, etc., cannot be attended to whilst the Bag is being made up for the Mail Cart at 6.

April 1885

A further entry in November 1883 records that flowers and produce from the Village Harvest Thanksgiving Service could be despatched from Cawthorne one day and arrive in good condition at a London Children's Hospital the following day to be enjoyed by the patients!

> The Bouquets collected at the Children's Flower Service on the 9th were sent the same evening in six hampers to four different London Hospitals, and were received the next day about noon 'fresh and beautiful'. As one of the letters of acknowledgment expresses it, "The patients appreciate them very much and they add greatly to the bright and cheerful aspect of the Wards." Another says, "They arrived safely at 12.30 on Monday, and were at once taken to the Wards, much to the delight of the little ones."

Richard Charlesworth and his wife Emma are chiefly remembered as pillars of the Wesleyan Chapel. The story of how they raised the money for the building of the present Methodist Church in Darton Road is told in the following extract from a Methodist newspaper of 1899:

In her Majesty's Service.
What a Village Postmaster did with a Dream
By John Cleeve

CAWTHORNE is a pleasant village not far from Barnsley, but, Methodistically, in the Denby Dale circuit. Our 'leading man' is the village postmaster, an interesting character, and one of the quiet heroes of whom there are many in the churches, and most of whom die unsung. Around his name centres the story of the building of a chapel, and it is this story that, briefly as may be, I wish to tell.

Until three years ago, Cawthorne could boast no proper chapel. For more than two generations services were held in a room made by uniting two cottages. All the land in the neighbourhood belongs to Colonel Spencer Stanhope, C.B., who has shown unfailing kindness

Richard Charlesworth's shop & post office, with his house, Holly Cottage adjoining.

to all his tenants and not least to those of them who are of the people called Methodists. The cottages were his, and to 'ask for more' might be to presume too much. Their hesitation does them credit, but at last they were obliged to seek a further grant of land to enable them to complete the comfort of their little meeting-room; in very wet weather, when the heating apparatus was used, the devoted old chapel-keeper had to wade through water to get to the furnace!

The first proposal was to adopt a new method of heating, and, at the same time, to erect a small vestry. A friend from a distance, discussing the situation, and seeing it as, perhaps, only an outsider could, declared that they ought to 'arise and build' a chapel. To the men on the ground this was a dream at first, but dreams, like prophecies, have a way of passing into fulfilment, and, in this case, that which at first seemed impossible, by and by took on a soberer hue. The first native who looked at the vision valiantly was my friend the village postmaster. It was a dream, but it was more. Mr. Charlesworth – for that is his name – found himself at Cannon Hall boldly asking Colonel Stanhope for land whereon to rear a Methodist chapel. And he came away with permission to measure out a piece of ground!

Listening to the story from his own lips, I was charmed and astonished at my friend's splendid audacity. But I remembered the story of his father's life, which I had chanced to hear that day, and I began to understand. This man, it was good to see, would not lay himself under obligation to any man for selfish, personal reasons, but he was ready to do a daring thing for the church that he loved. His faith was honoured on earth, as we may believe such faith is always honoured in heaven. It was a happy coincidence, and it assisted the progress of things, that just then the late Mr. John Dyson, of

The official opening of the Chapel.

Thurgoland, went to preach at Cawthorne, and was invited to Cannon Hall.

Soon it was clear that not only did Colonel Stanhope, but also his son and daughter-in-law, Mr. and Mrs. J. Montagu Spencer Stanhope, look with no unfriendly eye upon the aspirations of the Methodist people of their village.

The recital of the story had proceeded thus far, and I was thinking it over in the little parlour at the post-office, when my friend, who had withdrawn a few moments earlier, returned with a queer look on his face, to say, "We shall catch it if we don't come to us dinners." The young minister of the circuit, the Rev. David Rycroft, was with me. We had seen the 'Missis', and the fear of 'catching it' did not alarm us, but we hastened to 'us dinners,' for we had come from far.

The remainder of the story came afterwards. Now that the land seemed secure, what about the money – £1,200 or £1,600 – for the structure? Mr. Charlesworth thought again. The dream had not died with the opening day. Yes, one of the best friends of Methodism that he knew outside the village was Mr. Kenfield. He had helped the Cawthorne Methodists in many little ways. Would he in this great matter give them a start? This 'stranger,' who came on business once a month, called soon afterwards, and listened patiently to the appeal. His prompt reply was, "I will give a hundred pounds, if you will give a hundred pounds." The men gazed at each other across the counter.

That night uneasy lay the head of the village postmaster. He wore no crown, but in his dreams a bag of gold, a hundred bright sovereigns, hung suspended about his head; only not on a precarious hair, but on a springing elastic band that threatened to rebound too high unless weighted with another bulk of gold.

"I had never lain in bed before without going to sleep, but that night I did roll about, and it is a rare big bed! I could not see how we were to get a hundred pounds. But my wife said she would help, and in a bit it was settled, and after that I fell asleep."

That month, till Mr. Kenfield came again, passed slowly. After business, this was the conversation:

"You know what you said?"

"No. What do you mean?"

"About that hundred pounds."

"Oh, that was a bit of a nonsense. What would my family say? Still, if you are serious, I will give you twenty-five pounds."

Let it count to the credit of the Methodists postmaster that it never occurred to him that here was a chance of withdrawing from his own self-sacrificing intention. It was the chapel he was thinking about, not his balance at the bank. Mr. Kenfield spoke again:

"Well, I cannot stop bothering here; I want to be going. If you can find two more to give you £100, I will do in earnest what I really said in a joke."

The very next Sunday was propitious. A local preacher, Mr. John Townsend, was planned at Cawthorne, of which village he was a native. It was not Mr. Charlesworth's turn to entertain the preacher, but he 'borrowed' him that night.

First he and his hospitable wife gave the preacher the best supper they could have set before a king. Then:

"Mr Townsend, let me congratulate you. I hear they have made you a magistrate."

"Yes, Mr. Charlesworth."

"Praise the Lord. I hope you'll have strength and wisdom to

49

perform the duties of the office in accordance with the teaching of the Bible.''

"Thank you."

"I never heard you preach better than you did today. The Lord gave you those two texts."

"What makes you say so?"

"Well this afternoon you said we were to 'consider.'"

"Yes, 'Consider the lillies of the field, how they grow' – they are the Master's words."

"Well, we have something to 'consider' here at Cawthorne, I can tell you."

Then the postal official unfolded his project.

"At night you said, 'Whatsoever thy hand findeth to do, do it with thy might.' We folk at Cawthorne have gotten something to do 'at after we have 'considered' it.''

A pause in the talk, and then this from the visitor:

"Well, you shall not be fast, I will give you £100."

With even more enthusiasm than had marked certain of the earlier points of the story, the postmaster exclaimed in the cosy little room where the telegraph instrument stands, "I said to him again, 'Praise the Lord' – I could not help it. Then I scoured the country for the other £100, and with Mr. Kenfield's consent, I got it in parts instead of in one lump sum."

The two men were ready for one another when they met again.

"I reckon you want my cheque. I borrowed a blank one as I came along," saying which Mr. Kenfield took up a pen and filled it in. Handing the cheque to the beaming Methodist trustee, this generous man observed, "Put it in the bank; it will make you a bit of interest."

In due time all the money was raised. Colonel Stanhope, in addition to the gift of land, contributed £50, and his son £25; and from far and near the itinerant and well-worn "treasurer's book" gathered promises of help. It did its work in the usual three years' term. The postmaster's ingenuity, backed by his standing with the people, devised means also by which the trustees were saved the expenditure of a penny as interest on borrowed money. Of course there was a little harvest at the stone-laying ceremony, and at the opening services, and at the inevitable bazaar, but the substantial means of income was the careful and persistent circulation of the subscription list.

What has become of the old chapel? Through the influence of the honoured local family already referred to – and whose members, if any of them should chance to see this little sketch, will forgive these respectful and grateful references – it has been transformed into the Victoria Cottage Institute. One of the ladies was good enough to say that, seeing such good work had been done within the walls in past

The chapel that the Charlesworths built.   R.W.

days, good work, if of another kind, should continue to be done there. The building was opened by the Lord Bishop of Wakefield, who spoke to a similar effect.

You may visit the old and the new in five minutes: only the highway divides them. As I looked round the little hospital and talked with the nurse, I noticed a portrait of Peter Mackenzie, and before I could ask how it came to be there Nurse Nightingale had explained, "Mr. Mackenzie was my spiritual father; his photograph is worth exhibiting." It is a model chapel and school within and without. Over the entrance there is a statuette of John Wesley, executed by Samuel Swift, a clever sculptor, who volunteered to make this gift to the little Methodist chapel in his native village; and completing the appointments, an organ was put into the building quite recently. At last the postmaster is content, and if you would increase his satisfaction, you cannot do better than pray for the spiritual prosperity of the pretty place of worship which fulfils his dreams –

"Oft as they meet for worship here, God send His people peace."

The man who knows that God is with him is always a strong man.

Whilst, as the article says "not only did Colonel Stanhope, but also his son and daughter-in-law ... look with no unfriendly eye upon the aspirations of the Methodist people of their village", the same could not really be said of Rev. Charles Pratt who wrote as follows in October 1896:

A Letter

The following letter may probably be interesting to some of our readers:

"My dear –, you asked me the other day what I thought of the new Chapel that is being built here. I replied that, if there are Christian people among us who cannot for some reason or other worship with us in our Church's Services, it is at all events well that they should wish to have as seemly a building as they can to worship God and hold their meetings in.

But what you really meant was, I dare say, not what I thought of the building itself, but of the religious denomination to which it belongs. And I quite allow that you have a right to know what I think about our religious divisions.

In the first place, I quote some words from the Archbishop of Canterbury's recent Pastoral Letter, dated Aug. 30th. He says: "We know that our divisons are a chief obstacle to the progress of Christ's Gospel." We cannot but feel what a happy and blessed thing it would be, if all who believe in our Lord Jesus Christ could be of one heart and mind and worship Him together in spirit and in truth. This is what we should all hope and pray for.

As regards the Methodists, I always feel that they can only justify their separation from the Church by renouncing the most cherished principles of that good devoted servant of our Lord by whose name they call themselves. John Wesley, as you know, was a clergyman of our Church, as his father and brother Charles were, and never intended that those who were called Methodists should ever separate from it. He died March 2nd, 1791: the separation began in August, 1795. He regarded it as the great work God had given him to do, to establish an order of lay preachers in our Church. In a sermon he preached and printed within a year of his death, he says: "The Methodists are not a sect or party. They do not separate from the Religious Community to which they at first belonged. They are still members of the Church: such they desire to live and die. And I believe, one reason why God is pleased to continue my life so long is to confirm them in their present purpose not to separate them from the Church. I hold all the doctrines of the Church of England. I love her Liturgy. I dare not separate from the Church; I believe it would be a sin so to do. Ye yourselves were at first called in the Church of England: and, though ye have and will have a thousand temptations to leave it, and set up for yourselves, regard them not. Be Church of England men still." In 1790: "I never had any design of separating from the Church; I have no such design now. I declare once more, that I live and die a member of the Church of England, and that those who regard my judgment or advice will never separate from it." In 1772: "Our rule is, that, if any man separate from the Church, he is no longer a member of our Society." In 1785: "We do not, we will not, form a separate sect, but from principle remain what we have always been – true members of the Church of England."

I only quote these words to shew that what is now so generally called "Wesleyanism" was never intended to be what it is now become.

It is the bounden duty of us all to have no other but kindly feelings towards those who differ from us. The mind of our Blessed Lord on Christian unity is very distinctly revealed in the xvii ch. of St. John; the mind of St. Paul is clearly given us in such passages as 1 Cor.-J., 12, etc. We are each responsible to God for our religious faith and practice; and every true-hearted member of our Church must surely pray for God's blessing upon those who do not now worship with us, and that God will in His own good time and way heal all our religious divisons and separations and make us of one heart and mind within the fold of His Holy Church. Let us do all we can in Christian courtesy, kindness, sympathy, and love, to hasten that outward and visible unity. This we can all of us do, and ought to do, without in any way allowing it to be supposed for one moment that we "see no difference between Church and Chapel".

Many of the villagers did not share this view and their attendance at a variety of forms of religious worship seems to have more in common with the present-day ecumenical movement. A strain of Nonconformity had existed for a long time in Cawthorne as extracts from Oliver Heywood's diary show:

"1672. On Tuesday I went to Cawthorne, lodged with Will Roebuck, called of Mr. Thorp as I went on Wednesday."

"May 23rd and 24th 1679... went to Will Roebuck's, lodged there, God made me of some use... Nath Bottomley, Will Roebuck and I spent some time in prayer in the chamber about some solemne business and church, God wonderfully helpt."

One of the earliest Methodists must have been Richard Charlesworth's father, Joshua, who was born in 1805, the year of Nelson's victory at Trafalgar, and as a child was taken by his mother to services in a cottage given to the Methodists by Mr. Beatson of Cinderhill. This and the adjoining cottage were eventually united to form the chapel with accommodation for 120, which his son Richard's chapel was to replace. Joshua, who farmed at Hill Top, was a strict teetotaller who, in his 96th year, was taken ill, shortly after mowing the grass in his orchard. When offered brandy, he is reputed to have refused saying that, if he were to recover, he did not want the Devil to have any part in that recovery. When Joshua died, Charles Pratt entered this in his Parish Magazine:

> It is very seldom indeed that we have had to enter such an age as '95' in our Burial Register. In the present instance, it is after the name of one who had the great respect of us all, and will be much missed from his place at our Sunday morning services.

July 1901

Joshua Charlesworth dressed up – for church?

Joshua Charlesworth, his wife and daughter photographed outside their farmhouse in the 1880's.

The "farmhouse" as it is today: the home of the agent for the Cannon Hall Estate.

From this we gather that Joshua the Methodist attended Anglican services. This puzzled me, plus the fact that the names of the children of supposed Anglican families appeared in the prize winners lists at the Methodist Sunday School in the 1880's (and for that matter, some Anglicans still go to the Chapel Sunday School in the 1990's!) My puzzle was recently solved, however, by an old Cawthorner, who was born in 1903 and told me that the practice was yet another by-product of the feudal state of the village. "My mother told me", he said, "that Sir Walter went to Church on Sunday morning, and so they went to Church in the morning for the sake of their pockets, and Chapel at night for the sake of their souls!" [11]

After the opening of the Methodist Chapel in 1895, Richard and Emma Charlesworth spent the rest of their lives running it. It possessed a large Sunday School and extracts from the lists of prizes given to scholars throw an interesting sidelight on the heyday of late-Victorian Methodism. In addition to Bibles and Hymn Books, one finds such titles as "Beware of Idle Words", "The Hidden Talent", "Dialogue on the Need of Prayer". "The Irish Boy and the Priest," and "Every Cloud has a Silver Lining." Perhaps the most intriguing entry is the last one in the book, which shows Richard Charlesworth as a strong disciplinarian and the children of a century ago as being just as capable of mischief as their present-day counterparts. The entry simply says "Alfred Burgon, Wm. Fox, Edwin Jubb, Geo. Wm. Booth run out of Chapel." What provoked this we can only leave to the imagination.

THE CAWTHORNE OF REV. CHARLES T. PRATT (1866-1915)

Richard and Emma Charlesworth at their Diamond Wedding. Photograph by Rowland Wilkinson.

Even as shopkeepers, Richard and Emma Charlesworth stuck to their principles. One thing which they hated was smoking and anyone daring to do so in their shop came in for strong criticism and was probably not served. Similarly, workmen purchasing matches had not to let it be known that they were to be used for smoking. Their Christian charity, however, always triumphed when anyone needed a helping hand, and it is interesting to note in the account book that, in spite of the difference in their life-styles, when he was short of money, John Harrison (of whom more details come later) could always borrow from Richard Charlesworth.

Some village characters acquired their reputations as a result of the way in which they helped to correct a deficiency in the Cawthorne of 1871. At that time, the village had no lawyer and no doctor. William Moxon was Richard Charlesworth's predecessor as the village postmaster, but had before that been for a number of years the Schoolmaster at the Boys' School (now the Parish Room). However, his six weeks' training at college at York had been adjudged to be insufficient qualification and he had lost the job. He continued to help his successor by always being available to solve mathematical problems which defeated the better qualified man, but, in addition to his work as postmaster, he helped make up for the absence of a lawyer by doing such jobs as proving wills.

Also in 1871, John Fretwell was a young miner. He lived near his work at Barnby Furnace, but was later to move to a very old and distinctive cruck-framed cottage in Darton Road, where he

Joshua Charlesworth still harvesting at a very advanced age.

53

John Fretwell. The pencil drawing dated 1/4/1915 was done by a refugee living in Cawthorne, who worked under the name of Louis Stas. It was given to Cawthorne Museum by John Fretwell's grandson Wilfred Holroyd.

spent the rest of his life. In common with many of his contemporaries, at a time when the services of a doctor were hard to obtain and often costly, he acquired a very sound knowledge of herbs and natural remedies. Even when he was a very old man, anyone visiting him and daring to say that they were not feeling well was likely to be handed a handful of dried herbs with the instruction to "scald them with boiling water. Then, when it cools, drink the liquid and it will see you right". He was typical of the group of men of the village, who by their interests and collecting hobbies, were responsible for the foundation of the Village Museum Society. Although unable to write, he became a very enthusiastic and knowledgeable naturalist and was a founder committee member of the Museum.

He was a bee-keeper, and along with another villager, he annually had his bees transported to Board Hill, not far from the Woodhead Tunnel, to feed on the heather for the summer. One villager remembers going with her father and the two owners to fetch bees back by horse and cart. The return journey was punctuated by frequent stops at local hostelries for liquid refreshment, so that the final safe return to Cawthorne owed more to the homing instincts of the horse than it did to the skill and direction of the driver! [12]

When John Fretwell died in 1933, the following letter was sent to a local newspaper by Miss Winifred Pratt:

Cawthorne Memories

Sir – In the Cawthorne Parish Magazine is a notice of the funeral, on August 29th of John Fretwell, aged 84 years.

Those who remember the beginnings of the Cawthorne Museum will know that John Fretwell's collection of 'upwards of one hundred species of butterflies' was mentioned in the 'Barnsley Chronicle' report of the Museum opening in 1889.

Tales used to be told of his enthusiasm when he found a specimen he had not known before – how he flung his hat in the air in Sherwood Forest, shouting: "Isn't this worth more than three weeks at Blackpool."

His fellow miners told how every bird, insect or flower was noticed by him on the way to and from the pit where he had worked since early years, and in any natural history discussion, John Fretwell's intimate knowledge of birds and beasts was to be relied on to settle the disputed point.

He was also full of the old knowledge of the uses of herbs and in my recollection of the Cawthorne Flower Show his tray of herbs never failed to gain the first prize.

Such men are rare, and do honour to their village, and I should wish his grave to be known as that of John Fretwell the Naturalist – yours etc.

WINIFRED M. PRATT

(Formerly of Cawthorne Vicarage), Avondale Kings Road, Cheltenham, Glos.

Above: The cruck-framed cottage in Darton Road where John Fretwell lived. It would now have been a prime target for architectural preservation. N. F. M.

One great deficiency not only in Cawthorne, but in Britain generally pre-1908, was the lack of adequate provision of pensions for the elderly and the widowed. Some who had worked for a benevolent employer might be lucky enough to receive an annual sum plus accommodation, and one such person was Mary ('Polly') Fishburn (sometimes written as 'Fishbourne'), who, in 1871 lived at Norcroft and described herself as "Annuitant and cowkeeper'. Born at Woolley, she had worked on the estate of Coke of Holkham, later Earl of Leicester, who was the father-in-law of John Spencer Stanhope. Descriptions of her show a remarkable character, who would perhaps not have been out of place in the American Wild West of such as Annie Oakley.

> In his *Fifty Years of my Life,* Lord Albermarle speaks of 'Polly Fishbourne' as one of the gamekeepers at Holkham (Lord Leicester's) and Keeper of the Church Lodge. He adds, "She must be about my own age. She had large black eyes, red cheeks, and white teeth; her hair was cropped like a man's, and she wore a man's hat. The rest of her attire was feminine. She was irreproachable in conduct, and indeed somewhat of a prude. Polly was the terror of poachers, with whom she had frequent encounters, and would give and take hard knocks; but generally she succeeded in capturing her opponents and making them answer for their misdeeds at Petty Sessions. A Norfolk game-preserver once offered Polly a shilling a-piece for a hundred pheasant eggs. She nodded her head. Soon after she brought Mr. Coke (afterwards created Earl of Leicester) a five pound note. 'There, Squire,' said she, 'is the price of a hundred of your guinea-fowl eggs.' Of course the Squire made Polly keep the five pound note. One time I was staying at Holkham, a bull killed a labouring man in the salt marshes. The savage brute was standing over his victim, and a crowd was assembled at the gate, when Polly appeared at the opposite gate. There was a cry, 'Get out of my way, Polly, or the bull will kill you.' 'Not he,' was the reply, 'he knows better.' She was right. The moment he saw her he backed astern to the remotest corner of the enclosure. It turned out that the animal had once attempted to run at her, but she had lodged a charge of small shot in his muzzle. (Vol. II., pp. 232,3). Neither her fine looks of manly womanhood nor her anecdotes of Holkham and her own former powers with dogs and guns will soon be forgotten by those who knew her. She died at Norcroft in 1873, aged 80.

In 1871, Cawthorne had a variety of widows (aged 40 to 77), who were forced to provide for their families as milliners, dressmakers, laundresses, charwomen and even garden-labourers.

Mrs. Clegg in her garden.   S. S.

In addition to these jobs there were opportunities for employment in areas such as agriculture and the brickyard, areas which (with the exception of the periods of the two World Wars) subsequently passed out of the employment orbit of womankind, until the days of the Sex Discrimination Act. In the Housekeeper's accounts for Cannon Hall can be found numerous payments to Mrs. Elizabeth Clegg for mending linen, and, if her photograph is to be believed, she seems to have been a happy, well-cared-for person. In talking to older members of the village, who were members of families of ten and eleven brought up by a widowed mother, I have been struck by the apparent happiness of their childhoods. Indeed, they seem to have enjoyed a greater sense of stability and childhood security than is sometimes enjoyed by some present-day children with two working parents. One cannot, however, but wonder how these Victorian widows managed? In seeking the answer, I have found that they enjoyed two strong sources of support. Firstly, the family unit was important. Living in a small community in which families were intermarried meant that there were Aunts, Uncles and Grandparents who could help. The family pulled together, members helping each other, sharing the work and the enjoyments of family life. Secondly, many of the widows seem to have been sustained by a religious background and strong faith. Worship was a family affair and an important factor in keeping families together.

One commodity of which there was no shortage at all was alcoholic beverage. In addition to 'home brew', Cawthorne had

173. Badsworth Hounds At Cawthorne, March 14th, 1910.

The Spencer Arms, which was under the Wilcock family from the 1820's to c.1900, has played a central role in village life as headquarters of the Enclosure Commissioners, meeting place of the Friendly Societies, venue for the Rent Dinners . . .

headquarters of the Village Band . . .

three licensed drinking-places in the centre of the village: 'The Spencer Arms', 'The Golden Cross' and 'The White Hart'; plus 'The Jolly Sailor' at Barnby Basin, which catered for the canal trade and the miners of Barnby Furnace (or Stanhope) Colliery, and 'The Farmers' Arms', which served the passing agricultural trade in the lanes between Cawthorne and Penistone. Other drinking-establishments had opened and closed again over the years within the village. Such availability of drink at low prices, coupled with long opening hours (later to be severely restricted by the Defence of the Realm Act of the First World War) resulted in a good deal of drunken behaviour, which was frequently the subject of public condemnation by Charles Pratt, who was a strong supporter of the Temperance Movement:

...back-drop for countless photographs, and its Coach House (seen to the right of the newly-refurbished Spencer Arms) served as both Band Room and Home Guard H.Q.

The Report of the Select Committee of the House of Lords on Intemperance has recently been made public, and will doubtless be the groundwork of some further legislation on the subject. It is stated, that, whilst the population has increased by 4,000,000 since 1869, the number of drinking places has on the whole diminished. There is still one, however, to every 238 of the present population! The consumption of alcoholic liquors was 52 per cent. more in 1876 than in 1860. The actual expenditure is estimated at rather less than 3d. per head per day. Since 1860, the consumption of wine has increased 143 per cent., spirits 36½, malt liquors 38: of tea 67, of sugar 146. The growth of expenditure in alcoholic liquors is only part of the general advance in expenditure due to increased prosperity.

The convictions for drunkenness were in 1860, 88,361: in 1876, 203,789.

The Committee strongly recommends what is called the Gothenburg system, by which the local authorities have a monopoly and those employed by them no personal interest in the sale of liquors. They propose that all licensed houses should open at 7am and close at 9 in rural districts: that they should open on Sundays for two hours in the afternoon for consumption off the premises, and from 7 to 9pm. On a canvas being recently taken by paper in 201 Towns, no less than 443,406 householders voted for complete Sunday closing; 56,173 against it; 32,100 neutral. In Manchester and Liverpool there were 5 to 1 against opening.

We will only add for ourselves, that, after seeing what is meant by 'Saturday night closing-time' in our own village, on March 29th, we can hope more than ever for some means of saving the slaves of drink from its terrible bondage.

June 1879

Particular times of the year seem to have been associated with excess drinking, notably Cawthorne Feast, Haymaking and Harvest-time; the latter especially being associated with extra drinking because of the habit of some farmers of brewing their own beer and including it as part of the wages of extra hands recruited to help at these busy times. I have heard it said that Edward Lawson, who farmed Cinder Hill Farm, never had any trouble obtaining extra labour to get his harvest in because the men of the village thought that he brewed the best beer to be found in Cawthorne! In 1876, however the Vicar had his own ideas about how the raging thirsts experienced at work and play should be relieved:

Haymaking and Beer.

Everybody allows that haymaking is very hot and thirsty work and one which requires a good deal of moistening by a drink of some kind: the heat drains the body of its moisture, and there is said to be a dust arising from the hay itself which has an irritating effect upon the

A Cawthorne Inn of which Rev. C. T. Pratt, no doubt, approved. The Temperance Inn run by the Parkinson family in Darton Road.   R. W.

throat and makes it specially dry. We wish that farmers generally would give their haymakers the choice of a fair amount more pay and no beer, instead of their having in reality to "drink out" part of their day's earning in beer, whether they prefer it or not. Some few might prefer providing their own drinking: and to others, farmers might give the choice of some such refreshing drink as cold tea or ginger-beer. In the long run these would be found to allay the thirst better than beer, without producing the same heat and feverishness. We have had strongly recommended "Hedges' Ginger Beer Powder" which, with very little trouble indeed, makes 2 gallons of very refreshing beer. It is sold at the Shops in 3d. Packets. At all events, let haymakers be offered something else as well as beer to "sleck" their thirst with, and many of them will be thankful to the farmers for their trouble, and farmers themselves will – to say the least – have no reason to regret it.

June 1876

Thirsty work, this harvesting!

These two photographs remind us that agricultural work was no less strenuous nor thirst-provoking when they were taken shortly after World War Two. They are also a reminder of the part played years ago by the scythe at harvest-time. The father of Mr. James Holroyd (who is extreme left, right hand picture) died in 1903 after severing an artery with his scythe while climbing a stile: an agricultural implement to treat with care and respect.   N.F.M.

Feast Time.

Cawthorne people do not need their Parish Magazine to tell them that Sunday the 16th is what is called "Feast Sunday" here. We heartily hope the weather may prove favourable for the Monday and Tuesday's Cricket Matches, as there are few prettier and happier sights of the kind to be seen, than people taking their amusement cheerfully, sensibly, soberly, and innocently, around our pretty Cricket ground. If there are some who feel that cricket-watching, like haymaking, has an irritating effect on the throat, we recommend them to study what we have said on page 2.

June 1876

Above: Cawthorne Feast revelry early 20th Century. The "Lads" of the Village about to leave the Golden Cross Yard for a donkey ride – but one wonders how John Harrison would remain in the saddle once Jos Broadhead rode away? Mick Glennon is on the right hand donkey. Bandsman extreme left is Billy Machen. R. W.

One village "character" spoken of by Old Cawthorners as being synonymous with excess drinking was John Harrison. He made his living from a variety of jobs to do with carpentry (e.g. odd-jobbing repair work and funeral work, in which latter capacity of undertaker he was responsible for the funeral of the artist Abel Hold). He often got drunk and, before this rendered him incapable, he could turn awkward, as shown by newspaper cuttings telling of court appearances resulting from his refusal to leave "The Golden Cross". One Cawthorne resident told me in the mid-1970's that, as a young boy early in the present century, he made many a penny by supporting a drunken John Harrison the twenty-odd yards from "The Golden Cross" to his cottage at the top of Taylor Hill. "We weren't very strong and if he tumbled down, we went down with him." [13] Such behaviour naturally brought him into conflict with the temperate Charles Pratt, and two stories which have been passed down are as follows:

(a) Seeing John Harrison staggering home, Rev. Pratt took the opportunity to lecture him on the virtues of water as a drink. He finished his impromptu sermon by pointing out the wonders and power of the steam engine, adding, "You see how strong water is, John. Why don't you drink it?" The surprise on his face must have been worth seeing when the reply came back, "Nay, Vicar! Yon beer's strong enough for me"!

How did John Harrison, at the end of his life, manage to obtain a ride in the back of this 1907 Sunbeam?

59

(b) On another occasion as John progressed unsteadily through the village, Mr. Pratt said to him,"Oh dear, John! You are going to the Devil,'' only to be told, ''You're wrong, Vicar. I'm going to mend Mattie Batty's mangle.'' [7]

This review of village characters of 1871, began with the Spencer Stanhopes and it is, perhaps appropriate, that it should end with the man who was the link between them and their village tenants. Charles Wemyss succeeded his uncle as steward (a title later changed to ''agent'') of the Cannon Hall and Horsforth estates in 1852 at the age of only eighteen and continued to serve the Spencer Stanhope family in that capacity until his death during the influenza epidemic of 1900. His job would have been onerous in so far as he had to supervise a considerable estate workforce, now long-since disbanded, and to deal with a large acreage of land and the property which stood on it. Many of the old inhabitants speak of the days of former agents as if they were part of a ''golden age'', when criticism of the Spencer Stanhopes was never dreamed of. Perhaps what they mean is that criticism was not quite so open and so loud. Miss Alice Moxon, a life-long Cawthorner, who became a Headmistress, once said to me, ''It was a very paternalistic set-up under the Stanhopes... but villagers never said what they really thought. They always felt that they had to keep on the right side of the powers-that-be... Even now, the old people don't say anything and then, when they get outside, they say to me ''Why did you let them get away with that?' '' [10] One well-known local Socialist and rebel, J. W. ''Mick'' Glennon was a vociferous critic in the 1920's, when the agent was Mr. Hugh Pardoe, and is reputed to have coined the phrase that ''the trouble with Cawthorne is that it is Squired, Parsoned and Pardoed''. Nevertheless, when ''Mick'' Glennon lost his job elsewhere, it was Mr Pardoe who found him employment with the Estate! Nowadays, the agent for the Cannon Hall Estate probably has to put up with more overt criticism than his predecessors, because of a number of changed circumstances. There is no longer a member of the Spencer Stanhope family living within the village, and, therefore, the agent has become the sole focus of any discontent among the tenantry. Since so many of the properties are now no longer owned by the Estate, and their owners do not depend upon it for their livelihoods, the old barriers to speaking out do not exist... and the expansion of

Charles Wemyss, agent of the Cannon Hall Estate 1852-1900. He was one of the enumerators of the 1871 Census. He helped to introduce many ''liberal'' measures to the village and was presented with a watch from the workmen for introducing Friendly Societies into Cawthorne.

Gardeners at Cannon Hall photographed outside their bothy with their housekeeper

the village and increasing use of land for building purposes has provided controversy about which people want to speak out and make their criticism known. That Charles Wemyss' Cawthorne was not a paradise without grumbles is, however, made plain by this extract from Mrs. Stirling's book "Life's Little Day".

> With his tenants my uncle kept up the traditions of his family. My grandfather, for instance, forced to claim some tender of rent for his cottages, used to collect one shilling per annum from the old people, then give them a lavish public banquet, and return to each man the shilling he had paid. Many were the equally characteristic yarns connected with my uncle...
>
> Once after an electioneering campaign, he hurried back to Cawthorne to interview his agent. "Any news, Wemyss?" he asked.
>
> "Bad news, sir, bad news!" responded Wemyss with a twinkle in his eye. "Old Johnny B. has sent in an ultimatum; he wants a new fireplace put in his cottage at once or he threatens to leave."
>
> "Oh-ah," said my uncle. "By the way, what rent does old John pay?"
>
> "Rent?" repeated the agent. "He hasn't paid a penny of rent for seven years."
>
> "Oh-ah," said my uncle with a smile. Then, as he left the room: "See that the masons are sent to old John's cottage first thing tomorrow morning." [4]

Charles Wemyss and his wife Jane (née Maakson). They are said to have kept their marriage secret for some time because Jane, who was Lady Elizabeth's maid, had promised never to leave her mistress.   B.

Indeed it would be naive to pretend that any situation involving the acquisition and administration of property could be totally without controversy, and a recently-acquired photostat of a letter dated July 1891 seems to point to considerable acrimony concerning the acquisition by the Spencer Stanhopes of property previously owned by the West family. The Wests built The Red House in the 18th Century and owned the Malt Kilns, which were later converted into dwellings as Malt Kiln Row. The property passed in the 1870's to Joseph Bramah, who had married into the West family. When one of the descendants of the Wests wrote to Charles Pratt enquiring about her ancestors, his reply dated July 31st 1891 contained the following "I have seen Mr Bramah more than once: he was always very pleasant with me, tho' I know he had a great grievance against the Stanhope estate, and – if what he told me was quite true – not without reason... Mr. Stanhope bought all Mr. Bramah's property here about 12 years ago." An intriguing snippet which could provide interesting future investigation when time allows!

61

CAWTHORNE 1790-1990

Stanhope Colliery and Barnby Basin in the 1890's.

A piece of rail from the Waggon Road unearthed in 1953. It is now kept in Cawthorne Museum.   N. F. M.

A view of a line of stone sleepers along the Waggon Road photographed in 1968.

A stone sleeper from the Waggon Road photographed by Noel Moxon 1968.

Industrial Cawthorne.

Nowadays it is difficult to convince anyone that Cawthorne has an industrial past, but the fact remains that during the period of industrial expansion in England from the early 18th Century onwards, which in the late 19th Century was given the collective title "The Industrial Revolution" by the historian, Toynbee, much of the prosperity of the Spencers and then the Spencer Stanhopes came from first iron and then coal. By 1800 the iron-industry of the area, which had brought wealth and influence to the Spencer and Cockshutt families, and is still remembered in the name Barnby Furnace, was in decline, while the coal industry was embarking upon a period of increasing output. At the beginning of the 19th Century, coal-mining was widespread throughout the Cawthorne parish, but was carried out only in small-scale units, most of the workings being bell-pits, as shown by John Nattes, or shallow drift mines. Until the late 1820's there was a mine at Norcroft, reached by the kind of cage and shaft, which we now tend to associate with coal-mining, and this is well illustrated in one of the Nattes drawings. The Spencer Stanhopes ran their own drift mine into the embankment along the side of Tivydale, from which the coal for Cannon Hall came, but most of the major mining operations were to be found along the valley between Barnby Furnace and Silkstone, and beyond that to Silkstone Common. Here the Spencer Stanhopes had the role not of colliery-owners, but of landowners leasing out land and mineral rights to a variety of tenants.

One of the major problems with the coal mined in this region was not its quality, which was excellent, but its accessibility to its markets. The overland transportation was rough and difficult, and it was to overcome the increased costs which this entailed that a canal network was developed throughout England, linking centres of raw material production with manufacturing centres and their markets. From 1790 onwards, the canal companies built "railways" as feeders to their canals. These were the successors of the old "waggonways" or "tranroads", systems of wooden rails which

The Black Horse Tunnel at Silkstone Common through which coal-waggons were hauled before starting the descent to Silkstone by a self-acting incline.   N. F. M.

The track of the self-acting incline photographed in the 1940's by Noel Moxon, shortly before it was finally obliterated.   N. F. M.

A view at Silkstone Cross at the bottom end of the incline, which shows how the right-hand building was adapted to facilitate the passage of waggons (the porch was, of course, a later addition!).   N. F. M.

had existed in Durham and Northumberland since the 16th Century, and along which coal waggons had been hauled by man or horse-power from the collieries to boats operating on the river systems of the North East. When the rails had first been strengthened by iron-cladding and, ultimately, made completely of cast-iron, they came to be spoken of as "railways" (long before the advent of the steam locomotive). An Act of 1793 authorised the building of the Barnsley Canal, to terminate at Barnby Basin within the Cawthorne Parish, and to be supplied by certain "railway" feeders. The first of these came in 1802, when a section of metal "tramway" was laid down from a colliery near Barnby Furnace.

In March 1808 the Act became law for the building of what came to be known as "The Silkstone Railway". It followed the course of the 1802 tramway, along what is still known locally as "The Waggon Road", and extended it to Silkstone Cross. Along this were hauled waggons each capable of holding 72 cwts carrying coal to barges at the Barnby Canal Basin (the average load of a barge being around 50 tons). There is controversy about the type of rail used for this railway. One school of thought believes that the full length was fitted with double-flanged (ie U-shaped) rails of the kind which can still be seen in Cawthorne Village Museum, while others believe that these were only used at road-crossings, with the rest of the rails being of L-shaped cross-section (N.B. unlike today, the rails, not the waggon-wheels, were flanged). These rails were mounted upon solid stone sleepers, many of which can still be seen in their original positions. Some of the coal which made its way through Barnby Basin came from beyond Silkstone Common from House Carr Colliery (known locally as Husker Pit), which was the scene of the terrible disaster by flooding in 1838, which is commemorated on the memorial in Silkstone Churchyard. From there it was

THE CAWTHORNE OF REV. CHARLES T. PRATT (1866-1915)

Above and below: The warehouse and "Jolly Sailor" at Barnby Basin.

hauled up to Silkstone Common by a stationary engine (known as the Black Horse Engine) and through the Black Horse Tunnel which went under the present railway line, near Silkstone Station. From there it went downhill by a self-acting inclined plane to Silkstone Cross, where it was transferred to the Silkstone Railway and on to Barnby Basin.

The building of the Silkstone Railway contributed considerably to the expansion of the coal trade of local collieries and the volume of traffic using Barnby Basin, which was enlarged in 1810. The dues paid for use of the railway reached their peak of £2,999 in 1837, and, in 1820, the Basin was handling 114,353 tons of coal per annum. In those days Barnby Basin was a lively place, almost a community in its own right, whose inhabitants had a distinct feeling of separation from Cawthorne Village. Often large numbers of boats queued up to discharge their cargoes of lime-stone and take on coal. (Lime-stone was a valuable "back-cargo", which prevented one half of the journey being made empty and, therefore, profitless. This was burned in lime-kilns at the Basin and the resulting lime sold for use on the large tracts of moorland being brought into cultivation as a consequence of the Enclosure movement). To service these barges, the Basin had the "Jolly Sailor" Inn, which provided food and overnight lodgings for bargees, and horses, plus a large warehouse and its own boatbuilder. In the early 19th Century it is recorded that bull and bear-baiting used to take place on the green outside the "Jolly Sailor".

65

It now needs a considerable stretching of the imagination to appreciate the industrial past of this area, because so much has disappeared. The Silkstone Railway began a steady decline from the early 1840's onwards and, in August 1872, when the Barnby Furnace Colliery closed, the rails were pulled up and most of them sold for scrap. The Stanhope Silkstone Colliery opened in 1876, and, to serve this, a proper steam railway was built as part of the Lancashire and Yorkshire Railway, with extensive sidings. Stanhope Silkstone Colliery closed c.1928 and the railway-line, in common with so many others, was "axed" in the middle of the present century. Many valuable relics of industrial archaeology have been subsequently destroyed by open-cast coal-mining and the building of the M1 Motorway. Only a few reminders such as the stone sleepers and the ruins of an old iron-furnace remain, while just one of the four means of transportation which met at this point still functions. The Barnsley to Shepley Lane Head Road, which operated as a turnpike from the 1820's to the 1870's continues as the main Barnsley to Huddersfield road, but few who pass over it on the M1 can have any knowledge that below them stood one of those small industrial complexes which collectively contributed in no small way to Britain's 19th Century development as "the workshop of the World". The transport systems which served it in the past proved eventually to be mutually destructive. The steam railway killed the Silkstone "Railway", and went on to prove too strong a competitor for the Cawthorne stretch of the Barnsley Canal, whose trade dwindled until, during the First World War, a burst in the canal bank at Low Barugh robbed Barnby Basin of its water. The final stage for the canal was reported as follows in the "Barnsley Chronicle" on April 2nd 1937:

'Jolly Sailor' Days!
Century-and-a-Half-Old Cawthorne Building

> The large stone building – very much resembling a mill, standing back from the road in Cawthorne Basin – is being pulled down, and with its demolition goes an interesting piece of history.
> Built about 150 years ago, it was originally a granary used by the Aire and Calder Canal Company, the canal ending near the building. Later it became a public house known as the 'Jolly Sailor' Inn and afterwards served as the home of a family, who left about ten years ago, owing to its being considered unsafe for habitation.
> Early this week, writes a "Barnsley Chronicle" representative, I visited the district and was permitted to inspect the ruins. I was told that the building was being demolished for its timber and stone, which no doubt will be used again. The interior is perfectly dry, there being no dampness anywhere and the walls are of great thickness. The oak beams are practically as good as the day they were fitted, and, generally speaking the building is constructed with the solidness of a fortress. "It was never intended to be pulled down," my guide informed me "it would stand for ever."
> To ensure the floor's being absolutely damp-proof, it was built on puddled clay and then bricked over.
> In an effort to learn more about its history I interviewed various people in the district, and finally I learned more information as the result of a chat with Mrs. Parr, who had lived in one of the old cottages near by, all her life. When she was a child she remembered it as the 'Jolly Sailor' Inn. At that time barges used to come up the canal and bring cargoes, which were exchanged for coal at the Stanhope Silkstone Colliery, and the bargemen used to put up at the Inn. "I remember the sign – a sailor in his blue jersey and holding a glass of beer in his hand – as plain as day," Mrs. Parr told me.
> By all accounts it must have been a fairly popular rendezvous, for Mrs. Parr added that wagonette parties used to visit the 'Jolly Sailor' and the visitors used to have some good times in the well-kept grounds.
> She remembered two landlords, a Mr. Webster, who later went to keep a hotel at Normanton, and a Mr. Smith, who left to go to Wakefield.
> In later years trade slumped and the public house closed, the building then being used as a club for the men working at Stanhope Silkstone Colliery. Afterwards it was let as a house but the occupants left about ten years ago, and since then it has been empty except for two grey owls. Every night, Mrs Parr said, the two owls sit at the top of the building to send out their calls of ti-wit-i-woo. "And what they will do, or where they will go, when the building is pulled down, I do not know," she remarked.
> Following further enquiries, I interviewed an old man who had "supped a pint or two in the 'Jolly Sailor'," and he told me that there was not a brighter and better little house in the country about forty years ago.
> It is understood that a garage is to be built on the site.

The steam railway continued to serve the Stanhope Silkstone Colliery until that closed in the aftermath of the 1926

A bell-pit in woodland behind Cannon Hall drawn by John Nattes.

A copy of a very faded, retouched photograph of the Barnby Furnace Colliery which closed in 1872. The original was loaned to me by Sam Bagshaw.

Nattes' drawing of Norcroft Colliery shows an altogether more sophisticated set-up for the deeper mining of coal. Descent of the shaft and the bringing of coal to the surface appears to have been done by one of two methods – a hand-cranked windlass or a horse-gin. On the surface, we can see chutes for loading carts and a variety of weight-scales for weighing coal.

CAWTHORNE 1790-1990

Striking Cawthorne miners obtaining coal near Bentcliffe Hill during the 1926 General Strike. The Crouching man on the left is thought to be Fred Robinson, whose son operated a drift-mine near this site until the 1970's. Cawthorne did not experience much of the industrial unrest of 1926, but a group of Cawthorne miners did join with some from Higham in an expedition to shut down a drift-mine still working in the woods near High Hoyland. They advertised their intentions far too loudly and were ambushed and quickly routed by waiting policemen armed with truncheons. There were a few sore heads in Cawthorne that night!

Above: Hewing and filling. Sam keeps a supervisory eye on his son, Robert, and Neville Crossland.

In 1947, Noel Moxon took his camera down the Robinson family's drift-mine at Silkstone Bridge on the Cawthorne/Silkstone boundary and took a series of photographs which illustrate the difficult conditions and claustrophobic atmosphere which prevailed in many of these small pits.

Deputy Sam Bagshaw carries out an inspection of the pumps.

"Tramming" tubs looks comparatively easy in the main haulage road...

...but it was a much more uncomfortable and hazardous business as the roof became lower.

68

General Strike. The rail bridge disappeared during the last twenty years to be replaced nearby by a massive road-bridge carrying the M1 Motorway, while opencast-mining for coal has swept away all traces of the large railway sidings which stood there.

This was not the only coal-mining in Cawthorne. The drift-mine in Tivydale, which goes under what is now the St Julien private housing estate, continued to produce coal (mainly for Cannon Hall) until 1928. These workings were tested for gas and finally sealed by British Coal in 1987, when photographs taken by Wilfred Parkinson, whose father had been one of its last operators, showed the workings to be in remarkably good condition. The house, in whose grounds the entrance to the Tivydale Drift stood, was for many years owned by the Robinson family who, as the Tivydale Mining Company, operated at least three mines in Cawthorne: the Silkstone Bridge Drift (on the borders of Cawthorne and Silkstone), which worked until 1950, was one of them; the Norcroft Drift, which operated near the site of the old Norcroft Colliery was another; and the last one, which was in Bentcliffe Woods just off the Cawthorne-Hoylandswaine Road, continued to mine coal until the early 1970's. Their workforces were small because of a restriction to 30 men imposed by the terms of the National Coal Board licence for private pits. We are fortunate that, in 1947, Noel Moxon took his camera down the Silkstone Bridge Drift, providing a vivid picture of working conditions, which have since been recalled by one of the miners as follows: "The coal, which left big scales, was poor in quality for open fires, but was perfectly good for boilers and power-stations. The North Level was worked by the pillar and stall method (i.e. cutting out stalls of coal and leaving pillars of coal in every so far to support the roof). This Level was fairly dry, but the South Level was terribly wet. We did have trouble with water once on the North Level and so the manager and Sam Bagshaw (who was one of the mine's two deputies – Arnold Broadhead being the other) bored ahead and water came gushing out. They found that they had got into another old mine-working and it took a long time to get rid of the water. What they had broken into was an old shaft which it was possible later to look down into. (Author's note – this may well have been the shaft of the Norcroft Colliery shown in the 1807 John Nattes drawing). They tried to work the South Level by the Long Wall face method, but water made it impossible. This was not the only problem. They found a fault

The mine had a certain degree of mechanisation. Boring ready for shot-firing.

Laurie Morley operates a small, early coal-cutting machine.

Air-doors are an essential safety feature in mines to ensure an adequate circulation of fresh air throughout the workings. It is interesting to note the crude rope and pulley system to ensure that the door cannot be left open.

This shot shows the coal measures very clearly.

A welcome rest for Robert Bagshaw and Neville Crossland.

and, from time to time, there was gas. Once the manager was using a carbide lamp and a pocket of gas blew his hat off! The mine was a drift, which took seven or eight minutes to walk down, and the coal was brought out by a self-acting haulage." [14]

Various industrial establishments served the Cannon Hall Estate. It had its own brickyard, which was worked by the Acton family. The Acton brothers had crossed the Pennines in the 1850's from Ashton-under-Lyne. John, the elder, was the manager, while his younger brother, Samuel, whose toughness in the hot, dusty conditions saw him through over eighty years and earned him the name of "The Iron Man", worked in the yard. His toughness was shared by female members of the Acton family who often took their share in the work of the brickyard. The business was eventually acquired by the Acton family, becoming Acton's Stoneware until it passed from them to its present owners, Naylor Bros. In the 1870's the brickyard was supplying large pipes at 13s (65p) per 1,000, common bricks at 11s (55p) per 1,000 and pressed bricks at 13s 6d (67½p) per 1,000. Another establishment providing building raw-materials was the Jowett Saw Mill, a former water-driven corn-mill, which provided the cut timber for the Spencer Stanhopes for something like two hundred years and which was still in full operation in 1953 when Noel Moxon photographed it.

In 1987, British Coal checked the former Tivydale Drift mine for gas before finally sealing the entrance with a concrete plug. These photographs taken by Wilfred Parkinson show the state of preservation of a mine last worked in 1928.   W. P.

Sixty yards in from the entrance, the Tivydale Drift split. The left-hand way goes under the St Julien's Estate part of the village, while the right-hand goes towards the main Barnsley to Huddersfield Road. When the village by-pass was being built in the early 1930s by unemployed miners (each team working for ten weeks and then handing over to another team), their excavations collapsed into this part of the Tivydale Drift.

Brickwork intact and still bearing traces of its whitewash.   W. P.

Jowett Saw-Mill. . . . .

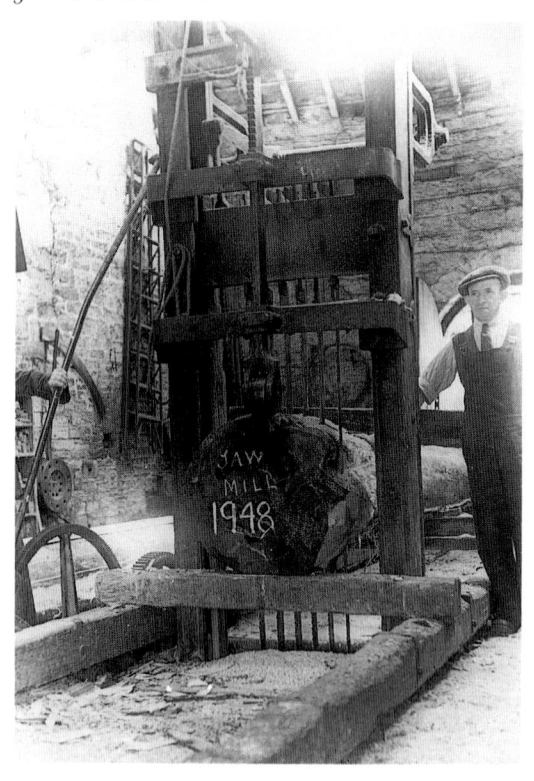

still working when Noel Moxon photographed it in 1948.

Benjamin Swift, builder of Cawthorne School and Hoylandswaine Church.

Much of the materials so produced were used by the Swift family, who were the masons (or builders) of the village for generations. The Stanhope papers contain bills and instructions given by Walter Spencer Stanhope to the Swifts in the first decade of the 19th Century for work carried out in the village. Ben Swift superintended the building of Hoylandswaine Church in the 1860's and "the family" followed on in the 1870's with the renovation and extension of Cawthorne Church to the designs of the architects Bodley and Garner, while Samuel Swift moved to London and acquired quite a reputation as a sculptor and mason. Many examples of his work are still to be seen around the village. A bill for what is usually known as "New Row" or "Brick Row" on Tivydale gives an interesting idea of the price of building materials and labour in Edwardian Cawthorne.

By 1871, the iron industry, upon which the fortunes of the Spencer and Spencer Stanhope families had been built, was dead and gone. All that remains of a thriving 18th Century trade, which gave the name Barnby Furnace to an area of the Cawthorne Parish, is the ruins of a furnace just off the Waggon Road between Cawthorne and Silkstone. In Cawthorne itself only small residual iron industries remained and were, by 1871, on their last legs. One such was the cottage industry followed at the top of Taylor Hill by Caleb Moakson, who in earlier surveys appears as an "iron warehouseman," but by 1871 was earning a meagre living as a "riddle maker", producing wire-mesh riddles for agricultural and horticultural purposes. The main metal workers, however, were the numerous blacksmiths who operated in the village. Their shops, in addition to the work that was done there, were meeting-places in the village where views, news and gossip were exchanged. The atmosphere is captured in old photographs and in one of the many Yorkshire Dialect poems written by Douglas Charlesworth, Cawthorne's farmer-poet. The grandson of Joshua and nephew of Richard, he was a man of many talents, whose natural curiosity made him a Cawthorne historian and led him to hold the office for many years of Secretary of the Museum Society. The Smithy, which provided the inspiration for his poem was George Wright's smithy at Raw Green.

The craftsmanship available in Cawthorne early this century is shown in the photograph on the left. The new pinnacle on top of the Church tower was carved and erected by the Swift family and Henry Puddephatt's son, George, with a young Philip Wilkinson seeing to the metalwork!
As the author's photograph bottom right shows, the pinnacle has now weathered to match the rest, but it was probably easier to identify in the 1930s when Alec Rusby was fixing a new rope on the flag pole.

Statement of Accounts paid for Materials &c.

	£	s.	d.
Lime for Mortar 1/10/= 2/14/= 3/9/8 11/10	8	11	6
J. Acton & Sons 8/12/10 11/14/6 16/2/6 14/8/- 10/12/- 1/12/3	63	1	9
Cumberworth Brick Co.	1	11	4
H. & F. Chamberlain 30/=/= 47/10/=	77	10	..
R. K. Micklethwaite Bricks.	4	7	..
Wostell Colliery Co. Tiles &c.	39	10	..
Jas. Smith & Son Stone 38/17/= 2/9/6 3/1/6	44	8	..
Robert Rhodes & Son Stone.	4	12	6
Free Stone & Doughty "	4	15	4
Tunstall & Co. Dampcourses.	2	7	..
Robson Cement Co. 1/=/= 3/13/4 11/1/8 3/4/=	19	2	..
Jere Kaye & Co Timber Accts. 30/5/= 50/14/= 41/15/1	122	14	1
M. Lawrance & Son Ironmongery &c. 18/4/5	19	..	4
Beaumont & Basille " 2/9/= 8/17/8 56/1/3	67	6	11
Herbert Wood Timber &c.	26	10	..
S. Walker & Co Flags &c.	2	10	10
John Scott Granite Sand.	3	17	2
J. Turner & Son. Sand.	2	..	..
J. Kilner & Sons Inks.	1	1	..
Barnsley Master Builders Finials &c.	1	2	..
J. Leeke, plaster, Laid &c.	3	3	2
H. Wilkinson 1/6/6 2/18/=	4	4	6
Rail Carriage accts. 12/7 15/10 1/1/= 5/1 19/= 1/4/=	5	4	3
Plaster Laths.	8	15	..
J. Holroyd &c. Cartage accs.	2	4	..
Geo. Wright Ironwork.		15	6
Accident Insurance Premium.	2	5	..
	£542	10	2

Cawthorne.
31 Dec. 1906

Messrs W. H. & A. E. Moxon.
 To Geo. B. Swift

1907		£	s.	d.
Feb. 6	To Cost of removing the old Buildings in Jugdale			
October	& building Six new Cottages, as follows,—			
	Accounts paid for Materials.	542	10	2
	Masons', Bricklayers' Tilers & Labourers wages.	292	8	8
	Carpenters' & Joiners' Wages.	105	19	8
	Plasterers' Wages.	43	4	6
	Plumbers' Account.	22	16	6
	Painters' Account.	18	..	..
		1024	19	6

Extra. Paving of front, with Kerb & channel.
  Accounts for Stone & Carriage 8- 3- 0
  Labour & Mortar 10/= 31/= 3-11- 0   11 14 ..
Own time making plans & supervision.   15 .. ..
                                            1051 13 6
Cr. value of old Stones & spare tiles.   17 .. ..
                                Total Cost £ 1030 18 6

Received Cheques on Account.   £   s. d.
  March 9th   100 - 0 - 0
  April 2nd   200 - 0 - 0
  May 18th   100 - 0 - 0
  June 1st   100 - 0 - 0
  July 13th   200 - 0 - 0
  Aug. 3rd   150 - 0 - 0
  Sep. 13th   100 - 0 - 0   950 .. ..
                  Balance £ 100 18 6

Settled 1907

THE CAWTHORNE OF REV. CHARLES T. PRATT (1866-1915)

George Wright's smithy at Raw Green which provided the inspiration for Douglas Charlesworth's poem. The photographs were taken by Houghton in 1905.

The Wrights posed for a family group outside their cottage for a photographer named 'J. Thorne of Higham.'

The Smithy
By Douglas Charlesworth

Neet sattles daan, an' ovver t'dale her dusky mantle nature thraws,
An' softly upo t'evening gale cooms t'distant saand o' t' hooamward craws,
An' stepping daan an' stepping eeast, t'greean skroggy hill ah leeave behind,
Then on past t' pooil wheer t' moorhens feeast, an' t' reeds an' rushes wave i' t' wind.

Affoor me far away i' t' neet, past waving boogh an' massive booal,
Ah see a breetly shining leet 'at seeams ta mak itsen my gooal.
Thus gently on ah tak my gate wi' t' buzzard clocks ta cheer my way,
An' t' hairvest-mooin ta be my mate, dipping its horn ta t'deeing day.

As ah draw near, t'leet breeter grows, resounding clangings fill my ear,
Enagh a country smithy shows 'at stands wheer t' brooklet ripples near.
As t' heavy sled on t'stithy falls, wielded by swithering airms an' strang,
T'clear ringing music to me calls, an' hastes my laggard feet alang.

An' sooin i' t' breet flames circle wairm ah finne'd mysen by t' smithy door,
Wi' chaps at's coom thru cot an' fairm ta kal for hauf an haar or sooa.
Wi' manly laugh an' rustic jest a'm greeted as ah step inside,
While t'smith, wi' pincers gripping fest, thraws a new-finished shoe aside.

Here tale an' legend howd their sway, an' wits are shairp an' feelings glow,
An' t'weary travellers often stay ta rest awhile be t'cheerful lowe,
An' as t' owd stithy sings a tune neyth t'steady ding o' t'busy sled,
It tells ta us the same owd rune it did i' days 'ats lang sin dead.

Daan dees the fire. Wi' a lang sigh ther vital breeath the bellows yield,
An' t'smith his leather brat flings by, then we gooa hooam across the field.
Fit for a thaasand morns an' moor t'stithy's saft ring all t'dale 'ill fill,
Though deeaf ta t' bellows busy roor t'smith ligs beneyth yon wind-swept hill.

Above and below: The Wilkinson family outside the Forge.   R.W.

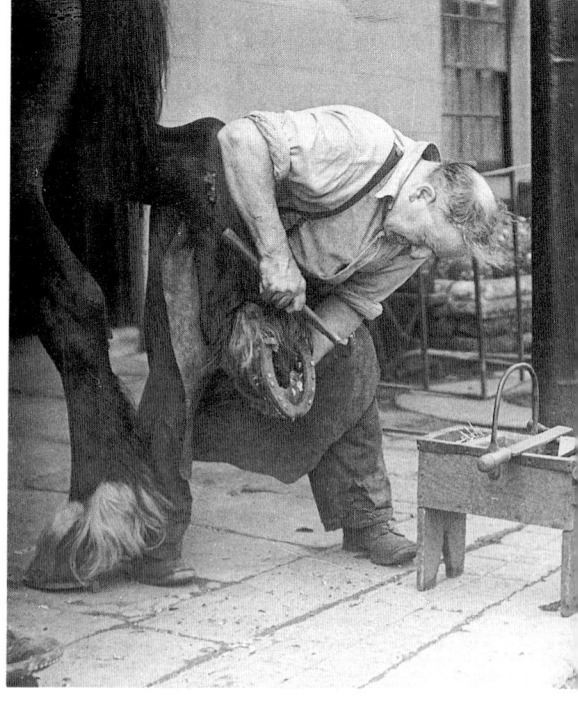

Philip Wilkinson the last blacksmith at the Tivydale Forge c. 1950.

Village Life and amenities 1860-1930.

Although only four miles from Barnsley, Cawthorne was for many of its inhabitants a relatively isolated place before the 1920's and the coming of regular motor-bus transport. In such villages there developed a high degree of self-sufficiency. Shops were small but such establishments as the Co-operative Stores and Richard Charlesworth's shop crammed a staggering amount and range of produce within their walls. What was not obtainable there could be obtained from hawkers – the two paraffin-men (the "Tuesday" man and the "Thursday" man) with their heavily-laden carts, the scouring-stone man (who used a donkey rather than a horse to bring his stones, which were considered so essential for keeping the front door steps looking "smart"), and the oatcake man. The butchering needs of the village were supplied by William Moxon, who began by bringing meat around on a hand-barrow, before moving to Clay Hall and having a shop by the Fountain House. "When women used to grumble to him about the meat being tough, his blunt reply was 'God sends the meat and the devil sends the cook'. ...If a customer came in saying that she had not much money to spend because her husband had had a short working week, he would offer her his oft-repeated maxim, 'Get some meat, missus. Never let your belly know that you are doing bad'." [7] Transportation caused its own problems for the butchers. Cattle for slaughtering at Clay Hall were brought from Wakefield to Barnsley by rail. Then it was the regular task of Jim Moxon and his cousin, Walter, to walk them to Cawthorne. During a rail strike they walked half a dozen bullocks from Wakefield to Cawthorne. There was nothing strange about this and it was a regular feature, when it was market day at Barnsley or Penistone, to see men with dogs driving cattle and sheep through the village street. These were the days when service to the customer was of paramount importance and Jim Moxon remembers having to get the horse out to take just a quarter of a pound of liver up to Banks Hall for someone who was suffering from anaemia. [15]

There were also in the village "house shops", private houses where people (usually widows) supplemented their slender resources by stocking and selling a particular specialised commodity. "Hannah Hawkshaw's sweet shop, which was where the hairdressers now is in Darton Road, was a particular favourite of mine. Here as boys we ate sweets, drank pop, and congregated outside to swap tales". [15] "Mrs Shaw was the widow of a butcher. She lived at Bank House on Taylor Hill where she made lovely teas for visitors to the village and sold home-baked bread and teacakes to the villagers." [13] Mrs Morley, who lived at the top of Taylor Hill from her marriage in 1884 until her death (and was followed in the same house by her son, Laurie, until his death in 1978), amply illustrates the survival instincts of Cawthorne widows in pre-Welfare State times. Her husband's great-grandfather had been butler at Cannon Hall until his death in 1813, and her own husband died in 1903, leaving her to bring up a family of six sons. To manage this she took in lodgers, the office at Cannon Hall often sending down workmen who had come there for short periods to do jobs. At Easter and Whitsuntide she catered for wagonette loads of visitors to the village or for cycling club outings, providing plain teas at 1s 6d or ham and egg teas at 3s. To do this she had 40lb hams and sides of bacon hanging from hooks in the house, a common sight in cottages of a village where many people kept their own pigs (e.g. there were back-to-back sties at the back of Collier Fold) and had men who specialised in killing them and salting the ham and bacon. To help their mother, the Morley boys had to be domesticated as Laurie Morley remembered: "We had no lasses in our family so we were brought up to do things. My mother was baking one day and put the mixture of yeast and flour etc. in a bowl on a chair and left it to warm in front of the fire. She then had to go out and told me 'Tha mun watch that bread'. I forgot and went out playing cricket, but after some time I suddenly remembered. It was through the rails of the chair and only three inches away from the floor. I had to wash my hands, get it back in the bowl and knead it up before she got back!" [13] Mrs. Morley's thrift was not unique, since a present villager remembers that, in 1929, his grandmother lived on 10s (50p) per week pension of which 2s 6d (12½p) was spent on coal, 2s 6d (12½p) on food etc. from the shop, 1s (5p) was put away for rent, 1s 6d (7½p) was spent at the paraffin-cart, and the rest was for clothes and "luxuries". Her cottage rent was £1 19s 0d per half year. [16]

Mrs. Morley and her family outside her home early this century. (NB. the tea-room sign).

In 1885 Charles Pratt wrote: "There are not many parishes, we venture to say, in which the good housewives more enjoy 'a right good cleaning-down' than they do in Cawthorne." Such an activity, however, was no easy matter when most of the amenities which we now take for granted did not exist, let alone the multiplicity of labour-saving devices which are part of modern life. Cawthorne did not acquire a gas supply until the 1980's and electric street-lighting only came shortly before the outbreak of war in 1939, and was immediately "snuffed out" by the black-out imposed to counteract enemy air-raids. Before this the people of the village lived in a world of cottages lit by oil lamps or candles, with just a few homes, whose owners or tenants had felt able to pay the installation costs, having electricity from c.1924 onwards. Running-water-taps (cold of course) were only installed in some houses around 1909, and before that water had to be carried. "Water was fetched in buckets from taps installed in walls in the village streets or from wells. Many cottages had a well in the cellar or in the garden.

You bathed in a large tin bath before the kitchen fire, and laundry was done in a 'copper', which was found in the kitchen or in a wash-house near the house. The 'copper' was filled with water, the fire lit under it and the clothes, which had earlier been consigned to the dolly-tub for the attention of the peggy-stick and rubbing-board, boiled before finishing off through the mangle." [8] All in all a hot, exhausting business! To carry out all these household chores, a carefully planned weekly routine was followed, of which the following was typical. "Monday was wash-day. After washing and drying, the clothes were folded and slightly damped down again ready for Tuesday, when they were ironed, using a box iron containing red-hot heating elements, a supply of which were kept hot in the fire or the oven. On Wednesday the bedrooms were cleaned, and Thursday was baking day, when a large supply of bread, teacakes, seed and fruit cakes etc. would be made in the coal-oven of the kitchen range. On Friday the kitchen was cleaned, stone-flagged floors scrubbed, and all the external windows washed. Shopping was

THE CAWTHORNE OF REV. CHARLES T. PRATT (1866-1915)

The paraffin-man calls on Tivydale.

Early examples of mechanised-farming in Cawthorne.

done on Saturday." [8]

The sights and sounds of the village were mainly agricultural, the main exception being the early morning clatter of miners' clogs on the dross roads as they walked to work at Stanhope Colliery or at Darton. Farm work on the many small farms which existed in the village before 1914 was labour intensive, hard work and involved long hours. "I remember my father sowing corn from a large flat basket, hung around his neck by a strap. Hay and corn were cut by an ordinary mowing machine and the edges of the field opened up by the scythe. Hay was cut, left in swathes, turned until dry, then cocked and led home on carts to be stored in the hay loft. Corn was tied into sheaves by hand and put into stooks. Potatoes were set by hand, and the job which was most disliked was spreading manure on the fields by fork. I think the time which I enjoyed most was haytime. I loved taking teas and bottles of drink to the men in the field, picnicking against a huge haycock, and the ride home on top of the hay or on the horse's back.

We had two horses. My father did a lot of carting for the masons on the Cannon Hall Estate; stone from the Quarry at the Sovereign, and timber from Deffer Wood. One horse was a trap horse and father used to meet people from trains at Darton and Denby Dale Stations." [8] The children of the family also had their work. "I used to take our cows along to the fields, sometimes almost half a mile away, as our farmland was very scattered. We had to deliver milk from a large can in pint and half-pint measures to many village customers, and also get the coal-buckets filled before going to school. We did other household chores in the evening. Cleaning spoons and forks was my weekly job and my sister cleaned the knives with bath-brick on a knife-board... From school we could hear the striking of the blacksmith's anvil and were sometimes taken down as a class to watch a wheel being made. I often accompanied my father when our horses were shod." [8]

Cawthorne never seems to have been short of itinerant visitors. "I remember an old 'Hedger' – we called him 'Old Norman' – who came annually to cut and lay the hedges around the fields, and a mole-catcher who came every year. The same Irishmen came over annually to help at the hay and corn harvests and stayed for the summer." [8] "A lot of farms had harness-rooms (they had one at Clay Hall). To keep the leather in good condition and free from damp, they had a fire in the harness-room. Certain vagrants, who came round doing jobs on the farms, used to sleep in the harness-room. Also there were always people passing through from Penistone Workhouse to the Barnsley Workhouse. Often they were men who had once had

Many farmers had other occupations in addition to their farming. George Edward Barlow is remembered as a superb craftsman cart-builder.

good family connections. There was George Hold, Abel Hold's son, one called Seth Haigh and one called Joe Fount, who many said was really one of the Fountain family of Birthwaite Hall. They slept in various harness-rooms in the village, doing jobs for a few weeks and then moving on'' [7] In addition there were street musicians with their monkeys, one of whom was captured for posterity by Mr. Houghton on one of his photographs. The same photographer recorded the annual visit to Cawthorne of the charcoal-burners, who built their rough shelters after a period of tree-felling and, using the cord wood (branches of 6" diameter and less), they made a conical-shaped fire. The pile was covered with soil and turf, with just a small hole at the top for smoke to escape and one at the bottom to light the fire. The idea was to produce a slow fire in which the heat and flames were contained by the soil and turf. Such control produced charred wood, rather than wood ash. The whole smouldering process could take up to three weeks, during which time the men lived in their rough shelters. The charcoal produced was sold to hotels or large houses for use in charcoal ovens (Cannon Hall had one), or sent for industrial use in the steel industry. By the time that Houghton photographed them, the visits of the charcoal-burners to Cawthorne were nearing their end. Another old country trade was dying.

When harvesting was a back-breaking, labour-intensive operation, pre-1914. Above, the Barlow family at harvest-time.

81

CAWTHORNE 1790-1990

The Charlesworth family similarly employed. One should note the involvement of the ladies of the family. Holding the horse's head below is Thomas Allott, while the two children are Rowland Wilkinson's son and daughter. The latter, Connie (now Mrs Moxon), delivered the telegram which told of Allott's death in action in 1918.

The Barlow Brothers (Jim, Alf, Harold and George Edward) also worked as contractors doing steam-engine threshing around the neighbourhoods as these two photographs from the late 1914-18 period show.

Charcoal burners near Cannon Hall, photographed by Houghton August 1905.

Tending the fire.

A break for refreshment.

A rough shelter, but it was "home" for anything like a three-week stretch.

THE CAWTHORNE OF REV. CHARLES T. PRATT (1866-1915)

The Victoria Institute when newly opened.

The opening ceremony of the Victoria Institute. The top-hatted Bishop of Wakefield stands beneath the garland. Colonel Stanhope (in "cowboy hat") is in centre foreground, while his daughter-in-law is on right giving instructions to a bandsman.

The paternalism of the Spencer Stanhopes has already been mentioned and is still recalled by old villagers. "When times were hard, they operated a soup-kitchen at Cannon Hall and the boys of the village were sent up with small milk-cans. Some of the more dare-devil ones among them fished out the meat with sticks, ate it and drank some of the soup. They made up the shortfall with water from the Cascade, with the result that their parents would greet the resulting mixture with the exclamation 'By jove, they've made some poor soup today'." [15] To encourage the tenants to keep their cottages smart, "white and green paint was dished out to any of them going with cans to the stable-yard at Cannon Hall", [15] while one family recalled that, when they moved to a different cottage in the village "Mrs Stanhope provided them with money to buy paint and wallpaper... but you know, after a decent length of time had elapsed, she paid them a visit to see that the money had been used for what it had been intended." [17] That "Mrs Stanhope" was Ida Mary Pilkington (1864-1920), the daughter of Sir Lionel Pilkington of Chevet, who from the time of her marriage in 1890 to John Montague Spencer Stanhope was a tremendous influence for good in the village right up to her untimely death. She was the moving spirit behind many of the schemes and amenities which led to Cawthorne so often being spoken of as a "model village".

The most significant village amenity for which she was responsible was the Victoria Cottage Institute which was opened in August 1898 to provide the village with a medical centre. At the opening ceremony Col. Stanhope, her father-in-law, had this to say: "If it had not been for Mrs. Spencer Stanhope, that building (the former Methodist Chapel) would very likely have been turned into two cottages. She, however, requested that it might be kept for something that might be useful to the village, and she had thought out that scheme." In opening the Institute, Dr Eden, the Bishop of Wakefield, said "For some years past, people of leisure and means had appreciated to the full the great blessing of having skilled nurses in their homes, but until lately it was thought such a blessing was out of the reach of ordinary working people, unless someone made it a matter of charity. But the great feature of that undertaking was that it was not a charity. It was not a thing that was being done for them, but a thing they were doing for

Mrs. J. M. Stanhope with workmen (those responsible for its conversion from a chapel?)

themselves. He had seen a long list of annual subscribers of one penny per week and they amounted to a good sum." For this, the patients received the attention of the resident nurse and invalid carriages were kept for the use of people who suffered broken legs or were too frail to walk. In addition, some patients were brought for convalescence from Barnsley Beckett Hospital and, when space was available, laundry and cookery classes were run there for the young girls of the village. The medical aspect of the Institute's work was especially valuable since, for a long time, the village was dependent upon visits from Doctor Rowley, who lived some five miles away in Victoria Road, Barnsley, but whose ancestors had been the Rowleys of Flash House Farm in Cawthorne. It was not until the early 1920's that the village acquired its own doctor, when Doctor Whincup came, as a young bachelor, to lodge with Ben Fish and his wife, and opened up a surgery in the sitting-room of a cottage in Church Street. He is remembered as a very good doctor, who followed the pattern of the times and performed minor operations in people's homes (usually on the kitchen table!). The village retained its own doctor until the 1980's, but now, although Cawthorne is home to numerous doctors and surgeons, the villagers have once more to go elsewhere for medical attention. After a year Mrs. Stanhope gave the following report on the Victoria Institute in the Parish Magazine:

Cawthorne Victoria Cottage Institute.

We have received the following Report from Mrs. Spencer Stanhope, and have pleasure in inserting it at her request.

The Victoria Cottage Institute has now been open for twelve months, and I am anxious subscribers should know of the work it has done. Mrs. Horton was obliged to leave in January through ill-health, but the Committee were fortunate in securing Miss Marsh as Caretaker, who gives every satisfaction. The Parish may well congratulate itself on the blessing of having such an excellent and good woman as Nurse Nightingale. She has worked hard and well, and endeared herself to all who have needed her services. Her ready and willing help is much appreciated. In the outbreak of measles last year she paid 844 visits in three months. She has made 112 this year, and averages 46 visits a week. There have been 12 deaths, and she has waited on 11 confinements, and been 39 nights on duty. She has had the care of six accident cases, one being a very severe scald, where her skill and prompt attention saved what might have been the loss of a limb, or even of life, as also in the case of a lad injured at the pit. The Cottage itself has proved most useful. Through the kindness of many of the Committee, Lessons in Practical Cooking were given to young girls. Soup was also made and sold. Two outfits of Baby-clothes have been made by the girls. The large room has proved most useful for the assembling of subscribers. One convalescent has been received, and one in-patient, in the spare room. My great desire is to make the Institute *pay its own way*. The funds are good, but they must be considerably increased if the Nurse and Institute are to be maintained. More subscribers are needed; and I strongly appeal to those who are now paying only the lowest sum asked, and could give more, to increase their subscription. I find from others who have organised District Nurses, that patients are charged so much a case for the Nurse's attendance, and that the charge for one visit is more than our lowest whole year's subscription. Our income is at present about £63 2s 2d; the expenditure, £97 18s 9d. This shows a deficit of £34 16s 7d. More money is needed, therefore, if the work is to go on. It is one which deserves to be properly supported and regarded as a trust for the general good of the Parish. All who can will, I hope, increase their subscriptions. They can be paid to any of the Committee: – The Misses Stanhope, Mrs. Kaye, Miss Kaye, Mrs. Sykes, Mrs. Wemyss, Miss Smith, and Miss Marriott (Secretary).

Yours truly,
IDA SPENCER STANHOPE,
President and Treasurer.
September 1899

The Institute Nurse and one of her deliveries, Connie Wilkinson (aged 3 weeks). The first Nurse encountered resistance from the village "handywomen", who considered births and deaths their provinces. R.W.

I have not, as yet, found when the medical activities of the Institute ceased, but was given the following explanation as to why it happened. "Needy, but poor cases who required attention were not turned away, but, as time went on, people who paid their subscriptions got to know of this and increasingly began to take the attitude 'Why should I pay when others are getting the same benefits for nothing.'" [13]

Early Motoring Years

Judging from his photographic coverage of them, Rowland Wilkinson was fascinated by the motor car. He sold petrol and oil at his shop.

Two shots of Dr. Rowley and his chauffeur on visits to Cawthorne. The car is a 1913 Standard Rhyl 10HP.

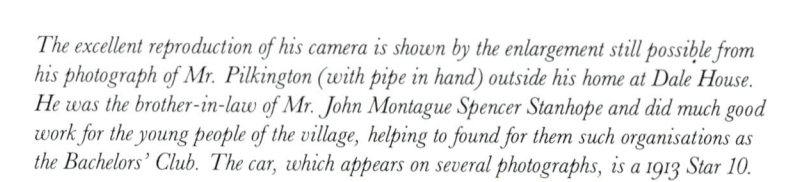

The excellent reproduction of his camera is shown by the enlargement still possible from his photograph of Mr. Pilkington (with pipe in hand) outside his home at Dale House. He was the brother-in-law of Mr. John Montague Spencer Stanhope and did much good work for the young people of the village, helping to found for them such organisations as the Bachelors' Club. The car, which appears on several photographs, is a 1913 Star 10.

Two further carefully-posed photographs of Mr. Pilkington and his car at Dale House.

91

This picture, taken outside Tower Cottage (then known as Ivy Cottage and the home of the Head Gamekeeper) poses problems. It is taken pre-1912 because one of the back-seat passengers is the Head Gamekeeper's wife, Mrs. Butler, one of the others being Mrs. Warren, the wife of the village Headmaster. The bare trees, the muffled horse, the covered car radiator and the dress of the chauffeur and his front-seat passenger (Fred Atkins, the Coachman to the Spencer Stanhopes) all point to a cold winter's day. Yet the ladies are lightly dressed – vanity for the sake of the camera?

Two Cannon Hall estate vehicles.   *pre-1919 Ford Model T*   *1910/11 Mercedes.*

Accidents were not unknown even on comparatively deserted roads and incidents such as this charabanc coming to grief on the road towards Huddersfield, just beyond Flash House, was too good an opportunity for Rowland Wilkinson to miss. The vehicle is a Dennis dated 1907-10.

CAWTHORNE 1790-1990

Accidents did not, however, deter intrepid charabanc trippers as is shown by this group setting off from the Spencer Arms. The charabanc was owned by George Booker of Barnsley who ran one of the first bus services through Cawthorne. One of his drivers was "Dick" Caswell, a Worcestershire man, who married and settled in Cawthorne, later running a successful garage and haulage business there.

Charabancs were not the only vehicles to have accidents, as these two photographs of an incident on Taylor Hill c 1905 demonstrate. The steam traction-engine which has "jackknifed" was bringing a load of bricks for the building of New Row on Tivydale. The man in the straw hat standing on the left of the top picture is Sidney Silverwood. In his 1915-19 diary, Douglas Charlesworth refers to his death aged over 90 and writes of him as the last man in Cawthorne to consistently plough with oxen.

CAWTHORNE 1790-1990

Even cycling had its problems, as this carefully posed photograph by Edgar Moseley, of his wife having repairs to her cycle wheel done on the Silkstone Waggon Road, shows.

Before Cawthorne had its own petrol-pump, the fuel was delivered and sold in two-gallon cans – and, of course, the place where this "Pratt's Spirit" was sold was Rowland Wilkinson's Post Office!

The motor-age had not yet caught up with the Royal Mail when this photograph was taken. Postmaster Rowland Wilkinson is standing extreme right.

97

A different method of transport was also sold at the Post Office.

An outing setting-off from Richard Charlesworth's shop.

98

THE CAWTHORNE OF REV. CHARLES T. PRATT (1866-1915)

By the time of this outing c 1946, transport had changed!

Another village amenity, which was provided by the Spencer Stanhopes and which was intended to be self-supporting, was the Reading Room. The reality of its continued dependence upon subsidy from Cannon Hall, plus the importance of Charles Pratt in running this venture are amply demonstrated by the following extracts from the Parish Magazine. (N.B. That Pratt always seemed to use the "royal plural" and wrote of himself as "we".)

The Reading Room.

At the Annual Meeting of Members, it was found that the Room had not quite paid its way last year. It was suggested that there might be some few in the Parish who would not be unwilling to assist it by becoming "honorary members," and giving some small subscription towards it. We hope there may be, for we can answer for the Room being a useful institution. Mr. Stanhope kindly provides the Room, coals, and Yorkshire Post.

February 1880.

The Library.

The Librarian's Report of his work for the last twelve months shows that there must be a fair amount of reading in the Parish. We could only wish that all the reading there is in it were of as innocent, sensible and improving a kind as that which is connected with our Village Library. The funds will now allow us to buy a few books which we included in the Catalogue when printed, but were not able at the time to purchase. We have often wished there was a Committee to manage the Library: but our own experience of Committees is not an encouraging one as regards the attendance of their members, and they generally end in the one man who is sure to be there having all to do, and we are not too modest to say that that one man is generally the clergyman.

February 1886.

Penny Readings.

We were certainly not prepared for such volumes of words as we received the other week made out of the word "Palmerston". There were 17 papers sent in, the lowest with 253 and the highest above 400. It was not intended that so many "Dictionary words" should make their appearance, and some of the words must have been almost as astonished to find themselves being made use of, as we were to make their acquaintance. After they had all been scrutinised by Mr. McWhan in addition to our own looking over, the paper of Charles Salvage, of Cannon Hall, is found to be the highest, with 417 words. The next are J. W. Gibson, 397; Willie Moxon, 393; M. A. Fish, 391.

Some who sent in about 300 words without ever using a Dictionary were really deserving, we think, of still higher commendation for their work.

Twelve papers have been sent with words from the word "Cawthorne." The highest is that of George Wright with 284: the next are George Fish, 279; J. W. Gibson, 249.

At a Meeting of Members of the Reading Room, held on the 21st, a Committee was elected for 1879. Though the Room is well used by those who are members, and the Chess and Draughts tables kept in almost constant use, still the number of members is not what it ought to be in a village of this size. The payments are 4s for the year, or 2s 2d for the half-year. A few Books have been added to the Library: among them, four volumes of Good Words and four volumes of Half Hours with the Best Authors.

February 1879

The Library.

The following Books have just been added to the Catalogue: Russell's Diary in the East, Life of Charlotte Bronte, Life of Robert Chambers, Work and Wages (by T. Brassey, M. P.), Palgrave's Journey through Arabia, Golden Deeds, Stanley's Livingstone, Things Not Generally Known (2 vols), Popular Errors, Rigg's Easy Chemistry, Science Lectures (2 vols.), Our New Vicar, Under His Banner, Edward Denison's Letters, Parley's Travels, Evelyn's Story, Sir Julian's Wife, Memoir of Mrs. Harrison (Miss Crawley).

November 1875

The Reading Room.

The contests in Chess and Draughts we mentioned in our last have been concluded, and have excited no little interest among the members who have played and those who have looked on. We give a full report of them, in order that those who have been beaten may keep it by them until they have so far improved their play as to wonder how it was they were defeated. Chess: James Fox beat George Fish; Joe Fish, James Fish; Tom Fish, Jos. Kitson; Mr. Pratt, W. Blacker. In second round, James Fox beat T. Fish; Joe Fish, Mr. Pratt. J. Fish beat J. Fox and won. Draughts: J. Blacker, jun; beat T. Thompson; John Louks, George Fish; James Fish, Mr. Pratt; James Inman, Joe Fish; W. Burgon, W. Blacker. Second round: J. Louks beat James Fish; John Blacker, J. Inman; W. Burgon odd man. Third round: W. Burgon beat J. Blacker; J. Louks odd man. W. Burgon then beat J. Louks and won. Some of the games were remarkably well contested. The volumes given to the winners were "Half Hours with the Best Authors". It is proposed having another set-to about the third week in January; and, as it has been suggested to us that one game each is hardly a fair trial of skill, it is intended that it shall be in each case through the game "twice out of thrice". We hope to be able to give a book of some kind to first and second next time, as a little memorial of their victories.

December 1878

We are hoping to take advantage of this month's Full Moon for a few Readings and Entertainments. We have arranged for the kind help of the Silkstone Handbells for one evening, and no doubt the Band, the Glee Club, our own Handbells and other native or foreign helps to an evening's recreation will be forthcoming, when required. *Author's note* (Note how, before street lighting, a Full Moon seems to have been essential to ensure a good attendance!)

January 1880

The oldest amenity enjoyed by the village (after the Church, of course) is the village school. In 1455 a chantry was founded at Cawthorne. Such endowments were common of chapels within, or attached to, existing churches and in which prayers would be said for the founders and for the souls of any relatives whom they nominated. The Cawthorne Chantry is given in W. E. Tate's "Index of some Yorkshire Schools founded mainly c.730-c.1770 A.D." as "the Chantry of Our Lady" and is said to have been founded by Henry and Isabel Langton. It came to be known as the Bosville Chantry, because prayers were said for the soul of Isabel's first husband, John Bosville. The Chantry was endowed with two acres of land "lying together in a croft between the land of Richard Waterton on two sides and abutting at the West end on the brook, and, at the East end, on the highway which goes to the middle of the town of Cawthorne, for the building of a house and the construction of a garden for the use of the said chaplain and his successors." This was the priest's house, which was no doubt used as a school by its occupant, most schoolmasters then being also priests, and which was later converted into a farm building when new residential premises were built. It continued to be used as a farm building by Joshua Charlesworth and his successors until it was finally demolished in 1962 by the present owner of the property and agent for the Cannon Hall Estates, Mr John Lees. On the plaster of the large upper room there were some crude murals of corporal punishment being administered to a boy by a schoolmaster, and Tate described the building as being "possibly the oldest school

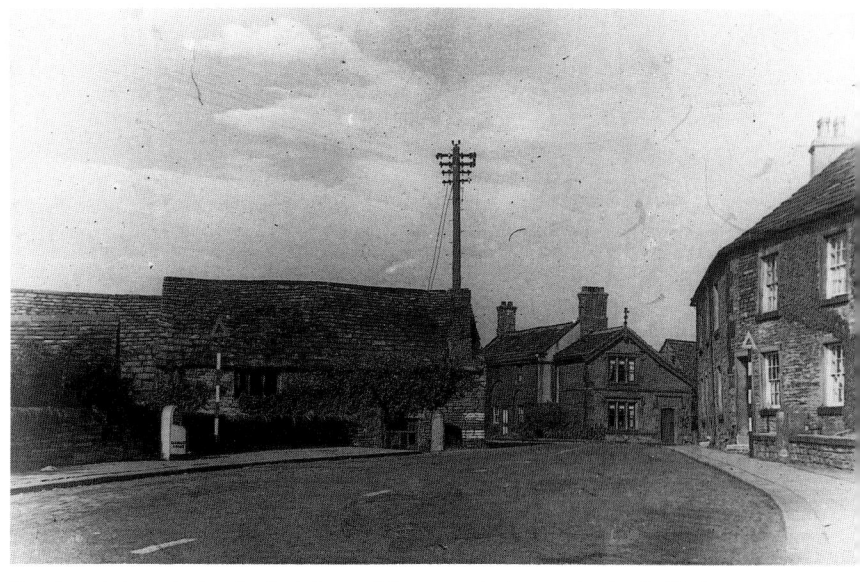

Cawthorne's first school and priest's house of the 1450s. A photograph taken by Noel Moxon in the 1950s.

building in Yorkshire." The chantry was abolished in 1547, but its endowments were given to the school for the setting up of a free grammar school with Richard Wigfall, the former chantry chaplain, as its first master. By 1578 the school had fallen into disuse, was without a schoolmaster, and, therefore, its endowments were passed by the Duchy of Lancaster to the school at Pontefract. They were successfully regained when, in 1639, the people of Cawthorne were able to point to a new school building (the present Parish Room) and a successful schoolmaster, Mr Peter Deane. This building, which consisted of one large room, over which was a loft in which the schoolmaster slept, continued as a boys-only school until 1872, having, in January 1862, been taken over by the National Society. The education of girls was, from October 1858, looked after by a school founded by Lady Elizabeth Spencer Stanhope in the building on Tivydale which now serves as the Village Hall. In February 1872 the present village school opened as a boys' school and the old Grammar School became the Infants' School. In 1906 the boys and girls were moved to the same school, the infants moved down into the former girls' school, and Rev. Pratt took over the old Grammar School as the Parish Room. In the early 1930's the Infants' School closed and became the Village Hall. After a long journey, all the scholars of Cawthorne were finally united under one roof. The previously mentioned establishments were not, however, the only educational establishments in the village: there was, at one time, a Dame School on Taylor Hill, which was demolished in 1886; in 1871 Mrs. Wood was running a private school for girls at the Manor House; and around 1914, Mrs. Annie Robinson, who had taught at the village school and was to do so again in the future, had fallen out with the village schoolmaster and gone into competition with him by giving private lessons. "Mrs. Robinson lived up Taylor Hill. She had taught at the school but had semi-retired. (She had probably fallen out with George Warren!). She took one or two private pupils. We paid 3s 1½d per week and we only went in a morning. As she taught, she used to do jobs such as bread-making (using the machine which is still preserved in the museum)." [7] Mrs Robinson provides a good example of Victorian/Edwardian teacher training – or the lack of it. She began work as a monitor in 1898 at the age of 13. She progressed to become an assistant teacher in 1904, retired upon marriage in 1912, but returned seven years later and continued until her final retirement in 1950. Her colleague, Mary Watts (née Fish), began as a monitor in 1903 at the princely sum of £6 per annum! She undertook 2 days per week pupil Teacher Training in Barnsley which led her in 1906 to Certificated status and three years later to Assistant teacher status. She retired in 1940.

Memories of schooldays in the early years of this century among the older generation of Cawthorners are many and

Miss Ashton in old age, pictured behind her cottage in Darton Road. She retired as mistress of the infants' school in 1890. She taught at the girls' school from 1848 to 1872, when she took over the infants' school. When she took over the infants, the school had 32 pupils, but, by 1882, numbers had risen to 85.

A Dame school on Taylor Hill. It was demolished in the mid-1880s. Miss Burkinshaw, who ran it, is standing left (leaning on a crutch).

A Cawthorne infants school class c. 1902/3. Seated left is Miss Evans. Wilfred Clarkson is sixth from the left on the third row back while Alice Moxon and her twin brother are in the centre of the second row.

varied. They always start with Miss Evans, who was in charge of the Infants' School for over forty years from 1890. "I loved Miss Evans, the Headmistress of the Infants' School. She was ideal with little children – she was very neurotic and the scent of eau-de-cologne even now always reminds me of her. She lived with her sister in the school house in Tivydale. She once told me, when I was older, of her appointment, a young lady from Wales making the long walk up the park to Cannon Hall for her interview with Colonel Stanhope." [8] Another said, "I think she was one of the nicest persons I ever met. She was very kind and gentle," [18] but her charm did not work immediately because, he continued, "I remember being taken at the age of five to the Infants' School (now the Parish Room). I didn't like the look of it and, while my sister and Miss Evans were talking, I slipped out and beat my sister back to the Basin." [18] She was, however, a disciplinarian and had a cane of twisted cardboard, which was not used for punishment, but for pointing at the blackboard and for poking inattentive children! One pupil at the Infants' School remembered that children "gave mimed performances of Nursery Rhymes and several times these were

CAWTHORNE 1790-1990

Mr. George McWhan and his family. He was Headmaster of the Boys' School 1870-97.

presented on a stage at garden parties at Hill House, when it was the home of Mr John Montague Spencer Stanhope and his wife. I was little Miss Muffet and sat on a wee stool with a hideous spider (made by either Miss Evans or Teacher Emma Charlesworth) hanging near me. Emma later told me, though I don't remember this, that we were invited to Cannon Hall to give these mimes when they had a house-party, and someone manipulating the dangling spider let it fall into my bowl of supposed curds and whey. My look of consternation caused guffaws of laughter from the audience, especially Sir Walter.'' [8]

When conversation switches to ''the big school'' (as it was usually known), two Headmasters are usually mentioned, Mr Arthur Senior and his successor, Mr George Warren. ''The thing I remember most there is Mr. Senior, the Headmaster. He brought the school round and made it a better place than when I started.'' [18] ''He was a great teacher, far above the average standard for a village school.'' [7] ''A Shakespearean scholar, he read to us from Shakespeare every week.'' [10] One feature which he introduced was the celebration of Empire Day (May 24th), which, since it was also Queen Victoria's birthday, was zealously observed. It became the custom for a few years to mark the occasion with a parade and costumed tableaux depicting among other things ''People of the British Empire'' and ''Scenes from British History.'' Of the former, one pupil remembered ''I had to black my face and be a colonial. I blacked up at Dale House, home of Mr Brown, the

Cawthorne School staff back row left to right: Mr. J. Woodcock, Miss Lisle (later Mrs. R. Caswell), Mr. B. Laycock, Miss Shoesmith, Mr. S. Bell. Seated left to right: Mrs. Annie Robinson, Mr. Senior (Headmaster), Miss Fish (Later Mrs. L. Watts). Mr. Senior was Headmaster 1904-10. Benjamin Laycock was killed in the First World War.

10. EMPIRE DAY 1909, CAWTHORNE.

Two of the Empire Day pageants organised among the school children by Mr. Arthur Senior, who is photographed with them below.   R.W.

Empire Day Parade 1907.

Divisional Education Officer, because I was a friend of his son, Laurie. During the parade we weren't allowed to touch our faces – it was a sticky time. All nations of the British Empire were represented." [18]

"George Warren was a bit of a tyrant, who did not spare the rod. He didn't half straighten some of the lads out – and some of them straightened him out. Some from the village and some from the Basin beat him up. They waited for him outside school and had a real go at him... One of his first tasks when he became Headmaster was to teach us to be courteous and polite to certain people; to raise our hats to the Squire, the Vicar, the Headmaster, and their wives. I did this for the rest of my life and Mr John Montague Spencer Stanhope always raised his in return." [7] The links between the "big house", the Church and the school(s) were always preserved, and, in return the Spencer Stanhopes gave generous financial assistance, but not without certain restrictions demanded by the morality of the time. "Lady Elizabeth usually paid the fees for the children of people who could not afford them, but this charity was not unbounded. A woman, whose daughter had an illegitimate child, asked for this concession for the child, only to be told 'Oh! No! We don't have illegitimate children in our charity.' [10] The "charity girls" were expected to work every afternoon at the school at needlework for Cannon Hall, as a return for their school fees and the teaching which they received each morning. This practice diminished and finally stopped after the Education Act of 1870 and the opening of the mixed school. The school-children were expected to play their part in other ways and pay their respects on special occasions. "When the Stanhopes went on holiday to Scotland, we all had to turn out from school and wave their coach off, then back to lessons...

Mr. George Warren, Headmaster 1910-1941, with his wife and another lady (the nurse from the Institute?) outside the School House, occupied by the Headmaster until the 1970s.

Three photographs of the upholders of the law in Cawthorne.

Mr. Coles near the Church and with his family outside the Police house in Darton Road.

Mr. Beanland, Douglas Charlesworth's father-in-law.

But I must say that they made a smashing Christmas Party for us in the Girl's School. It was a grand do that. Each one had to go up and receive an apple and orange. It might seem a little cruel, but what stuck in my mind as a child was that Miss Betty (John Montague's daughter, later Mrs. Fraser and the last of the Spencer Stanhopes to live in Cannon Hall) had difficulty in pronouncing the letter 'R'. We boys thought it was marvellous when she asked 'would anybody like any stwawbewy jam?'!''. [18] The children were brought out to line the route for Sir Walter's funeral in 1911, even the infants being brought to the lodge gates on Tivydale. The Church links were maintained by the Vicar himself. Each day, even in the Infants' School, began and ended with prayers and "We had our Scripture lesson most mornings, some of which Mr. Pratt took. He used to crack his fingers if he saw you weren't attending. He could make it sound like a whiplash." [18] "Success in the Scripture examinations usually brought a reward in the form of a half-day holiday and an orange." [7] There were tensions within the school between boys from different parts of the village. "There was a very great distinction made between Cawthorners and Basiners... It was usually a question of who was 'the Cock of the school', and from the Basin we put Albert Broadhead up, because he was the best boxer and fighter, who used to train at home. The contests had to be fought out on the green patch near the Spencer Stanhope mausoleum. I've shed some of my blood on there... When we were going home, we were often in time to see a funeral coach leaving the Church, and we used to ride on the axles down to the Basin, unless they stopped and punched us off... If there was any trouble in Cawthorne and the bobby, Mr Beanland, was called in, he would say 'I know who it is. It's those Basin boys again.' It was never the Cawthorners, they were angels. He would come down to the Basin and tell our parents... We were once out after some pears and came round the back of the Museum in the dark, when I ran straight into Mr Beanland with his lamp. He didn't catch me though, and he didn't get any of my pears!" [18]

Cawthorne Basin had a definite sense of separation, of being a community within a community, a small industrial community where life could be hard at the best of times, but especially hard when illness struck. "There was a man who went

Above: the Girls' School with chimney smoking. When the middle of the three buildings disappeared is not known. Was it, perhaps, the school which Lady Elizabeth's 1858 foundation replaced (or the school house which the one on the right replaced in the 1870's)?

The interior of the former Girls' School (now the Village Hall) photographed by John Marshall Photography for the "Barnsley Chronicle" on the occasion of a Victorian Tea to celebrate the Centenary of the opening of Cawthorne's present museum building October 1989. Something of the atmosphere of the schoolroom still remains.

off his head when he lost his job as a blacksmith at the colliery. He was a big, powerful chap and, stripped to the waist and armed with a hatchet, he would sit in a tree, preventing people going on the Waggon Road to the colliery. When he was in this frame of mind the only person who dared approach him was a boy, young Victor Broadhead, who could do anything with him." [18] Another manifestation of his illness was when he would lock his wife in an outhouse, sling a rope across the road as a makeshift toll-chain and refuse to allow travellers to pass until they had paid a penny to "see the monkey", who was of course, his imprisoned wife. "We entertained ourselves at the Basin, except on Saturdays, when we went into Cawthorne to stir up a bit of trouble. Lockwoods from the Golden Cross ran a bus (a horse-wagonette) from Cawthorne to Barnsley twice a week. On Saturday night we waited for W-w-w-w-William Lockwood (he stammered) bringing his bus from the Golden Cross. We kept watch level with the Church, but to stop us riding on the step, William Glover, the driver, followed the bus, whip in hand as far as the trough by the Village Green. We would hide and when we heard William Lockwood's voice shout "Right, W-w-w-w-William", followed by the crack of the whip, we darted out and pinched a free ride to the Basin... If we wanted a bit of real fun and drama, we went up to Higham. They used to fight over anything there. If it wasn't the beer, it was over the fish and chips." [18]

In days before meals were provided at school, pupils from outlying parts of the village had to make their own provision for

Pupils with Headmaster, Stanley Jackson c. 1946.

lunch-hour. "We took sandwiches. In the summer we played cricket in the park at lunch-time, but we could not leave our sandwiches in our jacket pockets on the ground or the deer, which were very tame, came and ate them. We used to tie them up in a tree in a handkerchief, but it had to be high up, because they could jump... Every Ascension Day we played St Mary's School, Barnsley, at cricket and hundreds came to watch. They thought it marvellous to see those deer running up and down. In time, however, the people caused problems by leaving behind broken bottles, which cut the deer's feet." [18]

Conditions at the schools left much to be desired. There were regular complaints of the atmosphere in the girls' and infants' schools as a result of a smoky stove, but, at least, this provided some heat, which was not always the case in the boys' school. The heating system there regularly broke down and, early this century, when the classroom temperature reached freezing-point, lamps were burned to try to help raise it again. Electric lighting did not come to the mixed school until 1934 and it was not unknown pre-1906, when it was the boys' school, for the timetable to be reversed in the winter months to make the most of the available light.

Nor were the schools the healthiest places imaginable with their stuffy atmosphere and children spitting on slates to wipe them clean. There is no wonder that childish ailments spread as the following table shows:

1880	Measles and scarlet-fever
1884	Coughs and colds – two deaths
1895	Scarlet-fever closed the school for 3 weeks
1898	School closed for a month because of a measles epidemic and re-opened with only 16 children
1900	One scarlet-fever death
1903	3 boys and 1 girl died of croup
1909	1 diptheria death
1911	School closed for 1 month (whooping-cough)
Dec. 1918 – Jan 1919	Influenza epidemic closed the school
1925	School closed as a result of chicken-pox.

Nowadays it is very interesting to read Charles Pratt's regular thoughts on education, from which he did not spare the readers of his Parish Magazine. In these days of equal opportunities and the attack upon sex-stereotyping, what would the author of the following have to say?

The President of the Board of Education remarked in his Annual Statement, "I believe it is essential for every girl, whether she is going into the dressmaking trade or not, that she should understand how to make her own clothes; and that their needlework should be really practical, such as would be useful to them throughout their lives." There are some of our mothers, we are afraid, who do not take all the pains they ought to do with their needlework. "It is less trouble to do it myself."

May 1913

It is sad to read that the Medical Inspection of West Riding Schools shows that more than half the children under five years of age are defective in one or more respects. Attention is drawn to adenoids being so prevalent. But what can be expected, when (as a Government

Report says) "one of the most noxious practices is the giving of india-rubber nipples to suck – a habit to be most strongly deprecated. It causes contraction of the roof of the mouth and the air passages at the back of the nose."

"The Education Department have inserted the following Note in their New Code (1879): 'The work of girls in Arithmetic will be judged more leniently than that of boys.' It hardly ought to have required all these years for 'my Lords' to discover that this is only fair towards those who have needlework to attend to. Mothers are hardly aware, perhaps, that the needlework required is all most fully given in the Code, with details of hemming, seaming, felling, pleating, gathering, stroking, setting in, making, button-holing, herringboning, cutting out, darning, patching old garments, running tucks, whipping, setting on frills, knitting, knotting, feather-stitching, knitting boys' 'knickerbocker' stockings and stockings with heels thickened, plain and Swiss darning, and grafting stockings. We give the list for mothers to see how perfect their children ought to be, and are sure they will agree with us that more time should be given to this useful work, and a little less to other things now required." *August 1879*

Or what about this in the light of "In-service training" and "The National Curriculum"?

There has recently been issued the Report of a Committee of Specialists on the education of children under five years old.
The recommendations for these nursery schools are enough to make a child's mouth water: large sand-troughs on wheels for making sand-pies, with a supply of small spades and buckets; swings, a rocking-horse, reins, balls, dolls, doll's houses, a Noah's Ark, a piano, etc., etc. Why should there not be a Commission on Infants-in-arms, to recommend mothers to keep those mischievous india-rubber things out of their babies' mouths, and to keep stewed tea, tinned goods, and "just what we have," out of their stomachs?
The abundance of recommendations about Education of every kind in these days suggests the idea that they are intended to find work for the unemployed.

An early example of attempted "parent power" was dealt with in 1882, which included part of a reply by the then equivalent of the Education Minister (A. J. Mundella) to a parental letter of objection:

I am at a loss to understand on what ground you object to your children being taught good manners, and to their manifesting that respect to their teacher which is due to him from every person entering or leaving the school-room, and more especially from his scholars. I hope, on reconsideration you will at once send your children to school, with instructions to do this. You will, of course, render yourself answerable to the law. (Signed) A. J. Mundella. It is a rule without an exception, that those who have most real self-respect never need teaching to show respect to others. This is true, whatever be their station in life, the highest or the lowliest. No better examples of this could be found than in our Queen and the Royal Family. *May 1882*

The terms for Education at Cawthorne's Boys' School were set out as follows in one of the very early editions of the Parish Magazine in January 1871:

The Boys' School
Mr. Butterworth, who is appointed to the Mastership of our Boys' School, out of more than thirty candidates, will begin his School duties on Monday, the 9th.
The Managers have made the following regulations for the conduct of the School, feeling sure that they are for the interests of the scholars' parents and the general good of the School:

1. That the School-pence, which will for the future be due to the Managers and not the Master, be regularly paid in advance on the Monday Morning or other first attendance of each week. (Much trouble will be saved to the Managers and Master, as well as the Parents themselves, by this Rule being strictly carried out).

2. That for the above weekly payment the Managers will provide Copy and Exercise Books, Slates, and all that the scholars generally require.

3. That at the beginning of each Half-year the Managers will arrange where assistance shall be given towards the weekly school-pence, taking into consideration the circumstances of the parents, the number of children they have at School, etc.

4. That, except under particular circumstances, Boys be not admitted to this School who are not able to read in the easiest book of single-syllable words and to form the letters and figures.

(It is much better for the children and for the Boys' School that those who cannot fulfil these requirements, if under six years of age, should be taught at the Infants' School.)

One of the constant problems to which Rev. Pratt drew attention was finance and especially to the reluctance or inability of some families to pay the "school pence," resulting in Colonel Stanhope having to pay the shortfall. He was also quite caustic in his comments concerning school attendance:

> An Act of Parliament was passed in last Session, which, although it does not actually come in force before Jan. 1st, 1875, is yet virtually in present operation. The Act provides that after that date no child shall be employed in agricultural work under the age of twelve, unless he or she has attended a Government School during the twelve months preceding such employment as under:
>
> "If under ten, there must have been 250 attendances: if above 10, not less than 150, unless he or she has obtained a certificate from a Government Inspector of Schools that they have reached the "Fourth Standard."
>
> *Feb. 1874*
>
> Although this Act does not affect our parish as it does an entirely agricultural one, yet there are a few families that will do well to keep it in mind. To make 250 attendances, taking account of holidays, Saturdays, and Sundays, it requires the child to be at school almost every day.
>
> Of the "Voluntary Contributions," a guinea each was given by Mr. J. M. S. Stanhope, Mrs. Stanhope, Rev. C. T. Pratt, Mrs. Hutton, late Mr. Kaye and Miss Kaye. This leaves £89 16s. 8d as Col. Stanhope's contribution, which is equal, we believe, to a rate of more than 4d. in the £ on the whole rateable value of the Township. It is by no means a pleasant task to ourselves personally to be so much responsible for the management of our Schools as we are at present, when such a sum as the above has to come from one individual subscriber.
>
> There is a School Attendance Committee, we believe, somewhere over in the Penistone country, but they hardly let us know at Cawthorne whether they are awake or asleep. There are districts in which every single absence from School has to be strictly enquired into and explained to the satisfaction of the Committee. There needs something more of that kind of strictness here, if school attendance is not to be played with as it is by some of our scholars.
>
> *August 1900*
>
> It is not without much consideration and regret that it has been found necessary during the past month to make an alteration in the schoolpence of many of the children. So general a change would not have been necessary, if all parents were as particular as some are about their children's regular attendance. By comparing the average attendance of the past year (149) with the number on the Books (206), it will be seen that one quarter of the children are regularly absent from school.

> The cost of each child in average attendance last year was, including schoolbooks of every kind, £2 2s 8d: the average cost throughout England, exclusive of books, is £1 16s 8d. Each child's payment in pence in our schools amounted to a fraction over 11s 9d, out of which we may say that 2s 5d each was returned in the cost of schoolbooks, copybooks, etc., which are all provided by the School.
>
> There are families in the Parish, no doubt, upon whom the payment of schoolpence for their children presses somewhat heavily in times when wages are low; but, when they consider what education is now made to cost by the requirements of Government, and that schoolbooks of every kind are provided by the School, the Parents of Cawthorne have no reason to complain of the share they have to take in the cost of their children's education.
>
> *October 1883*

Sometimes the problems were aggravated by industrial disputes:

> During the present stand-still of our Colliery, there are no doubt, some families in the Parish to whom the payment of their children's school-pence is an impossibility. In all such cases application should be made to the Local School Attendance Committee, who will take each case into its fair consideration, and will not refuse, we feel sure, to allow the school-pence where it is really needed. When our readers remember that everything in the way of Books, Exercise Books, etc., is provided without extra payment, they cannot think that our rate of school-pence is a high one. And the Managers wish it to be known that they believe it would be a mistake to allow children to attend and not be paid for. It has been decided that a child is not being "sent to School" in the meaning of the Education Act, unless the school payment is sent with it.
>
> With sincere sympathy for those who really wish for work and cannot find any to go to, we can only express our hope that times may soon mend, though it was not an unthinking person who lately remarked, "Do you think we have seen the worst yet?"
>
> *September 1885*

> No one whose opinion is worth noticing feels anything but kindly sympathy for parents who are honestly and thriftily doing their best to help themselves, but who, owing to circumstances over which they have no control, are not able to do all for their dear children they could wish to do without some temporary help.
>
> *January 1886*

Comparison between the village school of the 1880's and its present-day counterpart is ironic. A century ago the threat to the village school came from the poverty of the parents and their inability to pay the school fees. School fees only ended in 1904 when the West Riding County Council took over. Now numbers have fallen and worries are being expressed about whether it can remain viable and what will happen if it does not – but the reason is not a shortage of children in the village. Rather, the problem is created by the growing number of parents who feel that the village school is "not right" for their children and are sufficiently affluent to pay for education at fee-paying Junior Schools. The sadness is that, if the trend continues, the fleet of cars taking children out of the village each morning to private schools could be joined by a bus taking the less affluent children to the school of a neighbouring village, because their own school has been closed. There are a few encouraging signs that the village school is once again becoming fashionable as parents presumably recognise how much their children can benefit from its pleasant, family atmosphere. They must also recognise that, in days of stringent economy in Local Government, the same slogan applies to the village school as applies to other amenities (e.g. the Post Office and shops) – "Use it, or lose it."

The people of Cawthorne could themselves be endangering an amenity which their predecessors have enjoyed for the past five hundred years. The reply to this charge is always that, if the village school were to raise itself to such a standard of excellence, no-one would want to send their children elsewhere, but one cannot but feel that this argument is somewhat unjust and should lose any shred of validity which it may have as the National Curriculum becomes established. Also, recent legislation has meant that at no previous time have parents been so able to influence the village school as they do now. It was certainly not so when the author had close links with the school between 1968 and 1976, first as a parent then as a Manager. (Before anyone else comes back with this response, I must add that the children of Rev. Charles T. Pratt, corresponding manager dealing with both the Board of Education and the National Society, did not attend the village school, but were educated privately – a precedent subsequently followed by many local and national educationalists and politicians, who have spent their working lives extolling the virtues of state education! Miss Winifred Pratt did become a school helper and continued to help supervise school visits to the museum and give talks up to 1905).

Notwithstanding the problems to do with "school pence"

Houghton photographs taken in Cawthorne 1897-1907. These, though carefully posed, give a good picture of village life at the time.

Itinerant accordionist and his monkey.

113

CAWTHORNE 1790-1990

Cutting the bracken in Deffer Woods late 1890s.

THE CAWTHORNE OF REV. CHARLES T. PRATT (1866-1915)

The Butlers gathering sticks in Deffer Wood late 1890s.

Mr. Butler, the Gamekeeper (seated) pauses for a talk with his wife, daughter and Under-Keeper late 1890's. Mrs. Butler and her daughter can also be seen in one of Rowland Wilkinson's motor-car photos.

This cottage, known as Ivy Cottage, was obviously a favourite of Houghton's, featuring in at least three of his photographs. The picture of Mrs. Horatio Sales doing running repairs to her grandson Tommy's trousers always raises a laugh at slide-lectures. No-one like Granny in an emergency!

The road man at work 1906. The road is the Huddersfield–Barnsley road just beyond Dog Kennel Bar. Even at this time it was not a tarmac road.

Facing: Cottage on Tivydale not far from South Lodge. No deeds could be found by the Cannon Hall Estate and it is thought to have been a squatter's cottage erected in enclosure times. Old residents remember it as "Taff" Hudson's cottage.

116

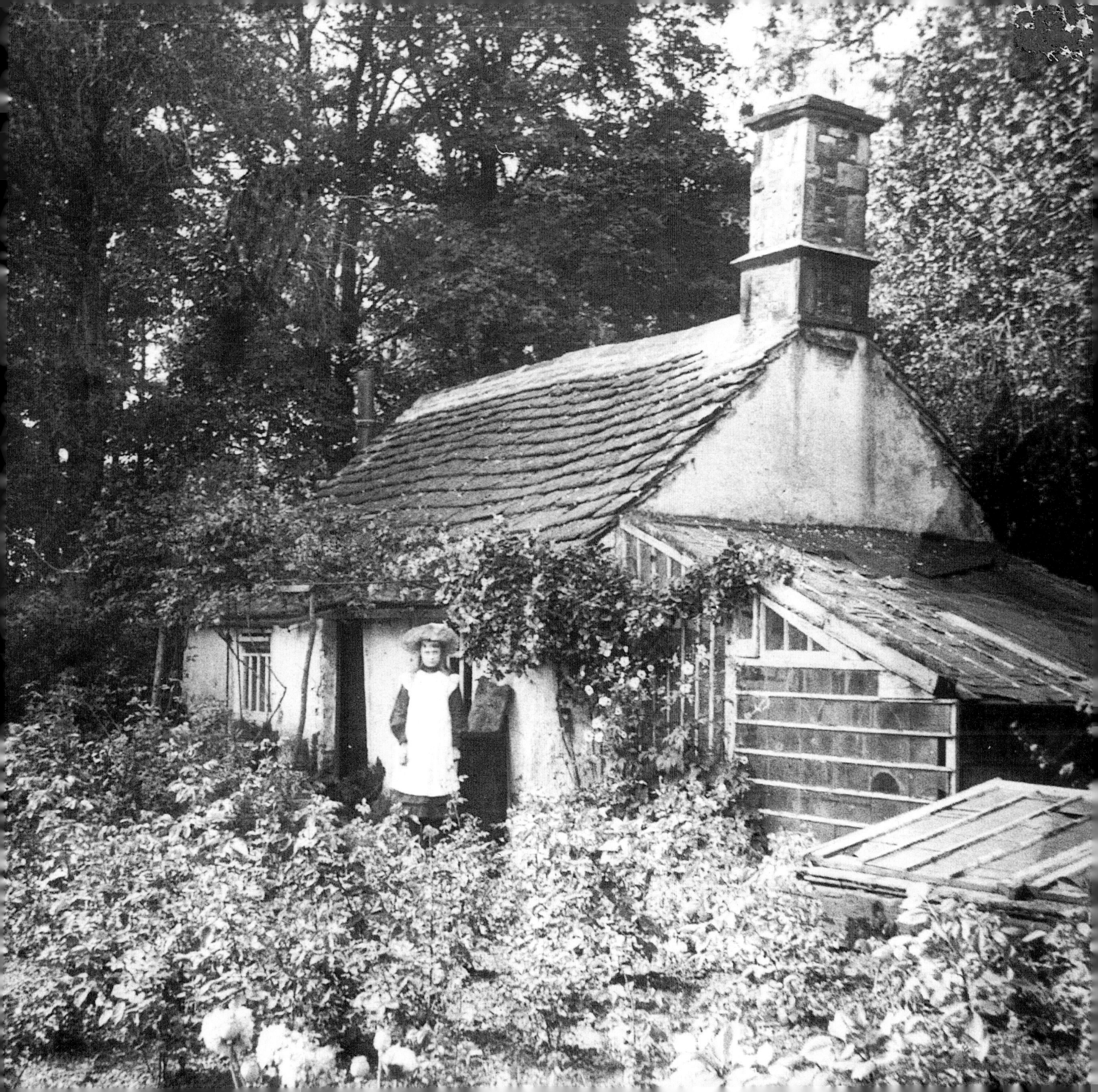

and school attendance, there was within Cawthorne a strong desire for education, and among the adults it engendered a spirit of self-education. It was from this spirit that there developed the Village Museum which, because the foundation of the present building was laid in the Golden Jubilee year of 1887, came to be known as "The Victoria Jubilee Museum." The following extracts tell the story of its foundation and show the part which it played in the village:

Cawthorne Museum

A circular has been sent round to every house in the Parish inviting people to join the "Cawthorne Museum Society" which has just been established with a payment of one shilling a year for membership. All who give in their names, male and female, younger or older, are desired to attend the next meeting in the Boys' School, at 7.30pm, on Monday May 5th. A Committee for the year will then be chosen by the members, and the Museum-room will be again open for their inspection. The small exhibition made on the 21st was, we thought, a very promising beginning.

May 1884

At the Meeting of members held on the 5th, a Committee for this year was chosen by those present, Mr Roddam Stanhope, at whose suggestion the Museum movement was begun, being elected the first President. The Members of the Committee elected are the Rev. C. T. Pratt, Messrs. J. Fretwell, A. Hill, S. Barraclough, C. Wemyss, G. McWhan, J. Dormand, J. Marsden, E. Clarke. Mr George Swift was appointed Treasurer, Mr. J. C. Wemyss, Secretary.

At the Committee Meeting on the 12th, the following general Rules were adopted: 1. That the Society be called "The Cawthorne Museum Society." 2. That the subscription of members, payable on admission, be one shilling each year ending with December. 3. That members be entitled to free admission to the Museum at such times as the Committee may determine it shall be open, and also, on showing their ticket of membership, to any Lectures which may be given in connection with the Society. 4. That until further notice the Museum be open on Monday evenings between 6.30 and 8, and on Saturdays from 4.30 to 6. 5. That admission to the Museum may be obtained by non-members on any week-day between 10 am. and 7 pm on application to the Caretaker, or in company with any member of the Committee at any hour. A box is to be placed in the Room, into which non-members are required to pay not less than a penny. Mr. Tom Chapple was chosen to keep a key as Caretaker. A Sub-committee was appointed to prepare the Museum for being open to members and visitors on and after Saturday May 31st.

It is the intention of the Committee that any Rules which may be made from time to time should be with the object of making the Museum as accessible and useful as possible to those who may be interested in it. The specimens will all be properly named, as soon as their permanent arrangement in cases can be finally made.

Many of our readers will be interested in hearing that among the present loans to our Little Museum are some Arab shields, spears, and knives, brought from the Field of Battle by W. Spencer Stanhope, Lieut. 19th Hussars. The Rev. H. Sandwith has kindly lent us some specimens of early Cyprian Pottery, found in ancient tombs in the Island of Cyprus. A most valuable collection of mineral specimens, with various other things, has been lent to the Society by Mr. Stanhope, whilst Mr. George Haworth has contributed among other things four cases of Brazilian Butterflies, etc., of marvellous brillancy of colour. Mr. Samuel Swift has sent a collection of Granites, Marbles, Alabasters, &c., and Mr. John Fretwell sends specimens of above a hundred different species of Butterflies, Moths, &c. It will take some little time to get all the things which have been already lent and promised arranged to the best advantage: but there seems every reason to expect that the small beginning already made will before very long outgrow the dimensions of our Museum's present lowly habitation.

June 1884

The Museum

IT is a peculiar pleasure to us to make known that Mr. John Ruskin has most kindly sent us some contributions for our Museum and promised us some more. "I shall have great pleasure," he writes, "in looking out some things for your Village Museum, and I have begun with a few minerals. * * I will look out later on some Prints and such things as are likely to answer your purpose." Those who know anything of Mr. Ruskin will very greatly appreciate his kindly interest in our Museum.

The Lecture on the 18th was in every way most successful, though we are afraid that those at a distance could not distinctly see the microscopic Lantern slides. It was just the kind of Lecture to open our minds to those wonders of God's creation by which we are every day surrounded without our knowing their wondrousness. We quite hope that Mr. Platnauer will come among us again.

Mr. Sandwith's Lecture will be in the Boys' School, on Monday, the 8th, at 7 pm. Admission free. Those who are willing to be members of the Museum Society for the current year, subscription one shilling, will be good enough to give or send their names and subscriptions to the Secretary, Mr. J. C. Wemyss, at the close of the Lecture.

The Museum and Malt Kiln Row at the turn of the century as photographed by Bamforth of Holmfirth. The quality of the original plate negative is demonstrated below by the degree of enlargement which it is still possible to make of a small section of the photograph.

On Tuesday evening, the 16th, there will be a Lecture on "Electricity." Mr. H. Burbury (of Dodworth Hall) will kindly bring over his Electric apparatus to illustrate the Lecture, and arrangements are made for bringing a wire down from our Post Office to the Boys' School and having some one at the Barnsley Post Office, to hold communication with the Meeting by Telephone. Admission one penny; seats will be reserved for those who are Members of the Museum Society. It begins at 7.

March 1886

The Museum

AT the Annual Meeting of Members, Mr. Roddam Stanhope was again elected President, and Mr. Montague Stanhope, Vice-President, of the Museum Society. The Committee was re-elected with the addition of Mr. J. C. Wemyss. Mr. McWhan was appointed Secretary. He will be glad to receive subscriptions of sixpence from those who are willing to become members. We are not without good hope that the Society will live and prosper. It does not seem to us impossible that it might some day have a more presentable habitation for its Museum. It was not altogether a dream, when we imagined the other day that we saw it established exactly where "Johnny Robert's old house" is, in a charming black-and-white one storey building, with a neat garden and iron rails open to the road, giving quite a pleasing look to the entrance to our Village. To assure ourselves that it was not an idle dream, we read over a letter received some time ago from the President, in which he most generously proposes "giving fifty pounds when wanted" towards a building of this kind, "and, should there be any further amount wanted later on, I hope I shall be able to help." It seems to us, that a very suitable building of this kind might "some day" be built on that site – all necessary permissions, etc., being granted – for some £130. In voluntary labour, teamwork, and donations, we believe we see our way at present to just about two-thirds of that sum.

May 1887

Mr. Roddam Spencer Stanhope and Cawthorne Museum
To the Editor of the "Barnsley Chronicle"

SIR – I have just read in your paper an account of the laying of the first stone of the Cawthorne Museum, at the Harvest Festival, in which you write in far too flattering terms of the share that I have taken in the scheme, which, owing to my living abroad had been a very small one.

To the vicar, Mr. Pratt, in the first place, to whose efforts the museum owes its existence, and the possession of the two interesting collections you mention; and to the efforts of the committee and a few others, in the second place, is the success which has attended it hitherto entirely due.

The collection has already outgrown its present quarters and my brother is now building for it the permanent museum of which the first stone was laid the other day; and, as now we shall have plenty of room, I trust that some of your readers may be induced to help us by contributing any specimens they may consider interesting, and which will be thankfully accepted by the committee.

I must crave space enough to add that I hope this may not prove an isolated attempt at lightening the increasing dreariness of country life, as the beauties of nature are gradually waning before the stern necessities of existence.

The English race has been hitherto in the forefront of civilisation, in all matters which concern, not only the necessaries, but also the luxuries and pleasures of life, and it is a pity that they should lag so far behind many other countries, in those things, that appeal to the higher instincts of mankind.

An Italian going for the first time to England, cannot fail to be struck with the air of comfort and neatness that universally pervades English home life, amongst all classes; or feel bewildered, as he sees out of the railway carriage the endless variety of arrangements, for the amusements of every class of its citizens, scattered broadcast through the country, from the racecourse, to the garden swing; a strong contrast to the too prevailing squalor and simple form of life he is accustomed to at home.

But he would have to go far and wide before finding any object of a sufficiently intellectual nature to attract in any way his attention or awaken his interest. Whilst in his own country there is scarcely a town or even a village that does not boast of something of the sort; whether it be ancient or modern, good or bad; and as regards museums in particular they are to be found everywhere; and in many a poverty-stricken town, no larger than an ordinary English village, may be seen the words "Musio," outside one of the principal buildings. Why it is not so in England is a question which I hope some of your readers may think worth their while to ponder over. I remain, Sir,

Yours obediently,
R. SPENCER STANHOPE
President of Cawthorne Museum.
Villa Nuti Bellosguardo, October 24, 1887.

Museum Lectures.

Canon Pigou has kindly promised to give a Lecture on Thursday the

An interior photograph of the Museum around the turn of the century taken from one of Houghton's stereoscopic plate negatives.

121

17th in Tivydale School at 7 pm on "Minute Organisms," illustrated throughout by the aid of a Lantern with Oxy-Hydrogen Lime-Light, of the power of 400 candles.

The Museum Committee have also arranged for a Lecture on Dec. 1st by Professor Arnold Lupton, Mem. Inst. C.E., F.G.S., Professor of Mining Engineering in the Yorkshire College, Leeds. It will be his Yorkshire College "Lecture of the People" entitled "A Mine," being mostly a description of Foreign Mines and Miners, illustrated by about 24 sq. yards of Diagrams and also by Magic Lantern Slides exhibited by Oxy-Hydrogen light, showing Views which he has himself photographed in his travels, and some of which were taken underground by electric light.

ADMISSION TO LECTURES. Members of Museum (to Front Seats) free. Front Seats, 6d.; Back Seats, 2d.; Day Scholars (on Gallery) 1d. If any members of the Museum are kind enough to give anything at the door, it would help towards the necessary expenses of these Lectures.

Mr. Stanhope expressed his desire that it should be regarded "as a commemoration in Cawthorne of the Jubilee Year of our Most Gracious Sovereign Lady, the Queen. The building would be contributed by the President of the Society (Mr. Roddam Stanhope) and the members of his family, but as far as the internal fittings were concerned – the cases and that sort of thing – they would be glad to have the assistance of any person who took an interest in the collection." He then called on Miss Mildred and Miss Winifrid Julia Stanhope "to lay the Foundation Stone, on behalf of their uncle and in his name."

The Collection is to be removed into the Manor House during the building of the Museum.

We can only express our great hope that the educational and other advantages to be derived from our Museum may be made good use of by the Parish, and that the young men may be encouraged by it to exercise their brains upon its collection and take an intelligent interest in it.

November 1887

The Museum.

No less than 464 visitors to the Museum signed their names in the Visitors' Book during the month of July. There were 310 signatures in August up to the 25th. There are always some whose names for one reason or another are not entered.

Mr. G. Pearson, of Barnsley, has given our little Museum Library the two interesting volumes of Mantell's "Medals of Creation", and Mr. G. B. Clifton, of Oxford and London, has presented a bound copy of the "Forth Bridge" Number of "Engineering." Mr. S. L. Mosley, F.E.S., Curator of the Beaumont Park Museum, Huddersfield, has been over to see our Museum more than once. He has expressed his great willingness to do whatever he can to help it on, and has given an evidence of his desire in presenting two interesting Cases. One is a case of "Injurious Insects," such as he has been engaged to do for the Kew, the South Kensington, the Dublin, the Edinburgh University, and other Collections. The second Case shows the caterpillar, chrysalis, and butterflies of several common species.

It is intended to occupy part of one of the new Cases with a collection of Coins. If anyone has interesting specimens they are willing to lend, the Committee will be glad to receive them. A Case of 20 Drawers is being made for a Collection of Moths and Butterflies which Mr. John Fretwell is collecting in the place of those who perished during the building of the Museum.

It will give some idea of the amount of rain that fell on Sunday the 10th, when it is stated that it amounted to upwards of 27,000 gallons, or something over 119 tons, for every acre. The measured rainfall was 119 inches. Mr. Symons' British Rainfall for 1889, as observed at nearly 3000 stations, has just been laid on the Museum Table.

September 1890

The Jubilee Museum.

At the Annual Meeting held on the 26th, the following were elected the officers of the Museum Society for 1891. President, J. Roddam S. Stanhope, Esq.; Vice-President, J. Montague S. Stanhope, Esq.; Treasurer, Mr. G. Swift; Secretary, Mr. McWhan; Committee, Rev. C. T. Pratt, Messrs. Fretwell, G. Hindle, Morrell, Hill, R. Charlesworth, R. Mosley, J. Marsden, C. E. Pratt, E. Clarke, E. Balme, B. Fish, Geo. Wright, and Miss W. M. Pratt. The very generous friend and supporter of the Museum, Col. Stanhope, C.B., is the Society's continuous "Patron." The Committee's Statement shows that there were 132 members in 1890, and that the Visitors' Box contained £14 19s. 2s. The New Year begins with a Balance in hand of £17 8s. 0d. after the Payments of 1890, amounting to £27. We hope that those who are willing to become members for the current year will lose no time in sending in their names and subscriptions (1s.) to the Secretary. For those under 14, the membership is 6d.

Mr. C. H. Hutchinson, of Barnsley Gas Works, will give a Lecture on "Coal and its Products," in the Museum on Monday, Feb. 2nd, at 7 pm. Mr. Frankland of St. Mary's Schools, Barnsley, will read a Paper on "The English Viper," on the 9th, at 7 pm. Members free; Non-members 1d.

The Rainfall registered here last amounted to 26.25 inches; ie., 26¼. It fell on 163 days: the greatest amount in one day was 1.19 inches, on Aug. 10th. Considerably more than one-fifth – 5.60 in. – of the total rainfall fell on 5 days. The Rainfall of 1889 was 27.12 inches on 153 days.

February 1891

The Museum.

The members of the Museum Society are about to hold a Conversazione in the Museum, from 6.45 to 9 pm, on Tuesday, the 8th.

Col. Stanhope, C.B., will very kindly allow the orginal Little John's Bow to be exhibited during the evening and Capt. W. Stanhope will show and explain his New Zealand Photographs, and give a short account of his Travels. Mdlle. Delabrosse will kindly give some Recitations. Miss Beatrice Pratt will play some Violin Solos. Mr. Jas. Balme's party will sing some Songs and Glees, and some short Recitations from Tennyson will be given by the Rev. C. T. Pratt. The Tickets of invitation are not transferable, and each Ticket will only admit the Member whose name it bears.

The Museum has just received from its President, Mr. Roddam Stanhope, a large Collection of Japanese arms, etc.

November 1892

The Museum.

Mr. George Hindle and Mr. John Fretwell will take charge of Field Classes of Members in Natural History as soon as the season is sufficiently advanced. We regret that Mr. W. Bretton has been prevented by illness from giving his further Lecture on Astronomy.

March 1894

Museum Committee, 27th, at 7 pm. Members' Meeting at 7.30 for Election of Officers. Subscriptions may be paid to Mr. James Balme. A Family Ticket may now be obtained for 2s. admitting all members of the family under 21 years old.

January 1898

In 1953 the Museum building was offered to the Museum Society by Mrs. Stanhope (as Mrs. Elizabeth Fraser tended to be known after her divorce and return to Cannon Hall) for the sum of £100, at the same time that the former Girls' School was being purchased as a Village Hall for £250. The sum now seems a small one, but it caused some problems in 1953, until an anonymous benefactor (later identified as Mr. Ben Fish) intervened, as related in a newspaper cutting of July 15th that year:

Surprise Ends Fight For Its Survival

The survival of Cawthorne's Victoria Jubliee Museum, which attracts 3,000 visitors every year, has been assured by an anonymous gift of £100.

The gift, which represents the Purchase price of the Museum from the Cannon Hall Estate, came as a complete surprise to the 60 members of the Cawthorne Museum Society.

They had been working hard to raise the money and had got £60 together as a result of exhibitions and other efforts. Then treasurer Mr. D. N. Stables was summoned to the bank and was told an anonymous donor had paid £100 into the Society's account.

A condition of the gift was that the Society should raise £200 in the next four years to guarantee adequate maintenance of the museum.

Estate Offer

Biggest threat to the museum lay in the likelihood of a breakup of the Cannon Hall Estate, which is now extensively affected by open-cast mining.

Mr. B. Harral, chairman of the society, told "The Star" today: "The estate were very generous and they offered us the museum for £100 freehold. We were trying to raise the money when this £100 was paid into our account."

Built by estate workmen in their spare time and opened in 1889 the museum, with its attractive half-timbered front, has grown considerably.

Looking ahead secretary Mr. N. F. Moxon said: "We could really do with a small annexe to house our surplus exhibits."

This last statement finally bore fruit in 1983.

The Cawthorne Victoria Jubilee Museum must now be unique in the museum world. A registered charity, it is owned by the villagers and administered on their behalf by a body of trustees. It is entirely self-supporting and opens on Saturday and Sunday afternoon (plus other times by appointment). It has volunteer curators and is manned during opening hours by members of the Society. Its character remains Victorian with its cruck beam construction and arrays of cases of stuffed birds. Offers of exhibits are seldom refused, resulting in the whole effect being one of a delightful clutter, where, however many times one returns, there is always something which has been

CAWTHORNE 1790-1990

Rt. Rev. Colin James stoops to sign the visitors book after opening the extension April 24th, 1983. Requesting him to do so is Chairman, Alfred Park, the driving force behind raising the money for the extension.

The doors are open and the visitors begin to stream in!

Television personality, Richard Baker and his associate, pianist Raphael Terroni, who gave a concert in 1984 at Nostell Priory to celebrate the Centenary of the Museum Society.

previously overlooked. The emphasis now tends to be local, but, because of the things which the Spencer Stanhopes brought back from their travels during the Museum's infancy, the range of exhibits on show are a geography lesson in themselves. As befits an establishment which was set up in a spirit of curiosity and self-education, nothing was too trivial to collect, nor too strange. Indeed many of the exhibits now border on the bizarre. Where else, for 25p per adult and 10p per child, could one see the stuffed remains of a two-headed calf and a two-headed lamb (both born locally – one in Victorian times and the other in 1988), or a horse's intestinal-stone weighing 9lbs 9oz, or a statuette of John Wesley carved from the vertebra of a whale? Where could one view the forerunner of moving pictures by spinning a zoetrope, or see three-dimensional views of Victorian and Edwardian times through a stereoscopic viewer; and in what other museum is one able to see as an exhibit the tattered remains of a boot being worn by a local boy, Tom Parkin, c1930 when he was struck by lightning (and survived)? To these can be added a collection of commemorative china, domestic utensils, farm implements, coins, photographs of village life, and much more. Such is the charm of this museum, to which people return again and again, bringing their children to look at some exhibits, to wonder at others (e.g. at the cruelty which allowed a fearsome man-trap to be set up in the Victorian orchards of Cawthorne) and to pit their wits against the "puzzle-lock": a lock (thought to be by Joseph Bramah) which was taken from the Church door in the 1870's, and which, to lock and unlock again completely, constitutes an exercise in instant frustration!

The museum has been fortunate in the continuity of service given by its main officials. Rev. C. T. Pratt was its guiding force from its foundation until his health forced him to retire to Cheltenham in 1915, Douglas Charlesworth served as Secretary from 1918 to 1940, with Noel Moxon continuing the tradition by serving in the same office from 1943 until his death in 1979. To honour this last period of service and to relieve the growing pressure for new exhibition space, the Museum Society, embarked upon a fund-raising scheme, raising sufficient money which, added to contributions from public bodies such as South Yorkshire County Council, enabled them to build "The Noel Moxon Wing" on the back of the building provided in 1889 by the Spencer Stanhopes. This extension was formally opened by the Bishop of Wakefield (Rt. Rev. Colin James) and the Chairman of South Yorkshire County Council in 1983. However, such is the Museum's tradition of not refusing offers of exhibits on gift or loan that it will not be long before it will be necessary to build the extra smaller room for which the foundations were laid at the time of the 1983 building work.

Jim Moxon and his grandson Andrew receive instruction from Stan Bulmer on the pose which he wants for a photograph of them cutting the first piece of turf for the Museum extension.

Members of the Museum Committee dressed up for the Centenary Celebrations, Oct. 1989. Photo by John Marshall for "Barnsley Chronicle".

A Methodist Sunday School treat consisting of a walk to Gunthwaite followed by a picnic.   R. W.

We are now so used to relatively-long periods of "holidays with pay" that we find it difficult to envisage what life must have been like when the only rest from long hours of hard work came upon "holy days" as they originally were known, religious festivals which had over the centuries acquired a very direct and practical meaning for people who lived by the sweat of their brows and the produce of their fields and gardens. There was "Plough Monday" when God was asked to "speed the plough" in breaking up the soil for the Spring corn, Rogation Day when blessing was asked for the growing lambs and calves and for the young corn, the first ripening of which was later celebrated at Lammas-tide, to be followed by Harvest Festival when "all was safely gathered in". The few non-religious festivals, however, were the times when the people of Cawthorne took full opportunity to enjoy themselves.

"Cawthorne Feast" is always remembered with affection by older people in the village. "It was always held on the third week-end in July. Many visitors came to see their families and Cannon Hall Estate issued tins of paint to cottage tenants so that most houses were smartened up for the occasion. The school had two half-day holidays (Monday and Tuesday) and the field bordering Silkstone Lane (where Kirkfield Close now stands) was taken over for the weekend by a small fair with roundabouts, swings, coconut-shies and stalls selling brandy-snap. As children, we loved most of all the donkeys, on which, for 1d. a time, we could ride as far as the quarry on Silkstone Lane and back. This fair kept on until midnight and we saved up our pennies for weeks to spend at it." [8] Charles Pratt was not entirely without reservations in his feelings about Cawthorne Feast and felt it almost to be an annual duty in his Parish Magazine to lament its departure from its religious origins and to regret some of the behaviour which took place!

"Feast-Time."

> After speaking of our Village Feast-time for so many years, it would not be easy, perhaps, to say anything fresh about it. Like most things it has its good and pleasant, and also its evil and painful aspect. There are not many Parishes, we venture to say, in which the good house-wives more enjoy "a right good cleaning-down" than they do at Cawthorne: and it is always a pleasure to see absent ones paying their home visits, bringing with them their happy tidings of "how nicely they are getting on." Still, there is a dark side to the picture: we do not wish to dwell on it: but let us all hope and pray, that Village Feast-times, here and everywhere, may cease to be times of Sunday desecration, instead of specially joyous Sunday worship, and that they may no longer be defiled by those sins which are contrary to Christian temperance, soberness and chastity.
>
> Our Services will have their special Hymns of Praise: and may our church be filled with those whose hearts are spiritually tuned to enter into the joy of praising God with such Hymns as "The Old Hundredth," and "Now thank we all our God!"
>
> *July 1885*

127

CAWTHORNE 1790-1990

Holidays away at the seaside were a luxury seldom enjoyed, but some families did find time and transport for full day outings as this delightful photograph of the Swifts at Wharncliffe Crags early this century shows.   S.S.

THE CAWTHORNE OF REV. CHARLES T. PRATT (1866-1915)

Two photographs of Cawthorne Feast festivities. Above a "scratch" cricket-team, probably ready to play in a match against a Ladies XI.   R.W.

A men's dressing-up and hat competition.   R.W.

"Our Feast-time."

It is always a great satisfaction to think that our Feast-time at Cawthorne is generally spent as innocently and sensibly as such a time is anywhere spent. We sincerely hope that it may be favoured by fine cheerful weather, and that it may leave behind it nothing but what is pleasant to remember. The older and more thoughtful among us cannot forget, indeed, that there are those to whom such a time is one of temptation. Let us remember that we, every one of us, have a special interest, even as a matter of Parish self-respect if from no higher motive, in its passing by us without leaving behind it a single memory that could or ought to raise a blush of shame. So far as one may judge at present, the early part of this summer will long be remembered for the good crops of hay that will have been gathered in with very little trouble before the Feast. Early hay crops have generally been light ones: happily that cannot be said of this year's crop. It is much to be hoped that the present good prospects of the farmer may all in due time be realised as the most important element in our national prosperity.

A good game at Lawn Tennis is always interesting. If the weather allows of it, some games will be played in the Vicarage Garden, after half-past five, on the Tuesday and Thursday evenings before the Feast (16th and 18th), where a seat and welcome will be ready for any who care to come and see them. If we cannot promise good play, we can promise the play of those who do their best.

July 1889

"The Feast."

There is an old custom which will never die out, we hope, of wishing each other happiness at our great Christian Festivals. Our village feast-times, as we have often said, had their remote origin in religion, and always in ancient times centred round the Parish Church. Few of our readers associate these times now with any religious observances. It would be better in every way, if we did. But we can always say in connexion with our Cawthorne Feast and its many pleasant family gatherings and meetings, may God give His blessing and much happiness to all our village homes, and may it be a time of innocent enjoyment.

July 1901

The Village Feast.

It is no use trying to say anything fresh about our Cawthorne Feast-time. One always tries to look on its *good* side, without trying to remember that many village feasts have a side that is not altogether good, and that it may be a time of temptation to some amongst ourselves. It is an opportunity for many of those who are living away to come and see those at home, and meet once more some of their old friends and school fellows of former years. It is a time that helps to keep up family affections and old friendships. But it should never be a time when the worship of God is neglected, because of visitors, by those who are accustomed to make the Lord's Day a day of public worship, as we all know it ought to be.

July 1908

129

CAWTHORNE 1790-1990

What Rev. Pratt would have had to say had he lived in early 18th Century Cawthorne is hard to imagine, since then times of village feasts and other such gatherings carried with them even greater dangers than those associated with excessive drinking. One old newspaper cutting contains the following story. "During the reign of George I, the press gang was very rife in Yorkshire. Village feasts were often troubled with surprise visits, and many a smart young fellow was abducted and pressed without any chance of escape. Cawthorne was celebrating its annual feast when the unsuspecting villagers were suddenly broken upon by the press gang, which had been hid in an adjoining plantation, opposite to the vicarage. Two young fellows were captured, the villagers sought retreat in every direction (some taking refuge in the woods), many shutting themselves up in their houses and drawing the blinds down. Scarcely anyone ventured out for some time after, and the feast so suddenly terminated was pronounced to have 'ended with a whew'. One of the pressed young men (Vasey) died in the Service abroad, and, after some years, the other (Beaumont) returned to his native village, where he ultimately died, and was buried in Cawthorne Churchyard".

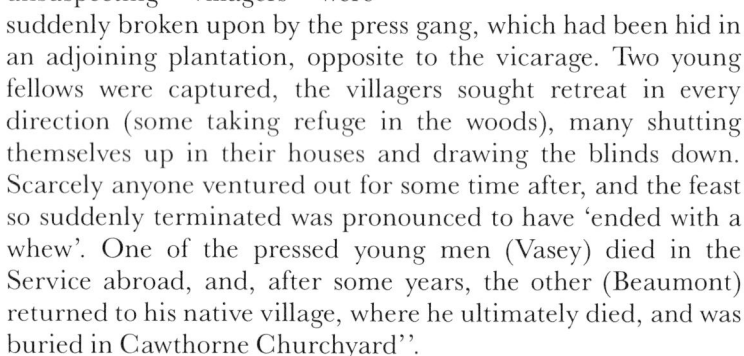

May Day was another time of festivities. Maypole-Dancing and May Day Games were encouraged by John Spencer Stanhope (1787-1873). Around 1900 the maypole-dancing in the village was in the hands of a Derbyshire-born miner, who lived at Cawthorne Basin. "Jos Broadhead was a character, a rumbustious miner, but he was a natural at teaching the kiddies to Maypole Dance." [18] Since his death, the tradition has been carried on first by his daughter and then by his grandson's wife. May Day was also a great day for the Friendly Societies, who

Another Feast photograph, since that was when donkeys figured prominently in the village.   R.W.

Maypole-dancing on the Village Green July 1st. 1989.   J.E.G.

Maypole-dancing at Cannon Hall late 1940's.   N.F.M.

held a parade of decorated floats populated by children. We tend to forget the part played by the Friendly Societies in the days before National Health Insurance in making sure that, through weekly saving, workers had some kind of provision made for them in the event of accident or ill-health. When the Liberal Governments of Sir Henry Campbell-Bannerman and H. H. Asquith brought in a system of social welfare benefits, Rev. Pratt was quick to warn his parishioners of the importance of the Friendly Societies in the administration of the Governments reforms:

The Insurance Act.

It is probably unnecessary by this time to warn those who are subject to the above Act against becoming what are called "Deposit Contributors," through the Post Office. Every insured person should become a member of an "Approved Society," or the consequence will almost certainly be most serious. Besides the schemes of our other Friendly Societies, that of the Co-op is well worth looking at, and seems to offer great advantages.

Sept. 1912

The three main Friendly Societies in Cawthorne were the Ancient Order of Foresters, the Cawthorne Labourers' Provident Society and the Rechabites. The activities of the first two are covered in two cuttings from the Barnsley Chronicle as follows:

Cawthorne Court Disbanded.

After being in existence for over 120 years, the Cawthorne Court, "The Lamb," of the Ancient Order of Foresters, is to be disbanded and absorbed into one of the Barnsley Courts.

The Cawthorne Court was founded at the house of Mrs. Sarah Bell, the Golden Cross Inn, in May, 1833, where it met for many years, moving later to the Spencer Arms, where it has remained until the dissolution this year.

The old rule book states that eight officers be elected. These included Chief Ruler, Woodwards and Beadles. The duty of the Woodwards was to inspect and pass the accounts and also pay benefits to sick brothers. The Beadles kept the door and executed menial duties. There was a rule to the effect that a dinner be held every second Saturday in August.

In the old book are some 50 names and ages of Cawthorne men showing that the Court had a good membership during the last century.

When new members were initiated it was performed with great ceremony. The recruit had to stand on the step of the meeting room, whilst a robe was placed over his shoulders. After knocking on the door he was admitted into the room, where he was greeted with a red hot poker for branding purposes. The new member was relieved to find that this part of the ceremony was not carried out in full.

The Foresters also had a team of bearers, who had to officiate at funerals of departed brothers or wives.

In the meeting room at the Spencer Arms is a large board on which are written the names of brothers who supported the Foresters'

A self-explanatory photograph of an entertainment at the Methodist schoolroom.   R.W.

cause some 80 years ago.

Mr. George Roberts, secretary, is desirous that the board be placed in the Museum for safe keeping, together with other records.

1954

CAWTHORNE LABOURERS' PROVIDENT SOCIETY – The above-named society held its sixteenth annual meeting for the examination of the accounts of the society and for the transaction of general business in Lady Elizabeth Stanhope's Girl School in Tivydale, on Tuesday evening, at eight o'clock, under the presidency of Walter Spencer Stanhope, Esq. – Mr. Stanhope, in meeting the labourers at the sixteenth annual meeting, congratulated them on the continued success and prosperity of the institution. If the funds of the society had been drawn upon this year to a greater extent than usual it was simply in accordance with the usual practice of dividing the funds at the end of each five years. The cash transactions of the society showed that £508 had been paid to members withdrawn; including the bonus paid at the end of the five years period, £106 14s. 10d. had been paid to members who had continued their ledger accounts with the society; and £115 4s. 10d. had been received during the year, which, with the balance in the hands of the treasurer, showed a total of receipts for the year of £745 10s. 10d., while the present state of the funds of the society showed that £16 14s. 8d. were in the hands of the treasurer, Mr. Wemyss, and £172 5s. 3d. invested in the Barnsley Savings Bank. A vote of thanks was moved by Mr. T. Kitson, and seconded by Mr. R. Charlesworth, to the president for his continued interest in the affairs of the society, and for his donation which he had announced of £5 to the reserve fund of the society. The auditors, as usual, were Mr. Longthorne, of Silkstone, and Mr. Barraclough, of Cawthorne, but now of Barnsley.

Date unknown

Noel Moxon had this to say about the Rechabites, of which he later became the Cawthorne representative: "When I went to work at Tivydale Pit, I was told to get an insurance card, which I got from a friendly society, from Sam Barraclough, the Secretary of the Rechabites... The amount that the society paid out if a member was sick depended upon its wealth. This led to the decline of the Rechabites in Cawthorne, because they only paid 15s. (75p) per week sick-pay, whereas the Co-op and Prudential paid £1. This district, being a mining district, had a lot of sickness claims and this affected the rate of sick-pay set by the society." [7]

A May Day celebration by the Rechabites.   R.W.

A further time for celebration and enjoyment, plus a good deal of hard work, was Cawthorne Show. It began in 1850 with the foundation by the Spencer Stanhopes of the Cawthorne Cottagers' Floral and Horticultural Society, the aim of which was to improve the appearances of the cottages and cottage gardens in the village by fostering among their tenants a spirit of friendly competition. (A spirit, which, as we shall see, did sometimes get out of hand!) During the hundred years or so of its existence it added the word "Agricultural" to its already long title and became one of the largest village agricultural shows in the North of England. Its demise in the early 1950's is still lamented in the village and it is remembered with affection. "It was always held on the first Saturday in September... and was then just a Flower and Vegetable Show, all displayed in one large marquee. There was great rivalry between vegetable growers especially, and I am not sure that all the exhibits were honestly grown by the exhibitors. I do remember tales to the contrary and well recall Mr. Pratt preaching on the subject. However, it was a very happy day. The school-children had a section for arrangments of bunches of wild-flowers. It is surprising how many were to be found so late in the year, and we took them to the school on the morning of the Show to arrange them in glass jam-jars. There was great excitement before the tent opened to see who had won the three prizes. The first prize was about 1s. 6d. (7½p) I think, which was a lot of money to a child in those days. As the years passed by the Show grew bigger, including in its events sheep dog-trials, horse-jumping etc." [8] As previously indicated, the Show did not always meet with the approval of Rev. Charles Pratt, although his daughter, Winifred, was closely associated with it. Indeed, written condemnation of certain aspects seems to have been an annual feature of his parish magazine as the following extracts show:

"October 1879. We should like to ask the Committee and subscribers of the Cawthorne Flower Show whether they were satisfied with our recent exhibition of fruits and flowers? In the interests of truth and honesty, we must enter our strongest protest against the present system of people exhibiting what they have never grown. It may make a better show, but it entirely discourages those who wish to do honestly and fairly, and defeats every object for which the Society exists. We should like to know where 'within six miles of Cawthorne' the sunshine was found which ripened certain apples, pears and plums we saw? If the Committee is going to allow this

An official photograph at Cawthorne Show early this century. Some of these are members of the Show Committee so often criticised by Rev. Pratt.
Back row (left to right) Willie Hoyland (Farmer at Barnby Hall), John Harrison (joiner), George W. Swift (Clerk of Works), Ernst G. Neumann (Spencer Arms), E. Chappell (Farmer of Flash House) and J. Milnes (Farmer of Jowett House).
Middle row, Unknown, Edward Lawson (Farmer of Cinder Hill), George Buckley (Farm Bailiff), James Wemyss (Estate Chief Clerk), Mr John Montague Spencer Stanhope, Mr Clarke (Head Gardener), William Lockwood (Golden Cross), a Cannon Hall Gardener.
Seated, Mr Hinchliffe (mason), George Puddephatt (stone-mason), Mrs Stanhope, Sir Walter, Samuel Swift (sculptor), Miss Winifred Pratt and John Fretwell.
Seated on the floor, a Cannon Hall Gardener and Herbert Hinchliffe (pupil architect Cannon Hall Estate Office).

A show Committee between the wars.

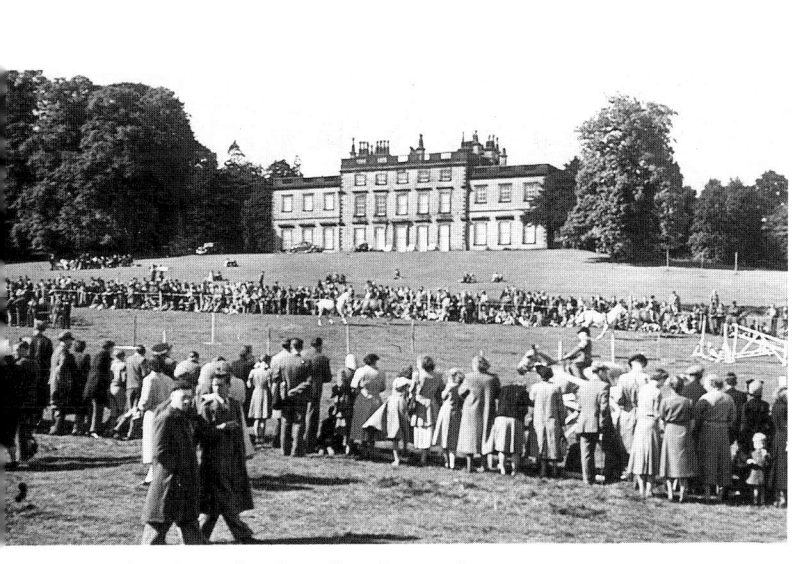

Crowds at a Cawthorne Show late 1940's.

Preparing the produce for exhibition.

The parade of the heavy horses.

Two "Barnsley Chronicle" Photographs of Cawthorne Show late 1940's. Failure and success.

systematic swindling to go on, we can only advise them to offer a prize next year for 'the best half dozen Cocoa Nuts grown in the Parish', and see whether exhibitors are found to compete quite as honest as some of those who have exhibited this year. Do they believe that the children's Bouquets are all honestly made by those whose names are given? The dishonesty seems to begin at about three years old and go up to well, we should hardly like to say what age.''

"November 1884. We are sorry to hear that our Cawthorne Flower Show has not yet been purified from those dishonesties to which we referred... some time ago... It would not be impossible, we believe, to trace some of last Show's onions to Stalybridge."

"September 1909. There is commonly felt a very strong and righteous indignation against one who robs a garden in the dark; there ought to be the same feeling about one who steals, or tries to steal, in the light, by showing what he has not grown in his own garden. It is equally wrong, too, in those who help to do this, by giving him what they know he is going to dishonestly exhibit."

CAWTHORNE HOSPITAL SUNDAY

IN AID OF THE
Beckett Hospital and Dispensary, Barnsley.

THE SECOND ANNUAL

MUSICAL FESTIVAL

Will be held in the CANNON HALL PARK
(Kindly lent by J. M. SPENCER-STANHOPE, Esq.),

On SUNDAY, JULY 16th, 1916.

CHORUSES & APPROPRIATE HYMNS

Will be Rendered by a FULL BAND AND CHORUS.

CONDUCTOR - - Mr. J. H. COOPER, of Darton.
LEADER OF BAND - - Mr. BUTCHER.

Selections will be Rendered by the SILKSTONE PRIZE BAND.

CONDUCTOR - MR. J. BOTTOM.

Chair to be taken at 2-30 p.m. by

E. M. S. PILKINGTON, Esq.

Supported by the Rev. Mr. COTTON, Vicar of Cawthorne, and Mr. FEASBY, of Barnsley.

IN THE EVENING,

SELECTIONS OF MUSIC will again be rendered by the SILKSTONE PRIZE BAND

IN CANNON HALL PLEASURE GROUNDS
(By kind permission of J. M. SPENCER-STANHOPE, Esq.)

The Gardens and Grounds will be Open to the Public from 7-15 p.m. till 10 p.m.

OFFERTORY SHEETS will be placed at the respective Entrances to the Park and Grounds, and the Committee respectfully solicit your support.

A PUBLIC TEA will be provided in the Parish Room.

PROGRAMMES - ONE PENNY EACH.

C. L. BURGESS, *Hon. Sec.*

J. E. VERO LTD., BARNSLEY.

CAWTHORNE HOSPITAL SUNDAY

In aid of the BARNSLEY BECKETT HOSPITAL.

THE ANNUAL MUSICAL FESTIVAL

WILL BE HELD IN THE

CANNON HALL PARK

(Kindly lent by J. M. SPENCER-STANHOPE, Esq., J.P.)

On SUNDAY, July 18th, 1920

CHORUSES FROM THE MESSIAH

And APPROPRIATE HYMNS

Will be rendered by a FULL BAND and CHORUS.

Leader of Orchestra - Mr. JAMES GRATION, of Barnsley.
Conductor - - Mr. A. NORRIS, Darton Road.

SELECTIONS will be rendered by the

CAWTHORNE SUBSCRIPTION BRASS BAND

Chair to be taken at 2-30 p.m by **CAPT. J. PARDOE**

Supported by the Rev. G. V. COTTON, Vicar of Cawthorne;
Mr. A. WHITHAM, of Barnsley, and
Mr. H. IBBERSON, J.P., of Mapplewell.

In the Evening, a

SACRED CONCERT

Will be held in

Cannon Hall Pleasure Grounds

By kind permission of J. M. SPENCER-STANHOPE, Esq., J.P.

Selections will be rendered by the
CAWTHORNE SUBSCRIPTION BRASS BAND.

Conductor: Mr. W. RUSBY

To Commence at 7-30 p.m.

On SATURDAY, July 17th, a **LADIES' CRICKET MATCH** will take place in the Park (kindly lent by J. M. SPENCER-STANHOPE, Esq., J.P.), consisting of Mr. G. Dalton's Team from Silkstone, and Mr. S. Crompton's Team of Cawthorne, to commence at 6 p.m. - Entrance to Park—SIXPENCE.

CAWTHORNE BAND will be in attendance and play Selections of Dance Music.

OFFERTORY SHEETS will be placed at all entrances to the Park, and the Committee trust that the Public will generously support the cause.

C. L. BURGESS, Hon. Sec.

PROGRAMMES 2D. EACH.

J. E. VERO, LTD., BARNSLEY.

THE CAWTHORNE OF REV. CHARLES T. PRATT (1866-1915)

Two shots of the Village "sing" early 1950's.

a more formal occasion with a choir mounted on a raised platform.

a more informal gathering on the Village Green.

The Cawthorne Show died in the years when the Spencer Stanhopes were engaged in selling off Cannon Hall and its park, and when the parkland on which the event had been held was being ripped apart by opencast-coal-mining.

In recent years the flower and vegetable show has been revived by members of the Tivydale Club, but whether this show will grow to the size of its predecessor is open to question. One of its great problems is the cost of staging it, since venues, which were once provided free of charge by the Spencer Stanhopes, can now only be obtained at considerable cost from the local Borough Council.

Music has always figured prominently among village recreations. The Cawthorne Singers, who were the bane of Rev. Phipp's life in the 1790's, have already been mentioned, and they were succeeded in the 1830's by another group. In addition to these, there was a strong tradition of bell-ringing which brought success in many competitions to the village ringers, a practice which did not altogether meet with the Vicar's approval. Groups of friends formed small singing and instrumental ensembles which entertained at concerts organised by such organisations as the Church and the Museum. One such group was run in the 1880's and 1890's by Mr. James Balme who was the Church choirmaster. The first organisation of singing on a large scale came with the First World War, and the establishment of the Cawthorne Hospital Sunday (usually known as the "sing") when a massed choir and accompanying band gathered in Cannon Hall Park. It was an occasion when, as the programme says, "Choruses from 'The Messiah' and appropriate hymns will be rendered by a full band and chorus", the object of the exercise being to raise money for the Barnsley Beckett Hospital. The first "Sing" was remembered as follows: "July 18th 1915 Cawthorne Feast Sunday, a glorious day. There was a "sing" in the park, the first ever held here. Over 100 singers and a number of players there. The hymns and choruses from the Messiah went well. I and Lily sat under an apple-tree in the orchard all the afternoon listening. They took over £60 in the collecting sheets." In 1917, on the day before the "sing", "Military Sports" took place in the park. These were given by members of the Royal Engineers from the Silkstone Camp, and consisted of "Bayonet fighting, Boat racing etc., etc." Out of the tradition of the "sing" (which is still held, but on the village green) there

The Choral Society photographed by Raymond Walker before a concert in 1987.

grew a village Choral Society. This was set up in 1927 and gave its first concert in March 1928. It continued sporadically through the 1930's with performances from the standard oratorio repertoire, but had lapsed by the time war came in 1939. The revival of the village "sing" in the early 1950's gave fresh impetus for the Choral Society to be reformed in 1955. It was not until 1965, however, that the choir began to rehearse on a regular basis, being for a short while affiliated to the local Evening Institute. Until 1976 it enjoyed close links with the music department of Bretton Hall College of Education, joining with their orchestra and choral groups in performances of "The St. Matthew Passion", "The Messiah" and Brahms "Requiem". The original membership of the choir was chiefly recruited from the village, but change came towards the end of the 1970's. The need to pay higher fees for conductors of the calibre of Peter Gould (now organist and master of choristers at Derby Cathedral) meant increased subscriptions and the necessity to find other sources of finance, such as grants from Yorkshire Arts and the National Federation of Music Societies. These, however, were not obtained without certain conditions, one being the inclusion in the repertoire of music of a less popular nature and with a more esoteric appeal. This brought a change in both membership and audience, both of which now come mainly from outside the village. One thing, however, remains constant. At the foundation meeting on October 19th 1927, it was decided that rehearsals would be held on Wednesday evenings in the Methodist Schoolroom, a tradition which is still adhered to as firmly as if it were laid down by Statute, but the subscription of 1d per week has not been subject to the same immutable law!

At most of the times of village celebration already mentioned, the accompaniment would almost certainly have been provided by the Cawthorne Brass Band, which has played an integral part in village life from mid-Victorian times to the present. It is understood to have been formed about 1875 in connection with one of the collieries run by the Charlesworth family. "It was originally known as the Cawthorne Subscription Band, having been started by public subscription with Colonel Stanhope providing £50 and every member £1 each. Within

THE CAWTHORNE OF REV. CHARLES T. PRATT (1866-1915)

A Choral Society rehearsal 1972, photographed for the "Barnsley Chronicle" by Stan Bulmer.

The band in full uniform early this Century.

seven weeks of its formation it did its first Christmas tour of Cawthorne and the surrounding district and has been self-supporting ever since. Circumstances have led to its name being changed several times. When it won a competition, it became 'Cawthorne Prize Band', and they added the word 'Silver' to the title when its instruments were refurbished.'' [7] Certain families have maintained long connections with the Band, and, when looking through old photographs, the family names of Machen, Rusby, Batty, Broadhead, Jagger, Bagshaw and Wood are usually recalled. ''The Machens were in the Band from the start. At one time there was in the Band Billy Machen, young Billy Machen, and his son, Billy. A Machen was usually in charge of the big drum... Harold Batty claimed to have played with the Band for Christmas in Cawthorne for 60 years... In its early years, because of its association with a colliery, certain areas of the village provided a disproportionate percentage of the membership. The ten houses which made up Norcroft at one time provided thirteen bandsmen, who often came into the village for rehearsals to the strains of a march.'' [7] A long-serving conductor of the band, (and before that a player) was Kenneth. H. Wood, who can be seen on band photographs from the 1920's to c.1955. A self-taught accomplished player, often sought by other bands, his work for Cawthorne Band was invaluable, involving long hours of transcription and arranging of music.

Christmas was a time when the band was very hard-worked.

141

CAWTHORNE 1790-1990

A less formal turnout when the football team won a competition (pre 1914).

the victorious team   R.W.

Not only did the playing of carols bring particular festive joy to the inhabitants, but money collected from the big houses was particularly welcome to keep the band's funds solvent. It is perhaps difficult to appreciate what Christmas was like in Victorian and Edwardian Cawthorne, but something of the musical flavour provided by itinerant bands and choirs is given in an extract from Douglas Charlesworth's diary for December 25th 1915: "Kexborough choir singing under the window by 5.30 a.m. They sang 'Christians Awake', 'While Shepherds Watched', and 'Hark the Herald Angels' to the tune 'Little Bilberry'. Our lot set off about 6.a.m. Going to Barnsley there were several brass bands out and one concertina band. It was a mild, sunny morning. We had two ducks for dinner and a plum pudding. In the afternoon, had a little rifle practice. Our lot went singing again at night." The Cawthorne Band ran into difficulties, the numbers of bandsmen dwindled as a result of deaths and illness, until it was disbanded around 1955. It was, however, reformed in the 1970's and, although it has had to join up with another band to keep going, it is still in existence and playing for the village "Sing", Remembrance Day Parades, Carnivals etc., and still makes its Christmas tour of the village.

CAWTHORNE 1790-1990

Photographs taken by N. F. Moxon in the late 1940's and early 1950's which show the importance of the band in the musical life of the village at different times of the year.

144

THE CAWTHORNE OF REV. CHARLES T. PRATT (1866-1915)

Late 1940's/early 1950's, Sunday School scholars sing around the Fountain.   N.F.M.

Celebrating 900 years of a Church in Cawthorne as recorded in the Domesday Survey.

The musical tradition continues. A village group, "The Skyliners" entertain members of the Luncheon Club in the Parish Room (the old Grammar School).

Singing Carols for Mrs. Fraser at Banks Hall in the late 1950's. N.F.M.

A sport closely associated with festive occasions has been cricket. Special cricket matches were held at the time of Cawthorne Show and a feature of Coronation Celebrations was a cricket match between the Ladies and the Gentlemen, with the Gentlemen being required to bat and bowl using their weaker hand. Photographs of such matches still exist and remind us that the Coronation of George V and Queen Mary was a time of great jubilation in the village. ("All the children were given celebration mugs by the Co-op. There was a big tea party and a special cricket match. There was a large bonfire on Bentcliffe Hill and hot-air balloons in the shape of animals were released. These were about four-feet-tall and made of paper, but, unfortunately, most of them got fast in the trees.") [13] The earliest record of cricket in the village was 1843, the club enjoying considerable success in the late Victorian and Edwardian periods, when prominent players were George Parkinson and members of the Fish and Sykes families. Charles Pratt thought highly of cricket as a sport, but had his own views regarding

147

"leagues" and the growth of too much competition. Characteristically, he did not shy away from voicing his criticisms or from enlisting the aid of the great W. G. Grace in support of his arguments:

> May we suggest to our Cricketers that playing for anything beyond the usual Club Ball is almost degrading Cricket to the level of Prize-ringing or even horse-racing? It introduces an element of excitement into the Matches. Cricket is far too good a game to need anything beyond "playing for love" to make it full of interest to players and lookers on.
>
> *July 1879*

Cawthorne Cricket Club.

> At a meeting held on the 23rd, the Cricket Club accounts for the past year were examined and a balance of £11 carried forward. We heartily wish the Club a prosperous season, and hope the members will muster well for practice. The Club Committee are C. Wemyss, B. Hold, G. Fox, G. Parkinson.
>
> We are requested by Mr. Spencer-Stanhope, M.P; to say, that, whilst he has no desire whatever to withdraw any privileges from the people of Cawthorne, he may feel obliged to place some restrictions upon the use of Cannon Hall Cricket and Play Ground, unless those who wish to make use of it take care to preserve good order. Ill conduct or any bad language will always be held sufficient reason for altogether prohibiting any one from the Ground, under pain of being summoned for trespass. He has the fullest confidence that such proceedings will never be rendered necessary.
>
> *April 1874*

The Cricket Club.

> The Secretary of the Cricket Club reports a very large increase in the number of members, and there seems much greater interest being taken both in Practice and Matches. As to whether our side wins the latter or not, we hardly "care" the proverbial "twopence", so long as our Elevens do their best to win and show they know how to take an honourable defeat. There are few things more to the credit of a place, than a cricket field on which anything approaching to drunkenness or bad language is never seen or heard. There is a Home Match each Saturday this month; St. George's, Barnsley, 11th; Penistone, 18th; Monk Bretton, 25th.
>
> *June 1892*

What "W. G." Says.

> One may take it for granted that every one who knows anything whatever about Cricket knows who "W. G." is. There is no one, we suppose, whose opinion on the Game is so entitled to consideration as his. We commend to the notice of our Cawthorne Cricketers and to all who take an interest in Cricket, the following extract from a Paper by him in our January number (Page 27) on "Cricket as a Pastime for the Working Classes." "One thing I am very sorry to see, and that is the great increase in League and Cup Matches. This is making too much of a business of the game, and leads to no end of disputes and quarrels, which did not occur when Clubs were playing merely a friendly match with a neighbouring Club."
>
> When a man says anything you entirely agree with he is called a "sensible man." We consider "W. G." most sensible in these remarks.
>
> *April 1896*

Cricket.

> From what we see and hear, there is as much interest taken among us in our County Matches as ever there was. But it seems nothing short of a disgrace to the Parish that there is no "Cawthorne Cricket Club" this year. We should have thought that an old institution like that would not have allowed itself to be put an end to in the kind of way it has been, by the cantankerousness of a few of its members, some of whom are, probably, not really playing members at all. Cawthorne has been singularly fortunate in the generous way in which Col. Stanhope has allowed its club for so many years to make use of his Park. Many of our readers know, as we do not ourselves profess to know, or wish to know, who are the ringleaders in all the miserable mischief that is now preventing the Cricketers of Cawthorne from enjoying their play, and from providing the usual pleasant amusement for us all in watching their matches. The real cricketers among us who love the game should never have allowed our Club to be temporarily put an end to by a few mischievous "wreckers" who cannot have the interest and welfare of Cricket at heart, or they would never have acted as they have done.
>
> *July 1903*

One very significant change which took place during the time of Charles Pratt was the re-organisation of Local Government. The last speech made in Parliament by William Ewart Gladstone as Prime Minister was on the Local Government Bill (popularly known as "The Parish Councils Bill"), which, when it became law in 1894 replaced the Vestries by Parish Councils. There had long been a strong non-conformist opposition to the Vestries because they were usually linked to the Established Church of England and presided over by the local clergyman. The new Parish Councils were seen as establishing a bulwark against the "Aggressive power of the vicar and squire". Charles Pratt announced them with approval in the Parish Magazine:

Parochial Councils.

"The Parochial Councils Bill," as it has been popularly called, has now become an Act, and takes its place among the many Laws of the Land which relate to elective bodies. We shall probably speak of its provisions so far as they affect our own Parish at this year's Annual Vestry Meeting, which will in some ways be the last of its kind. For our own part, we expect some improvements from it – we shall see, for example whose duty it is to repair Holling Lane and to keep public "footgates" of every kind in a proper state.

March 1894

However, his attitude cooled. He made the following announcement of the results of the election:

The Parish Council, etc.

The following were elected as members of the Parish Council at the meeting presided over by Col. Stanhope, C.B., on the 4th: – Mr. J. M. Stanhope, and Mrs. Stanhope, Messrs. Joe Armitage, Walter Holling, Joseph Hoyland, Edward Lawson, John Thomas Milnes, Frederick Shaw, John Henry Sykes. They have since elected Col. Stanhope, C.B., as their chairman. In such a Parish as our own, it would not be reasonable to raise our expectations too high of what the new "Parish Meeting" and "Parish Council" will do for us. As in most Parishes of the same kind, they will probably be more distinguished by what they do not do than by what they do.

Mr. Joe Armitage and Mr. Joseph Hoyland have been elected for the Rural District Council. A Public Inquiry into the Charities of our Parish was held on the 13th in the Museum (by permission of Col. Stanhope, C.B.) The Assistant Commissioner stated that his Report would be published by the Charity Commissioners early in the year. The only Charities to be inquired into here were the old Endowment of the Schools and the late Miss Stanhope's Charities.

January 1895

Fifteen years then elapsed before the Parish Council was deemed worthy of a further mention in the Parish Magazine:

The Parish Council.

For the first time, we believe, since it came into being, the Parish Council has given a public evidence of its existence, by publishing a request to "strangers and visitors" that they will be good enough not to scatter or throw about papers, orange peel, etc., etc. We are not alone in thinking that those to whom the request is specially addressed are not by any means the great offenders in this respect. It is a pity that even children are not brought up to see the untidiness of throwing papers about; and probably there are some older than children who are not so particular as they might be. One's idea of a village, and of the self-respect of its people, cannot but be influenced by this kind of thing.

June 1910

The reasons for this attitude were entirely personal, being a product of his sense of betrayal and resentment.

The first meeting to elect a Parish Council took place in the Boys' School at 6.30p.m. on Tuesday December 4th 1894. Colonel Spencer Stanhope was chairman and he put to the electors the names of eleven nominees who had been proposed and seconded to serve on the new Parish Council. These were as follows: Joseph Armitage, farmer of Hill House Farm, Walter Holling, miner of Norcroft, James Holroyd, farmer of Cawthorne, Joseph Hoyland, farmer of Barnby Hall, Edward Lawson, farmer of Cinderhill, John Thomas Milnes cashier of Tivydale, Charles Tiplady Pratt, priest of Cawthorne, Frederick Shaw, farmer and butcher of Cawthorne, John Henry Sykes, gentleman of Cawthorne, John Montague Spencer Stanhope, and his wife Ida Mary. When the proceedings opened, James Holroyd withdrew as a candidate. Questions were put to the ten candidates still wishing to compete for the nine seats on the Parish Council and, on a show-of-hands vote, the unsuccessful person was declared to be Charles Tiplady Pratt! Part of the intentions of the Nonconformist Liberals had been fulfilled, but the Parish Council in no way diminished the power of the Squire. Indeed from 1895 up to the outbreak of the Second World War, the head of the Spencer Stanhope household did not stand for election (although other members of the family did), but, at the first meeting after the election, he was co-opted onto the Council and elected Chairman. Thus the Estate influence was maintained in village politics and has been maintained since the family left the village by successive Agents serving as Parish Councillors. The tone of the meetings up to 1939 was strictly apolitical, the only reference to a political party in the minutes being during the General Strike of 1926, when "Mr. J.W. Glennon tried to introduce a letter from the Penistone Labour Party."

From the early years of its existence, some interesting extracts can be quoted from the minutes. In March 1896 we read from the Annual report that "The drainage scheme for Tivydale has been carried out. The discharge of raw sewage into the brook is now forbidden", and "Further steps are to be taken in the drainage of the upper portion of the village. The Parish Council is willing to be advised by the District Council but is strongly averse to borrowing money and incurring a debt, saddled upon the rates for the future." By 1898 much concern was being expressed about decaying footbridges with the Council resolving "to seek the advice of Mr. Dransfield (the Clerk to Penistone Rural District Council) regarding its powers to repair footpaths and footbridges." The answer was favourable, because by April 1900 a tender was being accepted for Mr. Heath of Denby Dale to make and erect a new footbridge in Tivydale at a cost of £2 8s. 0d. (240p). The tender must have been a case of "down to a price rather than up to a standard," because by November 1901 the bridge's foundations were giving way and Mr. Swift was being asked to repair it! One very puzzling minute occurs in September 1901. A communication was received from the West Riding County Council concerning the preservation of Ancient Monuments, to which a reply was sent that "there were no Ancient Monuments in the township"! Where I wonder did that leave the Anglian Cross unearthed during the restoration of the Church and subsequently reassembled in the Churchyard?

The end of Charles Pratt's time in Cawthorne came suddenly, at a time when he must have been looking forward some months to celebrating half a century of service there as Curate and Vicar. In his diary, Douglas Charlesworth made this note: "March 31st 1915 – Have heard that Mr. Pratt, the vicar, is going to retire and live at Cheltenham, he having been vicar here over 49 years. He was as tall and straight although 77 as at 30, until last Friday, when he was taken with a slight stroke going up to Banks Hall." Charles Pratt announced the retirement himself in the June 1915 edition of "The Parish Magazine" which he had begun back in 1870:

Personal.

> This June Magazine is the last that I shall prepare as your Vicar. It is "No. 541": the first was for June, 1870. That sounds a long time ago: and so it is. Since I came in October, 1866, there have been, of course, many changes in the family life of the Parish. I think I am right in saying that there is only one house in the Parish in which there are those living now who were there when I came, and in which there has been no birth, marriage, or burial.
>
> I am not going to write any farewell address, or preach any farewell sermon. My leaving here after all these years of ministry is in itself a sermon to myself, and also to those who are serious enough to profit by a sermon.
>
> I cannot personally say "Goodbye" to you, but I leave my blessing and all best and kindest of wishes to all who value them.
>
> Mrs. Pratt and Miss W. Pratt desire to take this opportunity of saying "Goodbye" to their many kind friends in the Parish.

A man who said what he thought and believed in, Charles Pratt was a big man in both his stature and his service to the community. Many may have disagreed with his views, but there can have been few over a period of nearly fifty years whose lives had not been touched and enhanced by the work which he did for Cawthorne. Nothing was too trivial for his attention and for comment, as this final selection of extracts from his "Parish Magazine" shows:

Earthquake.

> A slight shock of Earthquake was felt in the Parish on the 17th, about 11.30 pm. It was generally felt through the North of England.
>
> *April 1871*

> We believe there are six at present living in our Parish who were born in the last century: one was baptised here June 9th, 1794: and a sister of his, still living in an adjoining Parish, on July 18th, 1790. The greatest ages entered in the Register for many years back are Joseph Fish, (1863) 96: Joseph Clarkson, (1863) 90: Sarah Roberts, (1856) 91: Elizabeth Healey, (1875) 96: Martha Healey, (1872) 90. *February 1880*

The Queen's Jubilee.

"A Special Form of Prayer and of Thanksgiving to Almighty God for the protection afforded to the Queen's Majesty during Fifty years of Her auspicious reign" has been sent to all the Parishes for use on Tuesday the 21st day of June. The actual day of our Queen's Accession in 1837 was a Tuesday, and that day is appointed for the Queen's own Thanksgiving Service in Westminster Abbey and the National Holiday.

The special Service in our own Church on that day will be at 10.30 am.

It has been thought a good plan, that all who are willing to contribute towards our Cawthorne Jubilee Celebration on the 21st, should, without being asked, give their subscription to one or other of the following who are willing to receive them, and that there be a Meeting in the Boys' School on Thursday the 9th, at 7.30 pm, of all these subscribers, to settle what is best to be done with the money, according to the amount contributed. Among the objects likely to meet with favour are a Meat-tea for the poor and aged, a Tea for the School-children, a Public Tea for all at a small charge, a Display of Fireworks, a contribution towards the Jubilee Medals for the winning and losing Elevens of the Cricket Match. The decision, however, will rest with the Meeting. Messrs J. T. Milnes, Jos. Kitson, J. Fretwell, W. Blacker, A. Hill, H. Child, Jos Barlow, and B. Swift (Haddon), will receive donations, and no one will decline giving, we hope, because they can only give a little, "a copper or two," or forget that it must be given before or at the Meeting on the 9th.

June 1887

The Queen's Jubilee.

At three pm on December 26th, Mr. Stanhope was present at the planting of a Poplar tree, and several members of his family and others who cared to join in the ceremony helped to fill it in and then plant some shrubs in the little vacant corner at the north end of Church street, exactly opposite to the "Co-op," in celebration of Her Majesty's Jubilee. There was a goodly gathering of old and young. Mr. Stanhope made a short speech, explaining the object for which they were assembled, and expressed a hope that that place would be known in the present and in future generations as "Jubilee Corner," and that those who were then present as children would never forget in their old age the occasion of its name being given. The first verse of "God save the Queen" was then sung, and the interesting little ceremony brought to a close with "Three Cheers for Her Majesty."

The Lime tree in the corner, being of considerable size, had been previously planted on the 9th, in anticipation of the day's event.

It will not be forgotten, that, in laying the Foundation Stone of the New Museum on October 13th, Mr. Stanhope expressed his desire that the Museum should be regarded "as a commemoration in Cawthorne of the Jubilee year of Her Most Gracious Majesty the Queen."

Our readers will remember the "Woman's Jubilee Fund," for which there was a Collection of £6 12s. 7d. made here in the Spring. The Queen is about to devote the whole sum collected throughout the country to the "improvement of nursing among the sick poor," by means of some scheme which is not yet finally settled.

January 1888

St. John Ambulance.

A tea was held in the Boys' School on the 27th, after which the St. John Ambulance Association's Medallions were distributed to those who have passed their third and final Examination. Surgeon-Major Blackburn gave an interesting account of the practical use he had known such instruction to be in his own experience, and expressed a great desire that there should be another Men's and Women's Class ready for his instruction some time during the ensuing Winter. He was presented by his pupils with a sterling silver Hot Milk Jug, in recognition of his generous and gratuitous services in their careful instruction. The following is a list of those who have received Medallions, and may, therefore, be expected to be able to "render first aid to the injured," and in the case of the Women to be specially helpful in nursing – Men's Class: Rev. C. T. Pratt, Messrs. G. McWhan, Jas. Wemyss, Jos. Armitage, G. Swift, R. Charlesworth, W. Morrell, G. Hindle, Jos. and Chas. Clegg, Wm. and Cossham Robinson, Geo. Fish, T. Chapple. Women's Class: Miss and Miss Cicely Stanhope, Miss Rickmam, Mrs. and Miss B. M. Pratt, Mrs. and Miss A. Kaye, Miss Kaye (Hillhouse), Mesdames Padgett, West, Barraclough, Eliz. Clegg, Wm. Mosley, George Fish, Misses Yardley, M. Shaw, Mosley, McMillan, Ashley.

July 1888

It may be a matter of interest in some future years for the people of Cawthorne to remember that Prince Albert Victor, eldest son of the Prince of Wales, passed through their village on Jan. 29th, 1889, to be a guest for the evening at Cannon Hall.

March 1889

A Phenomenon.

About 12.10 pm on the 16th, a whirlwind suddenly caught up five or six large haycocks from a field of Mr. Joshua Charlesworth's in Tivydale and carried them up to a height of, we should say, quite 600 to 800 feet. It was a sight which those who saw it will not soon forget. Many hundreds of bunches were moving about for some time in the sky and then gradually fell, most of them within a quarter of a mile of the field, and some in the very field itself.

The Museum Members' meeting will be on the 19th at 7.30 pm. Subject: Cyclones, Tornadoes, Whirlwinds, and Earthquakes, Committee Meeting at 8.

August 1890

The Strike.
We give a few extracts from a Sermon preached on October 22nd.

"It is the most difficult thing in the world to free ourselves from our natural feelings and prejudices, and take what we call a calm, rational view of things. It is almost impossible, too, to have such an acquaintance with the facts on each side as would alone enable us to form a right judgment upon them. There are misrepresentations made about both masters' profits and men's wages. * * I do not myself believe, that, when all things are taken into consideration, a miner's wage, take one year with another, is more than he is fairly entitled to. And, unless masters received some large return for the investment of their capital, it would certainly never be invested in Coal Mines, with all the risks that attend a Pit, from its first sinking to its end. * * I believe myself that the masters never expected the men to accept the terms of reduction they asked, and that they never intended from the first to insist upon them to the last. I do not like that unprincipled system by which either men or masters ask at first about twice as much as they want, in order to make room for the other side to offer less, and then both of them split the difference. Surely the more honest way is to say at first what you mean, and show good and sufficient reason for it. * * The masters, I think, were wanting in consideration for the men, when they asked them to submit all at once to that very considerable reduction. But were the men altogether right in saying there is no need for any reduction whatever, and that they would only continue to work at the old rate of wages? Whenever husbands and wives quarrel, they are sure to say things that had much better not be said. And masters and men stand very much in the same relationship of dependence upon each other. God in His Providence joins them together, and it is a miserable misfortune to both when a misunderstanding puts them for a time asunder. * * I do not like to hear men talk of "clemming to death, before they'll go in at a reduction." It is not the men who suffer most, but the poor wives and children. Still, I could not say "always go in on the masters' terms, whatever they may be." But I do say this, that there is nothing noble or brave in a man standing out, if it is his wife and children who suffer most, and if they are allowed to beg their daily bread from their better-off and, it may be, more sober and thrifty neighbours. A man has a right to determine upon what terms he will work, so long as he is able to support himself and his family upon his savings or the Union pay to which he is entitled. * * Prices and wages must depend upon that varying demand and supply which make times called bad and good. No combination of masters and men to keep up the price, so as to allow a man's wage never to be less than so much a day, can ever ensure that the demand at that price will give the workman as much employment, or as good a total weekly wage for all the year round, as if the price is made to vary with the demand. * * We want more kindly sympathy between masters and men. We want the rule of each one's life to be, "I wish to do to others as I should wish them to do to me, if our respective positions were reversed." We want every master, employer, and landlord to act out that great Christian principle in all his dealings with others, and every working man to do his duty towards his neighbour, employer, and landlord, with a cheerful Christian conscience." (One or two other paragraphs are reserved for next month.)

November 1893

"Are we returning to Barbarism?"

The above is the heading of an article in the (London) Guardian of Feb. 23rd, on the horrors which are now being brought before us in disgusting and harrowing detail in the novels of the present day. We were reminded of this article by some large illustrated posters in the Parish in which a local newspaper is trying, we suppose, to increase its circulation by offering its readers some histories of local murderers. It may know what suits the taste of our neighbourhood, but it is certainly paying a poor compliment to the people's good sense and right feeling. It is surely degrading to the very lowest depths the honourable office of public journalism, when a newspaper panders to the coarsest tastes of its readers, by raking up the histories of murderers, with all their painful details, which it can do no one any good to know. The placards we have alluded to may well suggest the question asked in the article in the Guardian, "Whether we are not even now sinking into that worst form of barbarism – a rotten and diseased civilisation.'' If filth of this kind is what people care to read, it can only be because barbarism has either never got out of them, or is making its way into them.

April 1888
(a piece written following the "Jack the Ripper" murders in London)

The Truck Amendment Act, 1887.

The above Act will not so much affect our neighbourhood as many other parts of England, but its provisions ought to be everywhere understood. It insists upon every workman receiving his full wages in money, and forbids any allowance of beer or cider being given by any employer, whether the allowance be taken into consideration or not in the rate of day or weekly wage.

Such Acts as these, and those very important provisions about public-houses in the proposed Local Government Bill, may be necessary, but to our mind they bear humiliating testimony to our national intemperance in drinking – for there are other kinds of intemperance in drinking – and to our moral incompetence as a nation to keep ourselves sober. It seems to be treating grown-up people like little children: and yet, as long as grown-up people show so little self-control and self-respect, they must be treated so, whether they are ashamed of it, or not.

May 1888

A Trip Abroad.

The Exhibition at Brussels is causing the M. S. & L. Railway Co. to issue tickets to Brussels and back from Barnsley, via Grimsby and Antwerp, at 30s. This gives a capital opportunity for any who have some few brains in their head and some money in their pocket to have a pleasant little trip abroad. Antwerp is a most interesting Town and Brussels is a charming City. Could not some of our people make this run across to the Continent? Some could manage to do it, perhaps, by paying something into the Penny Bank every week for a time. If it were wished, we should not at all mind undertaking the whole management and conduct of a party there and back, each paying our own expenses.

June 1888

''October 1887. A course of Lectures on Political Economy will be begun in the Boys' School on Monday the 10th at 7 pm. The Course will include such subjects as Wages, Trades Unions, Co-operation, Socialism, Free Trade, Taxation etc: Admission free.''

In advertising a Defence Fund for two miners wrongly dismissed from work, he had this to say in August 1894:

''Most of our readers have heard of the two miners who were falsely charged with being drunk and disorderly. We took up their case with some earnestness, as we wish everyone to properly appreciate the value of 'Character'. The one who lives in this Parish had been a total abstainer for above three years. They were put to considerable expense and trouble in proving their innocence... It is quite as much everyone's concern that the innocent should not suffer, as that the guilty should not go unpunished. A miner's character ought to be worth as much to him as anyone else's.''

''September 1900. For the convenience of our neighbours we have complied with a request from the West Riding Local Authority that we would act as 'a Grantor of Licences for the Movement of Swine'. We have already discovered that there is much more locomotion among the pig tribe than we had ever imagined.''

Litter (of a different kind!) was obviously also a problem in late Victorian and Edwardian Cawthorne:

''October 1901. People who think as you think are always 'sensible'. It was a sensible old miner, therefore, who remarked the other day. 'Nowt looks war nor to see pieces o' paper tossin about on t' roads.' We are just having two Sanitary Pipes to stand on end near the Boys' and Infants' Schools, and both parents and teachers will, we hope, tell their children to always put their old dinner papers into one of these. We all have an interest and pleasure in seeing our pretty village look always neat and tidy.''

''March 1908. We shall give an address on 'Socialism' in the Parish Room on Tuesday, the 10th, at 7.5 pm if any are sufficiently interested in it to care to come.''

''August 1910. There is a growing sense among us that the younger generation is not made of the same grit as their ancestors, and that there is a spirit of indifference, slothfulness, idleness and want of self-discipline among us... Lord Roberts recently wrote 'There is a great need to instil into the minds of the people sense of patriotism, and to impress upon them that it is the duty of every member of our great Empire to endeavour to do something, however small, for the good of their country.' We ourselves hope that some measure of universal Military Service may soon be passed, not only as a duty of every citizen, but as a most welcome discipline of character.''

The Coronation.

It is no exaggeration, we feel sure, to say that there has never been, in the history of our village, such a day as the Coronation Day was made. If it were safe to judge of our loyalty and patriotism by the hearty enthusiasm with which everyone joined in the day's proceedings, Cawthorne would certainly hold a very high position among the villages of the country. Everything connected with the day's celebration passed off most happily and smoothly. Such a successful carrying out of every item in the programme was a splendid evidence of the way in which all the several Committees entered into the spirit of their work.

The following were members of the General Committee: Members of the Parish Council: Messrs. J. M. S. Stanhope (chairman) and J. Armitage (vice-chairman); Mrs. Stanhope; Messrs. Hoyland, John Milnes, E. Lawson, Jos. Hinchliffe, A. Hill, J. C. Wemyss, and F. W. Child. Appointed at the Parish Meeting: Messrs. W. Blacker, G. Wright, G. Buckley, Miss W. M. Pratt, E. Fish, R. Wilkinson, Mrs. Warren, Miss Marriott, Mrs. Laycock, G. T. Shirt, Jos. Smith, Mr. Falwasser (hon. secretary), and Mr. Warren (hon. assistant secretary).

Although the day was rather a wild one as regard the wind there was no rain whatever to interfere with the general enjoyment. The beautifully decorated "carriages," as we will call them, were a pleasing feature in the procession, and the tent as prepared for the tea looked remarkably pretty. The whole programme was, as we have said, a great success, and the bonfire and fireworks on Bentcliffe Hill brought the day's proceedings to a very enjoyable conclusion.

Sir Walter Stanhope kindly allowed the invitation to the Service at Westminster Abbey he had received from the Earl Marshal, "by Command of the King," to be exhibited in the tent. It was an interest to many of us.

It ought to make us very thankful for our fine day when we think of the much desired rain that followed it. In the more than 40 years during which we have kept a daily measurement of the rainfall we do not remember ever recording such an amount as fell on the Saturday. It was 2.03 inches.

It has been mentioned in the newspapers, we notice, that Sir Walter Stanhope has made a Coronation gift of land for an addition to our Cemetery to the District Council at Penistone.

July 1911

A Hint to Someone.

The tarring of the road through our village has been much appreciated. There are some parts that will be very dangerous indeed in frosty weather to both man and beast. Whoever is responsible will, no doubt, see to its being made safe.

Donald Laycock has gained an Agricultural Exhibition at Leeds University, we have pleasure in mentioning.

November 1914

Among all his other tasks, Charles Pratt also ran the Cawthorne Branch of the Yorkshire Penny Bank, to which he bade a reluctant farewell in May 1915:

"It has been decided that the accounts of the Cawthorne Branch shall be transferred to the Yorkshire Penny Bank on Market Hill, Barnsley, and the Branch at Cawthorne be closed after Saturday, May 1st... After Having established the Branch, and taken the chief part in its management ever since, I feel some regret that it is about to be closed."

Charles Pratt's forty-nine years of ministry in Cawthorne constituted an outstanding practical demonstration of what the present Church of England is preaching and striving for – the principle of outreach; involving Christianity in the community, and giving it a human face and influence seen and felt outside the four walls of the Church building. C. T. Pratt was a true shepherd and father of his flock.

1872.

A Congratulatory Address was presented to the Revd: C: Spencer Stanhope upon his having completed the 50th year of his membercy at the Harvest Festl, 1872 — He was not present: the Revd C.W. S:St: received it for him.
Collection £13·7·2 : Tea £ 3·17·5.

1874. Most unexpectedly at the end of Jany: Parliament was dissolved (by Mr Gladstone). W:T:W: Spencer Stanhope was re-elected after a Contest: he headed Poll with 9705: Starkey 9639: Leatham, 8265: Beaumont (Henry) 8148. We voted at Silkstone. Declaration at Wakefd on 11th.
On 25th Feby "old George Ashton" was buried: he died suddenly with me on the Sunday before — He was a good specimen of the "old sort" & much respected: we always

-1874-

went to ask him abt "things that had been": he had a remarkably clear memory & was fond of telling his stories of old days gone — When he was a collier "working for Thorp's": he remembered new bread one year at Lamth: T'east, Sheat so early: he was one of old "Cawthorne Musicianers": had stories of Mr Phipps (Vicar before 1799) "clouting old Thias Greenwood over his head at the Font wi t' Book & asking him that his ears were meant for if he cd n't say Amen at t' right time". Told of Wr Goodair living where Chas Hutchinson now lives whilst Parsonage was being made to fit for Clergyman & a residence under Gilbert Act. how he gave people their Registers in t°. of paying for odd jobs — much liked it' Parish. nearly ruined over the Vicarage.

Old Sally Ashton, his widow, died on March 8 — a Sunday too — & was buried on 11th, aged 76. She alw:s ? "It'll be wi' us just like Wr St & Lady Elizth: When one goes t' other'll not be long after. Whether even ours it may be as goes first".

The old Vicarage was pulled down this Spring.

Cawthorne in two Worlds Wars

1914-18 and 1939-45

"All the hills and vales along
Earth is bursting into song,
And the singers are the chaps
Who are going to die perhaps.
O sing, marching men,
Till the valleys ring again.
Give your gladness to earth's keeping,
So be glad, when you are sleeping.

Charles Sorley

"What the light and fire within us, men who march away." The Cawthorne "First Eleven" photographed behind the Spencer Arms, prior to leaving for Army Service, September 3rd 1914.
Back row left to right: T. Glover, A. Clarke, J. Sykes, H. Morley, W. Morley, C. Neumann.
Seated left to right: J. Batty, S. Bagshaw, F. Barrow, W. Heaton, G. Horton.

The War.

When we wrote for last month's Magazine we little thought that our Foreign Office would issue an announcement at 12.10 am on August 5th "that a state of war exists between Great Britain and Germany as from 11 pm on August 4th." We will not refer to what our newspapers have been and still are telling us about it. Never in the world's history has there been so awful a warfare, and never could a nation feel a stronger conviction than we do of its being a war forced upon us by obligations of international duty. It is 99 years since our country was engaged in a war so near to our shores, when our Duke of Wellington gained his decisive victory at Waterloo. We very well remember being in the Crystal Palace, in July, 1851, when "the Duke," as he was always called, paid his only visit to the Exhibition. And we remember reading the speech in the House of Commons in which war was formally declared with Russia, on March 28th, 1854. It ended with the words: "And may God defend the right." So may we say now.

Special prayers and Intercessions are offered in our Church every evening at 7.15. Copies of the Form may be taken home by those who would desire to make use of them, but are really prevented from being present at the Services. Would it not be well for everyone to offer a silent prayer when they hear the bell being rung for the Service?

There is another "Forms of Prayer for Public and Private use in Time of War," which those who would really wish to make use of it may take home from the Table in Church. Prayer and the neglect of Prayer and Worship are the two surest evidences of what our Christian faith is, or is not.

A special appeal has been made to Members of the Mothers' Union, that they would every day pray for our Soldiers and Sailors at Mid-day.

1914-1918

The "First Eleven" (plus others) in initial training camp.

THIS passage in the Parish Magazine of September 1914 conveys something of the surprise which must have been felt by most of the inhabitants of the British Isles that a distant incident in the Balkans, the assassination at Sarajevo of the heir to the Austro-Hungarian throne, should have led to war. It seemed incredible that the complicated system of alliances, which had, for over forty years, preserved a balance between the territorial aspirations of the major European nations and kept the continent at peace, should now have set in motion a chain reaction which inevitably ended in war. What cannot be conveyed, however, is the horror which must have been felt in Britain, an emotion engendered by a sudden blow to our self-confidence. For nearly a century we had stood supreme in trade and manufacturing industry, the veritable "Workshop of the World", backed by a massive merchant fleet and the resources of our Empire, secure in our island stronghold, and protected by the world's greatest navy. Now not only had the Americans and Germans overhauled us in coal and steel production, but the German navy had been expanded to a position of parity with our own, and their army, which had pushed relentlessly through Belgium into France, now stood menacingly just across the

A group photograph taken in front of the home of Mrs. West (seated centre). One of the soldiers is her son.

The spirit of "jingoist" patriotism showed itself even in children's pageants.

Channel. Despite the early euphoria, there must have been many who realised that this would be a very different military proposition from the series of minor colonial wars which had occupied our relatively small regular army over the previous sixty years. What does amaze, looking back to 1914 with the benefit of hindsight, is the fervour with which young men throughout the British Isles, and in Cawthorne in particular, rushed to supplement the resources of the British Expeditionary Force. We can only guess at their motivation, since none of our village volunteers survive and, as far as I know, no-one ever recorded their reasons for going. The reasons for the first Cawthorne men to see action was obvious. They were reservists, who simply answered the recall to duty which was expected of them, but what made eleven young men, ever afterwards proudly referred to as "Cawthorne's First Eleven", leave home on September 3rd 1914 as volunteers in the 9th Battery of the King's Own Yorkshire Light Infantry? To them, war still held visions of movement, dash and glory. They could not see the mud, the gas, the endless bombardment, the deprivation and the spiritual stagnation which came to be known as "The Western Front". Did they really believe that it would be a quick trip across the Channel and all be over by Christmas? Or were they of the same feelings as another young and, as yet, unknown Yorkshireman, J. B. Priestley, when he said: "To most of us the call was really little to do with 'King and Country' and flag-wagging and hip-hip-hurrah. It was a challenge to what we felt was our untested manhood. In centuries gone by other men who had not lived as easily as we had, had drilled and marched and borne arms – couldn't we? Yes, we too could leave home and soft beds and the girls, to soldier for a spell, if there was some excuse for it, something at least to be defended. And here it was. In those first months we believed that war still held movement, colour, adventure, drama?" [5] Or was it in some cases just a question of being bored, "broke" and looking for something to do, as it was for the author's uncle when he enlisted in Barnsley, thus beginning a series of escapades with the Black Watch in France, which saw him survive gas attacks before returning him, not to his native Monk Bretton, but to a thatched cottage in the New Forest where he finally died aged 87? For all of them, whatever their motives for volunteering to fight, the reality of warfare proved very different from their dreams, just as it did for the young J. B. Priestley: "Now came disillusionment for us who had joined up in a fine spirit of adventure. The frenzied butchery of this war, indefensible even on a military basis, was eventually to kill at least 10,000,000 Europeans. After being dressed in uniform, fed and drilled, cheered and cried over, these 10,000,000 were then filled with hot lead, ripped apart with shell splinters, blown to bits, suffocated in mud, or allowed to die of diseases, after rotting too long in trenches that they shared with syphilitic rats and typhus-infested lice. Death, having come into his empire, demanded the best, and got it." [5]

Judging by the following which appeared in the Parish Magazine during the first few months of the war, had Charles Pratt not been forced to retire, we would have had a very complete picture of Cawthorne's war contribution:

Signs of the War.

> The presence in our Parish of a Belgian family and of a convalescent wounded – one of our own army – must help, if we, any of us, needed help, to make us realise what the war is. It is really touching to see the most kind and generous feeling of sympathy that there is among us all for our guests from near Malines, in Belgium. We happen to know how deeply grateful they are for the hearty friendliness with which they are being received.
>
> *November 1914*

The War.

> The following is a correct list, we believe, of those in our Parish who are now serving their King and country in our Military Forces. We shall be glad to receive any corrections as soon as possible – before the 3rd – as the list is about to be placed in the Church Porch.
>
> Reservists: Osborne, J. W., L 4085, Royal Fleet Reserve, R.M.A.; Cole, A., 15825, Gunner, R.G.A.

Mr. J. W. Osborne, the village postman, who, as a Marine reservist, was one of the first men of the village to see action in the war.

> Midgley, R., 45th Battery, Royal Field Artillery; Chappell, H., 8961, 3rd Co., Scots Guards; Woodward, J. W., 3rd Batt. York and Lanc.; Bagshaw, S., Barrow, F., Batty, J., Clarke, A., Glover, T., Heaton, W., Horton, G., Morley, H., Morley, W., Neumann, C., Sykes, J. The above alphabetical eleven left home on September 3rd, after being passed at Barnsley, to join the Recruits at Pontefract. They are in the 9th Batt. King's Own Yorkshire Light Infantry. Evans, R. J., Sheffield Batt. of York and Lanc.
>
> Of the above, Osborne, Midgley, and Chappell are known to be on service at the war.

At our services of special Intercession, in the Prayer for the Sailors and Soldiers the words are added "and especially those from this Parish who are now serving at the seat of war."

Our readers are well aware, we feel sure, of all that is being done in the Parish for the various Branches of Relief.

Mr. Pardoe gives an address every Monday evening in the Mixed School, at 7 pm, on the present position of the war. The meeting makes an occasion for the mention of matters and questions in any way connected with the war, and also of what is being done here, and what still needs to be done. The poor Belgians are not to be forgotten. We very naturally ask the question, what might very possibly have been the condition of our own country at this present time if Belgium had not acted as it did?

October 1914

The War.

To last month's list of those in our Parish now serving their King and Country in our Military Forces there are to be added the names of F. Mellor, who has received the Commission of a Captain in the Pontefract Batt. of K.O.Y.L.I., and Frank Moxon, who has joined the Sportsman's Battalion. Reginald Midgley's name was given, but his brother Rowland's should be added, though not actually living here. F. Stayton, 8042 K.O.Y.L.I., reported "missing" on August 30th, has not been heard of: he is a prisoner, most probably.

November 1914

"1915."

As we write "5" instead of "4," one cannot help thinking what a very different year the old one has been from what we had hoped and expected it would be. It has been the most memorable year in our National History, and in the History of Mankind. And we enter upon 1915 little knowing what lies before us in it as a Nation and Empire, or in our own personal life. We have poor thoughts of God and His Goodness, if we do not feel that He would have us "learn the lessons of His Fatherly discipline" in this time of our national trouble, and pray that He would turn from us all those evils that we most righteously deserve, and give us grace to put our whole trust and confidence in His mercy.

If 1915 may not be a "Happy New Year" to us, such as we have been accustomed to wish each other, we can every one of us help to make it a year of great blessing to us all, by its bringing us spiritually "nearer to God."

January 1915

A Belgian refugee family in Cawthorne.

Belgium.

It ought to be deeply impressed upon our children as well as felt by their elders, how much our Country owes to the noble and brave King of Belgium, and to his Ministers and his Country. What they have done will be handed down in the World's history as a splendid example of a nation's sense of honour and duty. The extreme heartiness with which our present Belgian guests are welcomed among us is a striking evidence of our most kindly sympathy with them and their fellow-sufferers.

Writing to us in the name of all the family, Monsieur Van Thurenhout has asked us to be their spokesman to the inhabitants of Cawthorne, "to offer them," he writes, "our best wishes for Christmas, and to wish them a very happy New year; and to tell them that we feel an intense gratitude for and recognition of the attention and kindness that they do not cease to pour upon us, in order to make us forget the sadness of being far from our family, our home, and our poor oppressed Belgium. I can assure you," he says, "that we shall never forget the magnificent conduct of the people of Great Britain, and particularly on our account of the inhabitants of Cawthorne."

M. Van Thurenhout's French Class will be resumed in the Museum on Tuesday, the 5th. The charge for the course is somewhat less to Museum members.

January 1915

Our Lads.

We hope to give next month a full list of all in our Parish who are serving their King and Country, with each one's Battalion and Military Number. We have had a graphic description of a soldier's fighting in the Trenches from Herbert Chappell, of the 2nd Scots Guards, who writes the letters of a brave and trustful soldier. W. Morley and J. Sykes have been made Military Police. Several more recruits have just given in their names.

January 1915

Belgian Guests.

The Committee are arranging to receive two more Belgians in the cottage opposite the end of School Lane. They are sure to receive the same most hearty welcome that our former guests did whom we look upon by this time as quite "belonging to us".

March 1915

Additions to the List of our Soldiers.

Herbert Parr	Oliver Ibbotson	George West
Joe Launder	Albert Broadhead	Humphrey Adams
Joseph Moxon	H. Millington	William Wilkinson
Robert Hawkshaw	Luther Chappel	

Correction: Pte. S. Bagshaw's No. is 15,544

June 1915

Although the retirement of Charles Pratt resulted in the suspension for a number of years of publication of the Parish Magazine, Cawthorne is fortunate that a record has been preserved, which, although not providing much information about serving members of the Armed Forces, gives a good taste of the flavour of life in wartime Cawthorne. This record is in the form of Douglas Charlesworth's diary 1915–19. Grandson of Joshua and nephew of Richard, Douglas Charlesworth was a remarkable man. A farmer by economic necessity, he was a man of letters and a poet (especially in Yorkshire Dialect) by inclination. His formal education had been small, but his self-education through reading and discussion was vast. Memories of him usually refer to him sitting under a hedge at harvest-time reading a book, and yet the farming always seemed to get done. As Miss Alice Moxon observed: "I cycled to the High School at Barnsley and didn't mind the bike breaking down if I could ride to Barnsley in the milk-float with Douglas. This was especially so before exams, because he would recite poetry and Shakespeare to me on request. He always had time in summer to take his breakfast outside and read a book." [10] His books and meetings with his book-lover friends at Hudson's Bookshop in Shambles Street, Barnsley, must have been very trying for those who did not share his passion, as the following extracts show:

An, as yet, unidentified group photographed by Rowland Wilkinson at the rear of his Post Office (now Chantry House).

"March 30th 1915. Did this day buy 'The History of Worsboro' at Mr. Hudson's. Resolve that the growing habit of buying books must be checked, having bought 30 in three months."

"August 20th 1915. Went to Penistone to the vicarage... where the widow and son of the late vicar, Canon Turnbull, live. A rambling sort of house full of antique furniture and old pictures of great value... Bought about 200 books, the pick of some thousands, at 1d. per volume."

His capacity for completely absorbing himself in conversations and his pastimes must have been particularly hard upon the patience of his wife, Lily (daughter of Cawthorne's former policeman, Mr Beanland). One of his Literary Society friends wrote a dialect poem for him commemorating the time when he and his wife went shopping to Barnsley and arranged to meet. Douglas became so absorbed in his books (at Hudson's), in reading the proof copy of one of his poems and in conversation that he lost track of time, so that his exasperated

His home, Hill Top.

wife drove the pony and trap back to Cawthorne and left him to make his own way home. As his diary shows, similar things could happen even on holiday at Grange-over-Sands:

> "June 20th 1916. Got some beetles in the marsh near the home before breakfast. Then to Lake Windermere and up the dale to Rydal and Grasmere. Lunched at the Red Lion. Then to the church and Dove Cottage, after which we went up Silver How. While collecting beetles, I lost my wife and went to the top alone, from which there was a fine view. An interesting detail was my wife wandering about below. When I came down she was most angry."

He did not serve in the war, his attempts at enlisting making interesting reading:

> "Dec. 12th 1915. This morning I went to the Drill Hall at Barnsley to attest. It was crowded with men. I was number 2,009 and the previous day up to four-o-clock they had got over 6,000 for the week. I was put in group thirty-six."

> "Dec. 14th 1915. Got my money for attesting; a new half-crown and a threepenny bit. I am keeping the half-crown for a relic."

> "March 1st 1916. Today is the last day for young men to voluntarily enlist. Tomorrow they will come under the Conscription Act. Quite a number will have to go."

> "March 2nd 1916. The Appeal Tribunal sat today at Penistone. Most of our local farmers got put back four months from joining the army."

Douglas Charlesworth as a young man.

"May 11th 1916. In the afternoon to Penistone to the Appeal Court. Tom Milnes of Spring House, Wilf Milnes of Jowett House and myself all got 4 months exemption."

"Jan. 3rd 1917. To Pontefract to the Medical Board. Passed CIII to the great surprise of everybody as I have the appearance of being in hard training, but it is owing to a mishap of 4 years ago. Height 5ft 10¼ inches Weight 10 stones."

"Oct. 25th 1917. To the tribunal at Penistone. We all got 3 months exemption, the Chairman urging us to grow more corn."

"Jan. 31st 1918. Went to the Military tribunal today. We all got conditional exemption, on condition that we work hard and produce as much food as possible."

"Oct 9th 1918. Went to a Medical Board at Barnsley. Was given Grade I."

Had he been medically fit, Douglas Charlesworth would have been an asset to the Army, certainly with regard to his shooting:

"April 5th 1915. Easter Monday. Cawthorne full of visitors as usual. We were rather busy, eleven of us going hard the greater part of the afternoon. *(Author's note: this is obviously a reference to the tea-gardens which the Charlesworths operated in good weather at Hill Top.)* Horace Morley was home on furlough. Went out for some rifle practice, he taking the Greener and me the BSA. These Kitchener's army people can't shoot and yet they expect to go to France very soon. Bought a copy of Keats' poems to replace one that is lost or stolen. In the evening heard Mr. Pardoe give his weekly lecture on the progress of the war."

"April 14th 1915. Have been sent for to shoot in a team for the Barnsley Rifle Club against the 2nd Battalion on Saturday."

The local defence volunteer force in Cawthorne in World War One, led by the Vicar, Rev. Cotton. Mr. Cotton was an exponent of "muscular Christianity", who, when he caught two boys using thread, pins and buttons to do "window-tapping" at the Vicarage on Mischief Night, took them inside, put on the boxing gloves and made them spar with him in turn! This sort of behaviour did, however, occasionally rebound on him, since Douglas Charlesworth's diary records how, one April Fools' Day, some lads rolled the Vicar in the mud!

"April 17th 1915. This afternoon the rifle match with the sergeants of the 2nd Battalion. Nearly all the old rifle team have enlisted and the new ones have no experience of match shooting. Nevertheless we completely beat up the soliders, Sgt Bainbridge being the only one who could shoot properly, and, in his day, he was the best shot in Yorkshire. He it was who first taught me to shoot with a Lee-Enfield. Out of the 24 men who were shooting, I came second with a total of 131. In the first 8 shots I scored 7 bullseyes. In the second I made a very close group just off the bull, only one being through it, which was chiefly the fault of the marker. The soldiers were bitterly disappointed and are eager for a return match."

He was an active member of a volunteer force (a 1914–18 version of the Home Guard) of which Mr. Cotton, Charles Pratt's successor as vicar, was a leading figure.

"Dec. 24th 1916. The vicar took the Volunteers and Scouts to the Chapel today to a service."

"March 15th 1917. Tonight took part in night operations with the Royal Engineers from Silkstone Camp. They put up a picket line down Banks Bottom as far as Pell Mell and we had to break through. Personally I was taken prisoner of war while getting across the stream below Silkstone Bridge. They were sending a good many lights up."

"March 20th 1917. The Commanding Officer from Silkstone Camp came to watch us drill."

A reception for soldiers at Barnby Hall.

Interesting references are made throughout the diaries to events which have now passed down as landmarks in history, but which then merited a short comment as follows:

"May 3rd 1916. The Irish rebels reported all subdued, but a greater part of Dublin destroyed."

"June 3rd 1916. This morning came news of a great naval fight in the North Sea (the Battle of Jutland) we losing 13 ships and the Germans 11. They ran away before our main fleet could reach them."

"June 8th 1916. Went up the church tower to put the flag up half mast for Earl Kitchener, whose ship struck a mine off the Orkneys. Had to climb up the pole for the rope."

"May 21st 1916. The clocks all put forward one hour this morning according to Act of Parliament." (A short statement which does not do full credit to the long struggle by William Willett to get the idea of daylight saving passed through Parliament).

References to men of the village serving in France are relatively few, considering how many had joined the army, but thoughts of them inspired his poetry. The "First Eleven", whose photograph hung prominently in the village school, were the subjects of "A Yorkshire Song":

A Yorkshire Song

When t' grey leet o' t' morning crept far ovver t' dale,
An' t' sky lairk on heigh sang his wonderful tale,
Then gaily up t' gate at winds step alang t' hill,
Our lads they went marching wi' purpose an' will.
Chorus – Marching away, marching away,
Our leet-fooited lads
They went marching away.

An' far, far in Flanders, they faced a dree foe,
To save a brave nation thru' deadliest woe,
An' in t' height o' feight ther war nowt could prevail
'Geean 't lads at war bred in uz ooan bonnie dale.
Marching away, etc.

An' now t' war is ovver an' t' feighting's all done,
They'll come marching back ageean t' victory won.
An' winnet we welcome 'em? Trumpet an' drum
'Ll brust thersens ommost, if they'll nobbut come.
Laughing they'll come, laughing they'll come
Wi' song an' wi' dance,
And wi' laughter they'll come.

The impact of the war on the farming scene, plus remembrance of familiar faces never to be seen again, play their parts in "Harvest 1917":

Harvest 1917

Corn's weet ta neet lad
An t' sun gleeams red oer t' hill,
T' rain drips thru t' trees, lad,
An t' pooands begin to fill.
Dree sadness fills my heairt an all
Ah hear sum far-off speerit call.

Corn's weet ta neet, lad,
When sal we gerr it hooam?
Them at should be here, lad,
Far off i' Flanders rooam,
An yit just naa Ah must be fey
Ah thowt Ah saw em walk oer t' ley.

It's snell ta neet, lad.
An t' gabble ratches call;
Shades walk in t' dale, lad,
An hover raand t' laithe wall.
Sliving quietly back thru t' warrs
Bee t' leet o' t' scattered evening starrs.

Ahm starved ta neet, lad,
Goa festen t' aater dooar
An t' ghooasts in t' wind, lad,
Al moider uz na moor.
For them at's gooan are gooan ta stay
Happen till God's gret Hairvest Day.

The oak tree, the felling of which so angered Douglas Charlesworth.

For the rest of the time, Douglas Charlesworth's diary is the story of a community carrying on its life as near normally as possible and written by a man who loved and was a keen student of nature and the countryside:

"Sunday April 18th 1915. Glorious day. This afternoon went for a walk up Harry Royd Ing. Was much impressed with the invisibility of wood pigeons when feeding in the fields, their colour and creeping habits helping them greatly. Went past Raw Royd and into Shutts where they have felled a magnificent oak. Its branches are as large as trees and the timber is of the very finest right through. As it lays it looks like some great forest god fallen to earth. Although I am tall, I cannot stretch my arms across the widest part of its trunk. It must be at least 500 years old and was noted far and wide. May the man who caused it to be felled be cursed for ever. Coming home I saw the biggest stoat I have ever seen. Its marking was splendid. Watched the bees; they were carrying great loads of pollen in."

"November 29th 1915. This afternoon I went skating, taking my new skates. It seemed a quiet affair. All the fellows are abroad, either in Africa or Flanders, that I used to have great sport with."

"December 28th 1915. Two Miss Warrens came from Clayton West and were singing and playing the violin and piano the whole evening. I spent most of the evening reading... in the dining room, but went in and sang 'The Old Superb' and 'Drake's Drum'."

"January 26th 1916. Ploughing in Green Lane Close. To my mind, ploughing is the most pleasant work extant. The swishing music of the mould board as it goes through the ground and the

CAWTHORNE 1790-1990

Joe Fretwell, one of the Cawthorne butcher/slaughtermen mentioned by Douglas Charlesworth, photographed with his family behind their home in Darton Road. His son, Ben (standing right) visited his old home in the 1980's and marvelled how they all managed to fit into a "two-up, two-down".

clanking of the harness make a soothing effect on the system."

"April 26th 1916. Had breakfast and dinner outside for the first time this year. Saw two swallows and heard a whitethroat in the garden."

"January 29th 1917. Skating on the Fishpond. Saw some folks walk across the middle piece on the ice. Fred Robinson went through. If he had not been a strong swimmer he would have been drowned."

He was also a stout defender of the rights of the countryman, as the following extracts show:

"April 1916. Coming down Dark Lane, I found the stile railed up in Will Lockwood's field, but, it having been a public road for a great period, I knocked them down again."

"April 20th 1916. Coming down Dark Lane I found the stile railed up again, but broke it down. Young Lockwood said 'Our William put it up.' Heard the cuckoo."

"April 22nd 1916. Dick Crossland, the foreman roadman, very angry this morning about the stile being broken down. Told him that he had no right to stop a public road."

These were by no means the only inconveniences of country life. Animals had to be slaughtered for meat, but did not always provide the food which they were expected to:

"January 22nd 1917. Joe Fretwell (who was John Fretwell's son and one of the village butchers-cum-slaughtermen who killed and salted pigs etc.) and I shot the blue and white cow. We skinned her and when we opened her found her full of tuberculosis."

One mild annoyance to Douglas Charlesworth was the suspension of the rent dinners. These "feasts" where, according to one person who frequently attended them, "we had a joint of beef as big as a coal-scuttle", were given to tenant farmers on the day upon which they paid their rent to the Stanhopes; and, according to the same person "must have cost them a bob or two". [7] A frequent wartime note in the diary is "no rent dinner again".

Our farmer poet was not a superstitious man. A deeply-religious lay-preacher, one would not associate him with tales of the supernatural, but one incident of November 4th 1917 made sufficient impression upon him to record it in his diary:

"Rode up to Ingbirchworth to preach. Toward the top of Carr Lane my horse shied violently and seemed much afraid of something. At first I could see naught, but in a few moments I saw the shape of a great hound or dog, brown in colour and as big as a calf. The head was shaped like a foxhound with great ears which hung down. Its tongue was hanging out. Its body was more the shape of a collie's and it glided noiselessly past and was gone. The horse was terrified right to the journey's end, breaking out into a gallop and several times shying violently. I mentioned it to several people at 'Birchworth' but none knew of such a dog in the district. Preached on "Except your righteousness exceed etc." and, coming out of the service, I went to Benjamin Beever's to supper and stayed till ten. Down the lane again the horse was frightened. I wonder what it all was? Some folks said it was a token. Could it be the 'Brown Dog' which is said to haunt these dales?"

The weather often brought its own problems:

"March 13th 1916. H. Hinchliffe called and said that there are 21 motor cars, 9 motor lorries and 1 steam engine snowed up on Board Hill (on the Penistone-Manchester Road via Woodhead) and that, at Saltersbrook, Reuben and his brother have dug 55 dead sheep out of the snow. All the outside farms and villages are isolated. Some of the roads have not been used for a fortnight. Here at Cawthorne, being in the valley, we have not had it more than 8 or 9 inches deep and it has mostly melted as it comes, but even a few yards up the hillside makes a great difference."

"March 15th 1916. It is reported that the bodies of a man and boy have been dug out of a drift near Langsett."

"March 28th 1916. Today communication with the south was cut owing to a great blizzard, which happily missed us here. There were no papers, letters or telegrams. One report has it that 90 per cent of the telegraph-poles are down."

West Riding of Yorkshire Special Constabulary

No. 2 Staincross Division

Section Order for No 6 Section on receiving Air Raid Warning

No.	Name	District
1	Youell (cycle)	On receiving warning call Nos 2.4.8.9 also Section Leader and then patrol between Golden Cross and Low Mill Farm.
2	Hopcroft	Patrol centre of Village with No 3.
3	Fish	Patrol centre of Village with No 2.
4	Wilkinson (cycle)	Call out Nos 3.5.6.7 then patrol South Lanes as far as Elmhirst.
5	Moxon	Patrol from Stanhope Arms to Barnby Hall.
6	Blacker	Patrol Hill House and Norcroft
7	Wemyss	Take charge of necessary arrangements at the School in case of accident
8	Rigby	Patrol from Clough Green to Raw Green.
9	Barlow (cycle)	Patrol from Clough Green as far as North Lane

E. M. S. Pilkington
Section Leader

E. Moss
Section Leader

Dec 18th 1916.

Since these were pre-wireless days, telephones were not so common, and soldiers were only able to send home field-cards which contained just the most rudimentary message such as "I am well." Contact with the war came from soldiers on leave or wounded men on convalescent leave (e.g. "June 17th 1916. A fleet of motor cars full of wounded soldiers stopped in the village for tea"). One friend, whose leave visits to Cawthorne figure prominently in the diary was Frank Moxon, who reached the rank of Captain in the Sportsman's Battalion. His decoration with the Military Cross obviously created an impression in the village: "Dec. 22nd 1916. Met Lieut. Moxon today. He showed me his medal and told me how the King pinned it on him at Buckingham Palace." What brought the horror of war to everyone as never before, however, was aerial warfare. The threat of Zeppelin raids became a nagging worry at the back of most minds, a worry which occasionally became reality:

"November 28th 1916. This morning everybody talking about the German airships which came last night. I was fast asleep in bed all the time and saw nothing, but a great many people were up watching them and listening to the guns and bombs. They dropped three bombs at Dodworth but did no damage. Also they dropped bombs at Cudworth and other places, and, when I got to Barnsley, I saw that there were a great number had felt the fear of death, everybody being up all night fleeing to the fields."

Douglas Charlesworth, however, managed to turn even this into a positive advantage:

"January 16th 1917. Went to Silkstone Camp for two Zeppelin bombs, one for our Museum and one for the Barnsley Naturalists Society."

There was tremendous relief in the village when the Armistice was signed, but in the Charlesworth family this was overshadowed by its greatest sadness of the whole war.

"November 11th 1918. Armistice signed today. Received news of Tom Allot being killed in action last Monday at St. Quesnoy. He was in the 5th Battalion K.O.Y.L.I. 62nd Division. We shall miss his music."

Was Douglas Charlesworth remembering his brother-in-law as the organist of the Methodist Church, or as the friend who had accompanied him on the piano as he sang or played the violin or cello at many family gatherings? We shall never know, nor shall we know what thoughts there were of the twenty-one others who never returned to their village. Of the "First Eleven", three were killed (including Horace, one of Mrs. Morley's sons), George Horton lost a leg and Sergeant Sam Bagshaw suffered the privations of a prisoner-of-war camp.

Delivering the "War Spirit".   R.W.

Two victims of the war.

Above: John Fallas, when he was head choirboy at the Church.

Below: 2nd Lieut Donald Laycock, whose brother (a former teacher at the village school) was also killed.

Among others to die were the brothers Donald and Benjamin Laycock (the latter a former teacher at the village school), young Victor Broadhead from Cawthorne Basin, and former Head Chorister at the village church, John Fallas. For some of them, plaques were placed prominently in respective places of worship – Private John Watkin Woodward, Major Lionel Walsh, Corporal Elijah Herbert Chappell, and Second Lieutenant Thomas Allott. All twenty-two received public remembrance outside the Museum, when the War Memorial, designed by Mrs. Stanhope's brother, Mr. E. M. S. Pilkington, and sculpted by Mr. John Swift, was erected. Each year since, this has been a focus for a Remembrance Day parade of homage by those who returned, which was led, until he reached his mid-80s, by Sergeant Sam Bagshaw. Like so many of his contemporaries, he preferred to draw a mental shutter over what he suffered and saw on the Western Front, but one name which must have returned to him many times was that of the tall fair-haired young man who stood holding one of the Union flags on the "First Eleven" photograph. A bright, intelligent person, educated at Penistone Grammar School, highly thought of and encouraged by Mr. Pilkington, he may just possibly have died in France at the hands of a relative, because English-born Sergeant Carl Ernst Neumann M.C. was the son of a German-born, but English-naturalized couple, Ernst Gottlieb Neumann and his wife, who had kept the "Spencer Arms" since the beginning of this century. Such is the savage irony, the pity and the folly of war.

I like to feel that it was with all of these in mind that Douglas Charlesworth wrote one of his non-dialect poems:

When I must leave this world and pass away
I would be speeded by my dearest friends,
Who, full of life, of laughter and of love,
Beguiled the hours when I so weary lay;
So when the cord is loosed, to lull my fears,
Let me pass out with laughter, not with tears.

And, as the years roll on, and I still live
Within the thoughts of those who loved me well,
Think how I loved your life, and drank my fill
Of all its beauty, all that life could give;
So, dreaming in your happy after years,
Remember me with laughter, not with tears.

1939-45

Those who went to war in 1939 went with an attitude much different from the high idealism of the volunteers of August 1914. All ideas of glory had gone, having been banished by stories told them by their fathers of what "the war to end all wars" had really been like. From the beginning, most of them were conscripts fighting through necessity, not choice. As a result, the involvement of the younger men and women of Cawthorne in the Armed Forces was on a much larger scale than it had been thirty years earlier. They flew planes, went on dangerous convoys through Arctic waters to bring much needed supplies to the Russians, and took part in such raids upon enemy-occupied territory as the Narvik raid. They were active in all the theatres of war, but, surprisingly, only seven new names were eventually added to the Roll of Honour on the village War Memorial when it was all over:

On Active Service
August, 1941

Donald Acton	Leslie Fish	Colin Macnaught
Arthur Bagshaw	Raymond Fish	Stuart Marshall
Eric Bagshaw	Ronald Fish	Walter Millington
Maurice Barrow	Stanley Fish	Cecil Morgan
Alan Broadhead	Walter Fish	Wilfred Newton
Arnold Broadhead	Ernest Fretwell	Stanley Nichols
Irvine Broadhead	David Greenwood	Peter Pardoe
Austin Crossland	John Hall	Robert Pardoe
Herbert Crossland	Jim Hill	Henry Penrose
Joseph Henry Crossland	Joseph E. Hinchcliffe	Frank Price
Kenneth Crossland	Doris Hughes	Charlie Robinson
Stanley Crossland	Stanley Hughes	*Cyril Sales
Archie Cruickshank	Tom Hughes	Donald Sales
Bernard Dearman	Lewis Jagger	Leonard Sheard
‡John Dundas	Gerald Jones	Douglas Stables
Hugh Dundas	Wilfred Kitchen	Jimmy Stubbins
Frank Downing	Clarence Lindley	Frank Town
George Downing	Tommy Lindley	Arthur Warren
Donald Fish	Laurence Lonsdale	Irvine Woodward

‡Killed in action   *Prisoner of war

Second List – August, 1942.

Ida Batty	Simon Cruickshank	Peter Mason
Isa Buckley	Audrey Fish	Anthony Mason
Dennis Caswell	Ivan G. Hardinge	David Mason
Phyllis Chapman	Lawrence G. Hinchliffe	Jack Machen
Phyllis Child	Cyril Jagger	Marjorie Sykes
Amy Crossland	Roy Kitchen	Lilian Town
Emma Crossland	Hubert Mitchell	Lois Wood

All conflicts seem to produce their own "characters", their heroes. In the First World War, those who readily spring to mind are the young officers who led their men against German machine-guns, armed only with a pistol and a swagger-stick. They were "the wasted generation", young men of great talent and intellectual capacity, who could have played such a part in the affairs of this country in years to come. Their counterparts, who captured the imagination in World War II, were the fighter-pilots. The task of the fighter pilot was well described in the B.B.C. "Scrapbook for 1940" by the late Richard Hillary, as follows:

> "He has none of the personalized emotions of the soldier, handed a rifle and bayonet and told to charge. He doesn't have to share the dangerous emotions of the bomber, who, night after night, must experience that childhood longing for smashing things. The fighter-pilot's emotions are those of a duellist, cool, precise, impersonal. He is privileged to kill well. For, if one must either kill or be killed, as now one must, it should, I feel, be done with dignity." [6]

Cawthorne had two fighter-pilots, the brothers Dundas, whose parents lived at Dale House. In the memories of the older people of the village the younger of the two, Hugh, most fitted the popular conception of those who became fighter-pilots. A "tall, gangling youth", he is remembered as roaring around the neighbourhood on an extremely noisy motorcycle. When the noise of this machine caused the policeman at Barugh Green to stop him one day, Hugh Dundas is reputed to have shouted, "You'll have to speak up! I can't hear you for this thing!!" [7] – a situation worthy of a Will Hay comedy. He was once invited to join some of the villagers in a tennis tournament, but the invitation, given in a spirit of kindness, backfired upon them because he won:

"He was like a damned octopus, all arms and legs. You couldn't get anything past him at the net."* [7] His elder brother, John, was quieter and more studious. An Oxford first-class honours graduate, he had become a member of the Auxiliary Air Force whilst working for "The Yorkshire Post". As a result, he had been straight into action with 609 Squadron at the outbreak of war, flying Spitfires. When he was shot down and killed, aged 25, in November 1940, Flight Lieutenant John C. Dundas D.F.C. was in charge of B Flight 609 Sqadron and had just claimed his final victim, Helmuth Wieck, leader of Germany's crack Von Richthofen Squadron. Among tributes paid to him were the following:

> "He was undoubtedly one of the best air fighters this war has produced."
>
> "He was one of the rising generation whom post-war Britain could ill afford to lose."

His brother Hugh (now Sir Hugh) served in 616 Squadron under Douglas Bader, went on to become the R.A.F.'s youngest Group Captain at the age of 24, and subsequently was Chairman of British Electric Traction and then Thames Television.

One aspect which linked the two World Wars as far as the village was concerned was the blackout. The Cawthorners of 1914 were used to night-time walks through unlit streets, since there were no gas or electricity supplies, but the idea of lights from buildings etc. being of assistance to aerial raiders took some time to occur to those in authority:

> "February 16th 1916. This day is the first day of the lighting order when all windows and lights are to be darkened on account of the German Zeppelins."

By 1939, the experiences of the Spanish Civil War had demonstrated the full, horrible potential of air-power and, therefore, the immediate blackout, which war brought, extinguished the street-lighting and ended an amenity which Cawthorne had only enjoyed for a few months. In another respect, however, the villagers of 1939-45 were kept far less "in the dark" than those of the First World War had been. Information concerning the progress of the war, although carefully vetted, was plentiful and was readily obtainable at the

*Author's footnote: The organizers of the tournament seem to have underestimated an English public school education. He must surely have acquired some skills at racket games while at Stowe, especially since his older brother, John, won a half-Blue at squash at Oxford.

The Cawthorne Home Guard on parade. Above: on Tivydale, and below: leaving the Church.

flick of a wireless switch. The medium of radio was a powerful weapon, keeping the nation alert to the dangers of invasion in the early years of the war, a sense of alertness which was heightened and given an element of fear for those who turned their tuning dials too far and picked up the German propaganda of "Lord Haw-Haw", Bradford-born William Joyce. This fear

The Home Guard at the ready. I don't know whether the expressions on the faces of Laurie Morley, Noel Moxon and Joe Parkinson are the result of holding themselves still until the flash went or apprehension at the amount of powder with which Noel had loaded the flash!

Harry Fish (one of the officers of the Cawthorne Home Guard) entering the village church for his Civic Service as Mayor of Barnsley September 1979.

of invasion, especially by German parachute troops, gave an added importance to the Home Guard as a last line of defence. The platoon raised in Cawthorne, in common with its counterparts nationwide, contained a good cross-section of the village community, with officers drawn from local businessmen or members of the professions, some N.C.O.'s who had survived the 1914-18 conflict and were now above the age for active service, men in reserved occupations (e.g. farming and mining) or too old for the forces, plus youths gaining experience before reaching the age for "call-up". Characters and personalities also varied considerably: from one junior officer who could not wait to gain promotion to another rank and different sphere of activity, thus relieving him of having to take orders from a superior whom he resented, to one N.C.O. who thought orders applied to everyone else but him. There were always those with plenty to say on meeting nights, most of them offering helpful, constructive criticism, but there was always one whose comments were invariably carping and destructive. The majority were solid, reliable "soldiers", who did what was required of them with a minimum of fuss, but the platoon had its "dodger" whose artistry at missing parades, manoeuvres etc. reached new heights when his officers took out the punitive summons made necessary by his absence. [22] Cawthorne's Home Guard took its role very seriously and former members still talk of the rigours of training and drill which they underwent, involving long runs and wading through the water in Cannon Hall Park

Security and the scarcity of films in wartime made filming of the camp as an army base impossible, but these post-war football shots show remnants of it in the background.

– and the exercises grew even more rigorous when one of their officers, Harry Fish (later to become Mayor of Barnsley), returned from a training course with the Commandos! As one has come to expect, however, from subsequent writings and television presentations, the Home Guard seems to have often combined seriousness of purpose and intent with elements of high farce when intent was translated into practice. This was shown when a strange object was seen in the sky over the village. Philip Walker saw it, but preferred to continue planting his cabbages until he received an official phone-call for him to mobilise his men, thus causing his wife to draw a parallel with Drake on Plymouth Hoe. When the call came, every man was issued with five rounds of live ammunition and a thorough patrol of the area made to ensure that an airborne invasion had not taken place. Cars and pedestrians were challenged, the local A.R.P. feeling particularly threatened since they knew that the rifles being stuck under their noses were, for once, loaded. The excitement, however, subsided when official confirmation came

176

that the airborne invader was nothing more than a barrage balloon which had broken loose from its moorings on the hills over towards Manchester. One present Cawthorne resident, Stuart Fish, remembers further incidents which illustrate the humorous aspect admirably. As a boy in his early teens, who was too young for Home Guard Service, he witnessed an "exercise":

"They had been divided up into two separate forces, one defending and one attacking. The area being defended was the old cottages in Lower Collier Fold where old Henry Crossland used to live, but which were now derelict. It was all very serious with hand-grenades being thrown about. These were not loaded, but I can remember one of them knocked a big piece off the plaster-rendering on the side of our house. The attackers had plenty of smoke-bombs which they kept hurling into the cottages, until one of the defenders, Anthony Barker, was overcome by fumes. He was a big lad, and to get him to the Home Guard Headquarters in the old band room behind The Spencer Arms, they knocked a door off and used it as a stretcher.

Having nothing else to do, I walked along with them and saw them leave the wounded man's gun against an outside wall before taking him upstairs to H.Q. On walking back down Hollin Lane, I was called to by one of the attacking force, Angus Broadhead, who was in position behind our coalhouse and said, "I wish I had a gun – I should feel much more like a soldier." "I know where there is one," I replied, and ever ready to help a pal, I went and fetched it from the wall of The Spencer Arms. Of course in a village it is very difficult to do anything without being spotted by someone and so, when a "hue and cry" was raised for the missing weapon, they weren't long in finding out what had happened to it. As a result, I was marched under arrest to Home Guard H.Q. where I underwent a lengthy interrogation by Sergeant Sam Bagshaw."

It would seem that the fear of the Fifth Columnist was very real even in Cawthorne!

One factor which added to this fear from 1939-45 was the physical presence of the Army in the village. In the first World War, "the Army" had meant people from elsewhere, the nearest contact being when soldiers from the Royal Engineers' Camp at nearby Silkstone came to practice building pontoon-bridges across the water in Cannon Hall Park; and a young Noel Moxon, at his lessons in Mrs. Robinson's house on Taylor Hill, heard their marching-songs and tried to calculate how far they would get up the hill before breathlessness would compel them to stop singing. From 1939, however, the Army were in the village. A camp was built inside Cannon Hall Park, which brought significant changes. A new sewage system had to be built for the village to enable it to cope with the enlarged population, a population which came and went throughout the war years: the King's Royal Rifle Corps, the Royal Ulsters, the Canadian/Scottish, who came and then left to go on the Dieppe Raid, and members of the Polish Army in exile; all these and more found temporary lodgings in wartime Cawthorne. Their presence placed restrictions upon villagers living in the immediate vicinity of the Tivydale entrance to the park. Anti-aircraft guns and vehicles were often parked along Tivydale when they did not have enough room for them inside the camp; and it was disconcerting for residents walking to their homes in the black-out to find themselves facing the bayonetted rifle of a

Above: this post Second World War photograph shows mothers and children enjoying the winter on Cannon Hall's frozen lake, but a full printing of the negative shows members of the Polish Army, the last inhabitants of Cawthorne's camp.

One of the village fund-raising efforts ("Wings for Victory" or "Save the Soldier").

sentry, who sometimes took quite a lot of convincing of their identity. Some villagers had passes which allowed them into the camp (e.g. Pat Blacker collected boots for repair work and returned them each week), but for the rest the only access now to an area, which had always been open to the villagers by permission of the Spencer Stanhopes, was when they were invited to dances or whist-drives. Even such limited social contact, however, produced some lasting results, since at least six of those men, whose first contact with Cawthorne was through the army camp, married local girls and settled in the village. Even the local Home Guard C.O., local builders' merchant A. J. Taylor, could not have guessed that the war would bring him a Canadian Officer son-in-law.

One feature of the Second World War in Britain was the way in which the whole population was mobilised to help with the war effort. This was more of a "People's War" than the conflict of 1914-18 had been, although even then the children of the village school had regularly been taken out to pick blackberries, which were then sent to a central depot for making into jam for the troops in France, and much meadow land was ploughed out. The farms worked flat out to produce food, with the labour supply being supplemented by wives and by land girls. Evacuees came into Cawthorne, old properties such as Raw Royd and John Fretwell's former home in Darton Road being placed at their disposal by the Estate. Above all, the villagers combined to raise much needed funds, and produced comforts for the Armed Forces. Between October 1939 and August 1946 the Cawthorne Working Party and W.V.S. produced 2,917 garments for soldiers, refugees etc. The fund raising capacity of the village twice received a mention in B.B.C. broadcasts:

The board showing the progress of Cawthorne's efforts for "Wings for Victory."

Sunday 4th July 1943: Extract from a broadcast following the Six-o-clock news concerning the "Wings for Victory Campaign".

"Among the many small places with fine achievements are the parishes in the Penistone Rural District, whose population of 6,500 collected over £74,000. One of them, the village of Cawthorne, where there are 942 people, actually collected £83 more than the £25,000 target for the whole district."

From a similar broadcast about "Save the Soldier" Week, 18th July 1944 "Cawthorne, near Barnsley, collected nearly £30 per head," (i.e. £27,686).

When National Thanksgiving Week came at the end of September 1945, everyone felt that they had reason to celebrate. A new life was beginning – or so they thought. In fact, a way of life, aspects of which had existed unchanged for over two-hundred years and would have been in parts recognised by Fielding, George Eliot, Thomas Hardy, D. H. Lawrence, Flora Thompson and many other chroniclers of English rural life, was reaching its last days. The days of Cawthorne, the semi-feudal, model Estate Village were numbered.

Even the children got involved with the "Save the Soldier" campaign.

Kathleen Ellis helping husband, Norman, by driving the tractor at harvest, while, below: Ernest Shirt had some young helpers.

CAWTHORNE IN TWO WORLD WARS 1914-18 AND 1939-45

Group at Cannon Hall. Mrs. John Montague Spencer Stanhope is standing extreme right and her daughter sitting extreme left.

The latter years of the Spencer Stanhopes in Cawthorne.

Mrs. Elizabeth Fraser Spencer Stanhope as a girl, when the villagers knew her as "Miss Betty."

181

The indoor staff at Cannon Hall pre-1914.

A prize bell-ringing team. Of especial interest are "Ned" Dearnley (standing extreme left) and Henry Crosland (seated extreme left) who had 57 and 63 years of service as bell-ringers respectively.   D.

182

Alec Hughes feeding the young pheasants in 1937.

The days when hunting was much more common in the village than it is today. A group photograph (probably taken by Houghton early this Century) outside the gamekeeper's house when Mr. Butler held that position.

183

21. February 1912.

To Mr James Staylock, Easton Hall, Grantham. Game-Keeper.

The Terms & Conditions incidental to your appointment as Head-Keeper on the Cannon Hall Estate by John Montague Spencer Stanhope Esquire are as follows:—

1. Your engagement to take effect as from the fourth day of March 1912.

2. Your engagement to be subject to determination by one month's notice to expire at any time during the first or any succeeding year.

3. Your remuneration to be at the rate of Twenty five shillings per week together with one suit of Clothes to be provided for you once in every year during your engagement free of charge.

4. You are to reside in the house provided for you free of rent rates and taxes, and are at liberty to avail yourself of not more than five tons of Coal per annum free of charge for use in the said house.

5. You shall keep no pigs or poultry except so far as the latter may be necessary for the breeding and rearing of game, or any dogs for which licenses are not held at the Estate office without previous permission in writing to do so.

6. The duties to be undertaken by you are the management of the Shooting at and around Cannon Hall with all duties connected therewith usually undertaken by a Head-Keeper, including the breeding and rearing of pheasants ducks and other game as required, the supervision and management of the fish ponds and fishing, the management of the Deer in the Park, the keeping and cleaning of guns, and such other duties as may be required of you on the days set aside for shooting on the grouse moors.

Signed: J. Hubert Pardoe
agent acting for & on behalf of
J. Montague Spencer-Stanhope Esq

CAWTHORNE IN TWO WORLD WARS 1914-18 AND 1939-45

The Spencer Stanhopes were never Lords of the Manor of Cawthorne, but did own the Manor House before selling it to its present owner. This building appears to be of 17th Century origin, but an earlier house is mentioned in a 16th Century law-suit involving the Barnby family, who were very influential pre-17th Century, but suffered because they would not renounce their Roman Catholic faith. The cross to the left of the picture is a memorial to Charles Pratt. N.F.M.

Banks Hall, the Dower House of the Spencer Stanhopes, to which Mrs. Elizabeth Fraser Spencer Stanhope retired for the remaining years of her life after the sale of Cannon Hall. Subsequently, it became a student hostel and is now a residential home for the elderly. R.W.

Mr. John Montague Spencer Stanhope with his daughter and his grandson, Simon Fraser.

185

CAWTHORNE 1790-1990

She remained active in village affairs and is seen (late 1940's/early 1950's) presenting prizes to children who had taken part in the Museum Society's Wild Flower Competition. This competition was discontinued in the 1970's to encourage conservation rather than the collecting of wild-flowers.

The Village in Carnival mood

Cawthorne has never needed much excuse to celebrate with a carnival. To begin with, these celebrations relied heavily upon horses and carts, whether it was for patriotic pageants around the First World War period....

or honouring Belgian refugee families.

187

By the time of the 1953 Coronation, the lorry had taken over... N.F.M.

and by the time "The Slipper and the Rose" won the 1979 Carnival, the size of the lorries used and the structures built upon them had matched the growth in size of the village itself. G.B.J.

At most of these celebrations over the years, the Village Band was always ready to provide entertainment. N.F.M.

CAWTHORNE IN TWO WORLD WARS 1914-18 AND 1939-45

The centenary of the opening of the present school buildings was an opportunity not to be missed – and all the scholars made the most of their celebrations in June 1972. B.C.

CAWTHORNE 1790-1990

A Sketch Map (based upon Cawthorne Pre-1930) to show the approximate position of places mentioned in the text (not drawn to scale).

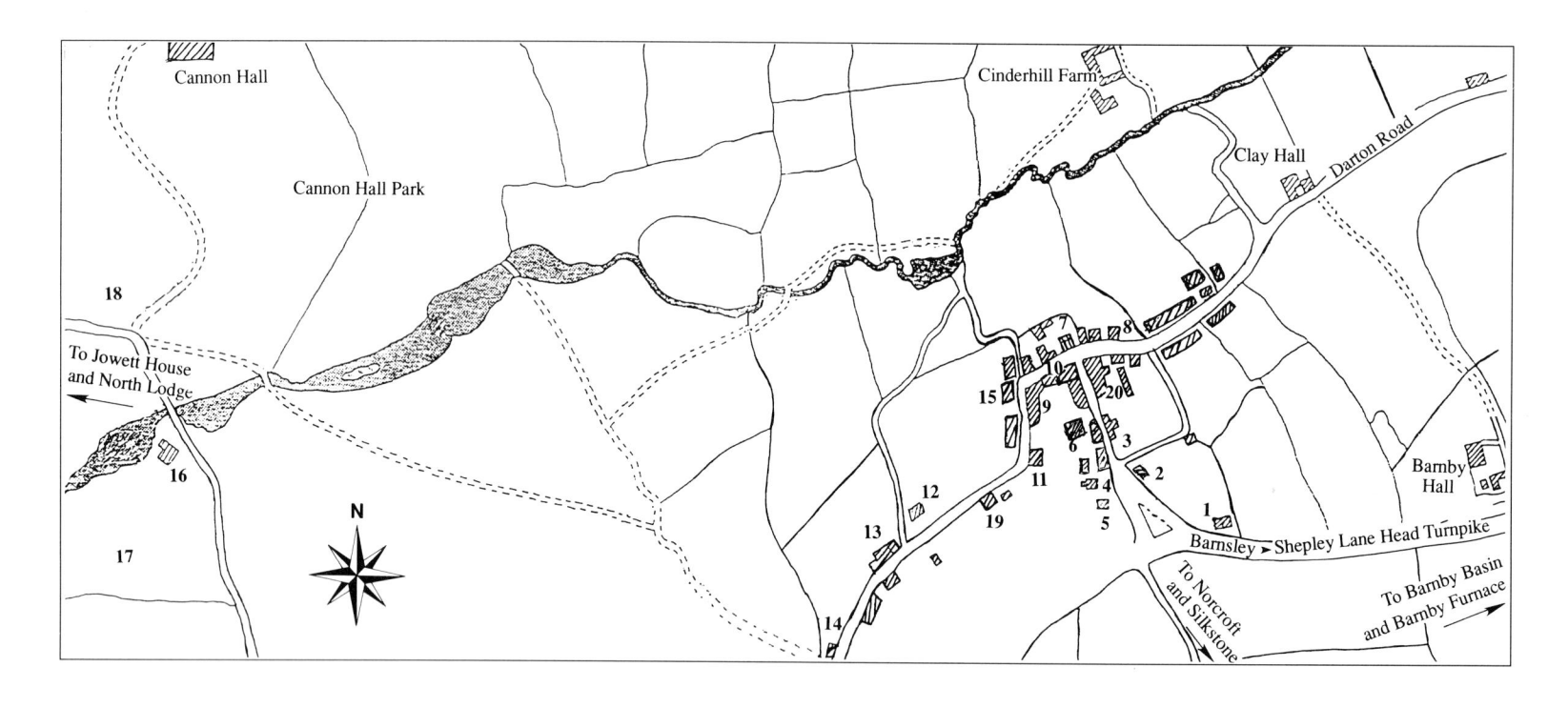

1. C. T. Pratt's Vicarage
2. Toll Cottage
3. Spencer Arms
4. Church
5. Grammar School (Now Parish Room)
6. Red House (Home of The West Family)
7. The Golden Cross
8. The Methodist Church
9. The Malt Kilns (Now Malt Kiln Row)
10. Richard Charlesworth's Shop
11. The Museum
12. Brook House – Abel Hold's Home
13. The Forge
14. South Lodge
15. Home of Joshua and Douglas Charlesworth
16. Jowett Saw Mill
17. Site of Killamarsh Windmill
18. West Lodge
19. Boys' (now mixed) School
20. Chantry House (Rowland Wilkinson's Post Office)

The Years of Change

1945-1990

CAWTHORNE 1790-1990

CHANGES had taken place at Cannon Hall from the time of Sir Walter's death in 1911. As one villager put it, "Life quietened down." Sir Walter, as a former soldier and Member of Parliament under Disraeli, had been known nationally and had played host to visitors from far and wide, including members of the Royal Family. His son, John Montague, appears to have been a quieter, more private person, increasingly so after the premature death of his wife in 1920. His sphere of activity tended to be local rather than national; he was the country squire, living a quiet life and entertaining a restricted circle of friends; a dignified gentleman to be seen in the village, driving to Church in his Renault car or walking on a tour of inspection of his property, accompanied by his faithful West Highland White dog. "He did not encourage visits to the Hall by societies and once said, 'If I showed everybody what was in Cannon Hall, I would have all the sneak-thieves coming up from London'; a maxim, the truth of which has been subsequently learned by the owners of many stately homes. He was operating on a good old Cawthorne principle which was somewhat differently stated by old Harry Crossland when he said: 'If you want to lose owt, show it to somebody.'" [7]

John Montague Spencer Stanhope died in 1944 and was succeeded as head of the Cannon Hall Estates by his daughter, Mrs. Elizabeth Fraser, who, after her divorce, added her maiden surname, to be known as Mrs. Fraser Spencer-Stanhope. She in turn passed the Estate in 1954 to her son, Simon Fraser, who is still the owner. During the 1970's he maintained a residence in the village, but now prefers to live on the West Coast of Scotland, where his grandfather and great-grandfather had always maintained a holiday home.

Ancestral home with its own deer herd. The deer were casualties of the war years and opencast mining.

The staff at Cannon Hall had diminished during the Second World War and was never built up again. The hall, described in the press as "a 50-roomed mansion standing in 150 acres of Parkland", was sold to Barnsley Corporation in 1951 for £15,750 to be turned into a museum and country park. Mrs. Fraser Spencer Stanhope moved to the nearby family dower house,

Museum and country park.

The Park fell victim to opencast mining in the late 1940's and early 1950's. N. F. M.

Banks Hall, which, during the nineteenth-century, had been home to the unmarried Spencer Stanhope daughters.

From 1947 onwards the coal, which had been an important part of the foundations upon which the Spencer and Spencer Stanhope fortunes had been built, became attractive to the newly formed National Coal Board and brought opencast mining to Cawthorne. Over the next seven years, a substantial percentage of the farmland owned by the Cannon Hall Estate, plus the parkland of Cannon Hall itself, was torn up to provide much needed coal for post-war Britain's fight to recover from the effects of the conflict with Germany.† The end of this particular period of change was reported by the "Barnsley Chronicle" on 29th January 1955 as follows:

> By the end of March the Cannon Hall Park, Cawthorne, should have recovered from the scars of opencast coal-mining. This news is given

† *60% of the land in the Parish has been subjected to opencast coal-mining.*

in a letter from a National Coal Board official to Mr. W. J. Taylor, C.B.E., D.L.,J.P., and M.P. for Bradford North, of Brentwood, Cawthorne.

The N.C.B. spokesman is Mr. V.J. Drummond, deputy chairman of the Board. In a reply to a letter from Mr. Taylor, he writes: "As soon as there is a spell of good weather, four weeks should suffice to complete all the work that remains to be done.

"By the end of March everything should be finished." Explaining the delay in restoring the opencast coal-site – known as the Cascade site – in the Park, Mr. Drummond reports that it was intended that the site should be available for cropping in the autumn of 1954. This was not possible because there was a lot of rock in it and extensive rooting had to be done to ensure that no large stones or boulders were left near the surface.

Then the very wet weather during the summer and autumn of last year delayed the restoration programme; indeed, the site was for some time water-logged.

Mr. Drummond continued: "In September, the Agent to the Estate asked specially to have a part of the site re-graded so that it could be used later as an agricultural show and sports ground.

"Two schemes were prepared to meet this request, and the Board's Opencast Executive are at present obtaining a quotation for the work on the one chosen."

Much Pleasure

The news that the Park is to be restored will give much pleasure to the people of Cawthorne and in a wider area, commented Mr. N. F. Moxon, of Green Gables, Cawthorne to a "Barnsley Chronicle" reporter this week.

"Once again we hope that the Parkland will give pleasure to people in the district on the same scale as in the pre-war years. Although privately owned the Park has, for four generations been available to the public for cricket, football, golf and a picnic centre." Mr. Moxon posed the question: "Can the present generation rebuild this fair place for the future as the 'Georgians' built for our pleasure?" It is sad to relate that through opencast working the work of nearly 200 years has come to naught." Planning of the parkland was carried out by William Spencer. He died in 1756 without having commenced his scheme and it was left to his son, John, who four years later began by rebuilding the stone bridge at the Saw Mill end of the stream. During the next five years great strides were made, for the three stretches of water with waterfalls were constructed together with an additional bridge.

It was during this period, 1760-1766. that many trees were planted in the Park and about 100 deer were introduced. Further improvements must have followed for in 1777 it is recorded that Capability Brown, the renowned landscape gardener, visited the Hall.

The open-cast mining, coupled with the establishment of the Army camp during the war had several effects. The village lost its nine-hole golf-course, its open-air swimming-pool, and its cricket field, while the Cannon Hall deer herd, which had been purchased in February 1762 by John Spencer, gradually disappeared. Various agencies have been blamed for the latter; the Army opening gates, thus allowing animals to escape, the devastation of the Park by the National Coal Board and so on. Legends abound concerning the deer and some people are willing to swear that a small herd descended from the Spencer Stanhope deer still roam the neighbouring woodlands, but times and dates of sightings are so vague that one is forced to conclude that the Cannon Hall herd is now phantom rather than fact.

Above: Cawthorne swimming baths were built by miners during the 1926 strike. They too closed down as a result of the effects of Army occupation and opencast mining. R.W.

Before the baths in the village, some baths had been built at Barnby Furnace, but, although popular as a venue for a swimming gala (above), they were not long-lived. Neither baths would have stood up to present-day health regulations.

From the beginning of the present century, a cricket match was played every Ascension Day between St. Mary's (C. of E.) School, Barnsley and Cawthorne School, when all the scholars of both schools thronged Cawthorne Cricket field. The fixture died with the loss of the old cricket field to the Army Camp and then to opencast mining.

The sixth green of Cawthorne's nine-hole golf-course, which went as a result of opencast mining. All that remains is the club house or "Old No. 10", the "Bottom Club", on Tivydale. The photograph was supplied by Raymond Fish, who played Minor Counties cricket for Lincolnshire.

Some of the fields which Douglas Charlesworth farmed and where, from time to time, he sat in the shade of the hedge-row to read one of his many books.

Present-day view looking from the top right-hand-side of the above photograph. What a difference! Cannon Hall can just be seen in the top left-hand corner.

It was inevitable in the post-war years, when taxation and death duties increased, that a rationalisation of the Cannon Hall Estate would become necessary. The Estate was too big for a dwindling family to support, hence the sale of Cannon Hall. The residential development of land in Cawthorne which was surplus to requirements was the next obvious step, and plans for such work had been drawn up pre-1939 and been placed in "cold storage" as a result of the war. The rate at which residential development now took place was regulated to a large extent by the political and economic state of Post-War Britain. The immediate post-war year saw restrictions placed upon private house building, even down to the size of houses permissible (a regulation which was rigorously enforced, as some Cawthorne residents found to their embarrassment). The supply of building land and land values were virtually rationed by regulations which were not relaxed until the mid-1950's. The Town and Country Planning Act of August 1947 gave Local Authorities three years from "the appointed date" to prepare development plans for particular areas and such plans were to be reviewed every five years. Attlee's Labour Government was badly hampered in fulfilling some of its objectives by a dollar crisis in 1948-49 and biennial sterling crises (1947, 1949 and 1951) which resulted in Treasury cuts in house building programmes. The economic position stabilised from 1951 to 1955, in which year another sterling crisis occurred. From 1955 onwards, the economy began to pick up. All of this greatly assisted the now famous Harold Macmillan house-building programme of the 1950's. Cawthorne followed the national pattern. Private building had taken place during the 1930's on selected single plots sold by the Estate, situated mainly on the outskirts of the main village, and other similar

THE YEARS OF CHANGE 1945-1990

The old houses in Lower Collier Fold, built to house local miners, came vacant during the war years and were pulled down (to be replaced by Swedish timber houses). These were the setting for the Home Guard exercise described in the book.

developments took place in the late 1940's. In the immediate post-war period there was a limited amount of Local Authority house-building (the Rural District Council having by now replaced the Cannon Hall Estate as the provider of new accommodation in the village), but larger scale privately-funded residential development of land sold by the Cannon Hall Estate did not really begin until the late 1950's, with the building of the small Tivydale Drive Estate to the West of the South Lodge entrance to Cannon Hall Park. Immediately adjacent to it followed the building of a Local Authority Estate of houses and old people's bungalows jutting right out into the Green Belt of the Park. The siting of this latter owed far more to political prejudice and expediency than to sound planning, since it requires its elderly inhabitants to climb a steep, and, for many of them, insurmountable hill to reach the village shops, places of worship and social meeting places.

The pace of private development really quickened in the late 1960's and early 1970's. In the mid-1960's 9.5 acres of land were sold to James Miller and Partners, to finish off an estate which had been thought of since 1935 when Tivydale Close had been started. Unfortunately, the sale took place at a time when there was an abundance of building land as landowners rushed to sell to beat the 30% Capital Gains Tax announced by Chancellor of the Exchequer, James Callaghan, in November 1964 and imposed by him in April 1965. As a result, the St Julien's Estate was not subject to the same stringency of control, which the Cannon Hall Estate had imposed elsewhere by restrictive covenants relating to building materials and density of building. The village, which in the Second World War had been home to 942 people living in just over 300 houses, had by 1971 expanded to a population of 1,251 living in 440 houses.

During this period, the village lost some of its old properties as a result of demolition. When one talks now to older residents, one is told in no uncertain terms that certain properties should have been preserved; John Fretwell's cruck-framed cottage being one usually singled-out for mention, and Raw Royd being another, despite its isolated position, with access only possible across several agricultural fields, and its complete lack of services (mains water and electricity). The agency usually singled out for blame is "The Estate". It is, therefore, interesting to read the minutes of a public meeting held on January 13th 1956 at which it was said that there were 18 sub-standard houses in Cawthorne (some of which, fortunately, survived and were renovated) bringing frequent calls for "slum clearance". The voice consistently raised in opposition was that of the Estate's Agent, Mr Hugh Pardoe, who asked why they could not be brought up to standard; and maintained that Darton Road was a better place for old people's houses than the proposed site in the Park!

A further change deplored by many of the older residents is the decline in the number of tenant farms on the Cannon Hall Estate; and it is easy to point to quite a large number of old farm houses which have been sold off, renovated and are now very desirable homes. Such concern with numbers of farms could easily blind one to the fact that a high proportion of the land farmed in Cawthorne in 1939 is still being farmed but in larger units and by a smaller number of tenant farmers. An essential and successful part of the rationalization of the Cannon Hall Estate has been the creation of efficient farming units of sufficient size to maintain two generations of one family, thus ensuring that the sons of farmers do not have to move elsewhere to seek a living.

The impact of these changes was considerable and, initially, very deeply felt. The problem was one of integration. Cawthorne had always accommodated "comers-in", but these had in the past been brought in gradually as workpeople by the Spencer Stanhopes. As a popular song of the 1940's said, "It aint what you do, it's the way that you do it. That's what gets results." The influx of people into the new private housing estates was on a scale much larger than anything hitherto known. Some of those who moved in were aggressively vociferous in saying what amenities the village needed, but were surprised when they received an equally aggressive reply from old Cawthorners, who felt aggrieved that pleasant open fields through which they had walked were now built upon, and were quick to ask, "Why have you come to our country village if you want to live in a mini-town?" In some respects, the newcomers' demands were justifiable. The extension for which they agitated proved a great asset to the village school (even though its designers made no attempt at architectural integration), but it did little for the cause of communal harmony to see some of the coverage given by the Press. Old Cawthorners and at least one young "comer-in" felt a sense of outrage at seeing their school written about under headlines which proclaimed "Dickensian conditions at village school." For a while in the early 1970's there was a definite possibility of a split in the community and the author can vividly remember how this upset the late Miss Mildred Holroyd, who, although born in the village and capable of writing about her childhood and adolescent years there with the utmost affection, was no blinkered reactionary, having spent most of her working years in Health Administration away from

Perhaps the greatest change in the character of the village streets has resulted from the removal of farms from the centre of the village, with all their attendant machinery, livestock and smells. The last of these, the Golden Cross, is clearly seen as a working farm in the aerial photograph above.

South Yorkshire. One evening at a Choral Society meeting she said that she had heard of the possibility of some people starting a Cawthorne New Residents' Association, but hoped that they would not do anything so stupid, because, if they did, she would start an Old Residents' Association and really split the village!

Time, however, brought its own solutions. People moved on, among them some of the more aggressively critical newcomers, and those who stayed came to realize that the Old Cawthorners were not "country bumpkins with straws behind their ears." For their part the Old Cawthorners began to recognize that many of the newcomers really wanted to be part of the community and were willing to work on behalf of it and its institutions. Over the past twenty years, the vigour and new ideas which the "comers-in" brought has mixed with the affectionate pride in the past felt by longer residents to form a well-integrated village society. It is a very different Cawthorne in which the socio-economic balance has shifted from Working to Middle Class, but the social mix and the mix of "old" and "new" families is still a good one. It is a village with a strong community spirit, where, at such times as the biennial Cawthorne Carnival, people are willing to roll up their sleeves and produce a show of which they are rightly proud. Their environmental pride is evident in the number of times that they have carried off the trophy as "The best kept village in South Yorkshire," while the spirit of communal caring and self-help sustains thriving Over-60's and Luncheon Clubs.

One is forced to conclude that the degree of expansion experienced by the village was beneficial, despite the fact that some life-long residents still answer the compliment that Cawthorne is a lovely village with the reply, "It used to be." Without the economic sustenance once provided by the Cannon Hall Estate, a small Cawthorne of pre-war size would by now have been well on the way to being a dying community. In addition to new vigour and ideas, the influx of population brought increased parish rates for the upkeep of such amenities as the Village Hall; and it brought children to what could easily have become a village for the retired elderly. Without these children, the village school would by now almost certainly have followed along the closure path already trodden by the schools of other villages in the neighbourhood which did not expand. Cawthorne is a thriving community, but it has its problems, some of which it shares with many other rural communities throughout the British Isles. Much of its property pre-dates the motor-car, and its builders, therefore, made no provision of space where these "necessary" adjuncts of modern life can be stored (and the necessity increases as the frequency of public transport decreases). If the social balance of the community is to be maintained, a heavy moral burden rests upon the Local Authority and the Cannon Hall Estate, as the two agencies with property to let to young people who were born in the village but who cannot afford to pay the high prices being asked for houses offered for sale. This burden is not made any easier by government legislation, which has eased the restrictions on the size of rents which may be charged. This could start a rent spiral, which in turn could put even rented property out of the reach of the children of the village.†

Who knows what future changes await Cawthorne and similar villages? In so many spheres of modern life we have seen planners pursuing the ideal that, for institutions to be efficient and viable, they must be of a scale, the enormity of which our grandparents could never have envisaged – and we have also seen the social problems created by the impersonal and, often, prison-like conditions of inner-city high-rise flats; or the disciplinary and learning problems experienced by some large comprehensive schools. Such is the present ecclesiastical law of supply and demand that some Church leaders would even suggest that it is not possible to run as single units parishes with populations lower than 8,000 – but what better example could one hope for of Christian outreach in a pastoral flock tended by a caring shepherd, than the Cawthorne of Charles T. Pratt?

Enjoyment of life in a village community seems to increase with one's willingness to be involved in that community and its life. Village life does make demands of those who choose it, in terms of communal discipline and tolerance, and they need to educate themselves and their families. Church bells will not cease to ring because someone moving into a house near the Church does not like the noise which they make; nor should new residents expect villagers to stop using their halls and meeting places just because they object to the noise and vehicular congestion which meetings and concerts sometimes bring. It is very pleasant to wake up near green fields full of spring lambs, but it is pointless to then object when the farmer decides that the same fields should be ploughed up and heavily manured. It is now less safe for unaccompanied children to enjoy the countryside as much as their predecessors were able to do, but a little careful education by their parents could go a long way towards showing them that country life is not boring, and can, in fact, be very interesting. It would be sad if future generations were to grow up knowing more about the beaches and bars of Benidorm than they do of the delights of Deffer or the other woodland walks which surround Cawthorne.

It would furthermore be ironic if we in Britain, who condemned the Ceaucescu plans for the obliteration of villages in Romania, were in the future to condemn to death so many of our own village communities, where people know and are known, by allowing pressure from those who build and sell houses to erode the Green Belt. It would be doubly ironic if Cawthorne were to be so condemned, since it was quick to adopt the Romanian village of Valea and mount its own relief expedition there in March 1990 – and yet the loopholes in planning control are such as to raise fears that it could happen. Instances are increasing of a considerable volume of local opposition being overruled in the granting of building planning permission; or of permission being granted for something which constitutes an asset to the village community, only for a "change of usage" application subsequently to transform it into something which simply exploits the tourist value of the village for private profit. This is not to decry such exploitation, but rather to re-emphasise that anything which makes possession of a car a pre-requisite for living in the village must substantially change the structure of the community. As a former village plan, prepared in accordance with the 1947 Town and Country Planning Act, states: "The aim of the village plan now should be to preserve the attractive landscape around the village and to ensure that the village does not develop beyond its present capability of maintaining a balance between rural character and environment, and regulated development." Village life has contributed a richly varied historical, architectural and cultural heritage to our national life. Aspects of this heritage are still being rediscovered in Cawthorne. Village dwellers should increasingly be conscious that they are custodians of an ancient tradition, who must ensure that what they pass on to future generations is worthy of transmission. In planning for the future, the past should be kept in sight: "He who knows not whence he comes, cares not whither he goes," or, as former American Presidential candidate, Adlai Stevenson, put it, "We can chart our future clearly and wisely only when we know the path which has led to the present."

†*Author's footnote: 1991: The Parish Council, in an attempt to address this problem, has entered into discussions with the Local Authority and a Housing Association to try to measure the need for and possibility of supplying reasonably priced rented accommodation.*

The entry to the village from Barnsley as seen above by Bamforth of Holmfirth, late 1890's. Facing the old Toll Cottage is what is still remembered as "the tree", where the men of the village sat (usually in the typical miners' squat position) and talked in good weather — a sort of unofficial village parliament.

Cawthorne then and now.

How the scene has changed by 1989!   G.B.J.

Above: Cawthorne Toll Cottage, known to Rev. Pratt as "Johnny Roberts' House" and thought of originally by him as the cottage in which to house the Village Museum. Shown outside it are two Belgian refugees, housed there 1914/15. It was later incorporated into the bottom floor of what is now one of the village shops (below).

Two views from the top of the Church tower, looking towards Barnsley – probably taken by Bamforth and Rowland Wilkinson respectively.

The same view as seen by the author in March 1979.

203

CAWTHORNE 1790-1990

The Fountain and the Church then and now.

204

The old cottages (above right) were demolished late 1930's and the farm (above left) made way for the Co-op in the early 1930's.   R.W.

G.B.J.

CAWTHORNE 1790-1990

Caleb Moakson's Riddle Shop at the top of Taylor Hill. Demolished 1900.

Below: the same view in 1990.   G.B.J.

Two views of the Co-op and the Post Office. It is interesting to see how the Co-op frontage changed.

Above: Old cottages at the top of Cliffe Hill photographed late 19th Century.

Below: A complete transformation by 1990.   G.B.J.

Above: members of the Swift family photographed early this century.   S.S.

Below: taken about 50 yards away from the same spot in 1989.   G.B.J.

THE YEARS OF CHANGE 1945-1990

Edwardian Cawthorne, looking towards Cannon Hall.   R.W.

209

Servants near South Lodge, returning to Cannon Hall from Church (early 20th Century).

First the camp, then opencast mining and then building, have completely transformed the area around South Lodge. R.W.

G.B.J.

G.B.J.

The picturesque "Squatters" cottage on Tivydale has completely disappeared.   *H.*

Two aerial views taken by David Broadhead vividly illustrate some of the post-war development which has taken place in the village.

CAWTHORNE 1790-1990

One of Noel Moxon's photographs c. 1939 shows the wide-open spaces and the A635 by-pass when it was fairly new.

How the spaces had been filled up by 1979.   G.B.J.

The village has spread since the top photograph was taken in the mid 1930's.   G.B.J.

These houses stood at the edge of the village at the beginning of this Century.

215

The town houses in Darton Road, in which, in the 18th and early 19th Centuries, those poor people in receipt of Parish Relief were housed. They were provided with employment – the men often doing work on road-mending and women doing knitting. They were demolished in the 1950's.

216

In 1971, Mildred Holroyd wrote the following piece for the Cawthorne Carnival programme:

"Life Before 1919"

What wonderful years they were! Or so it seems to me, looking back maybe, through rosy spectacles. My earlist recollections start when I was 3 years old, when I commenced attending "Infants' School" – situated a good quarter of a mile from home – we had a dear old school mistress, and many happy hours were spent there preparatory for transfer to the "Big School" at the age of 6.

I remember the lovely summers, long days of sunshine, picnics, and such happy freedom in the fields and park. My Grandma lived on a farm and at the age of 7, my family moved into the old house. The remaining years to 1919, I remember with nostalgia, so happy helping my parents, fetching the cows from the fields before and after milking, they ambled across the fields in answer to my childish call of "Cush, Cush" from the gate: taking milk around the village in a large can and pint measure – taking teas in a large basket to men in the hay-fields, and playing amongst the tall hay-cocks, riding home on top of the hay-load or on the back of old Boxer, the grey carthorse.

The winters too, I loved, heavy snows, and using a small hand-plough to make paths. Skating on the Cascade in the park, and on moonlight nights what happy times we children had sliding on the ice and watching skaters gliding gracefully on long stretches of ice.

A great treat was to go to Barnsley in a little waggonnette, covered in winter, owned by the landlord of the village inn; we mounted by the two steps, and it was illuminated by a candle lantern; the passengers sat facing each other. The horses were stabled at an old inn whilst the shopping was done – what a treat too, to be taken to a cafe for tea! The cakes were far more exciting than Mother's home-made ones. Christmas time was a special treat as the shops were open very late and then, most shopping was left until Christmas Eve.

The village had several red-letter days, Shrove Tuesday, half-day holiday, when hoops, shuttlecocks, whips and tops were first brought out. How we gaily sped along the roads! No traffic fears then. The tops were prettily crayoned: hopscotch too we loved; we chalked squares on the causeways. Then Cawthorne Feast, the third weekend in July, was a great joy to us, with two half-days' holiday: a fair with roundabouts, swings, coconut shies, shooting gallery and best loved of all, donkeys (1d. a ride) in a field at the top end of the village. Seeing Brandy Snaps even now, fills me with nostalgia for the sound of hurdy-gurdies again.

Half a day holiday on Ascension Day and watching cricket between our school and St. Mary's, Barnsley.

We never had seaside holidays; it was difficult to leave a small farm and money was scarce; our lovely countryside was sufficient. I never remember longing for a holiday: one yearly treat was going with the choir trip to the seaside. Oh! the excitement getting up at 4.30 am, packing sandwiches, going in our dog-cart to Darton station, the train journey and a day by the sea.

Another great annual treat was a visit to the pantomime at the Grand Theatre, Leeds, and afterwards tea at my Grannie's, who lived there.

At eleven years of age I went to High School and felt very important, cycling with older pupils – we used to read as we cycled along, so quiet were the roads.

Life in our village centred round Church and Chapel; there were Girl Guides, a Girls' Club, which I joined. Sunday School and Church Choir – what happy dances we had, organised by the Church and held in the Infants' School, real family affairs they were, our only music being a piano! many times we were danced off our feet in the Lancers! The Chapel Band of Hope gave concerts and lantern lectures. These were a great treat in the winter evenings. How I loved too, the Chapel Harvest Tea, followed by a "Service of Song".

I remember vividly, the lovely aroma in the old farm kitchen on Thursday baking day – a large batch of bread, scones, seed and fruit-cakes, tarts, sandwiches – the bread never tasted stale, kept in our lovely cool cellar.

Our only lighting was by lamps and candles, a beautiful soft light. The lamps were filled and trimmed daily – water was heated in a boiler at the side of the range and replenished by lading-can – cooking was all done in iron pans on the fire and baking in the oven, which took endless wood underneath to get it hot – looking back I marvel at the wonderful meals we had and wonder how Mother cooked under what now seems such primitive conditions.

What hard wash days too! Getting up early to fill the 'set pot' and light the fire, peggying, and at the end of the day, mangling and mangling with a great mangle, but, oh! the spotless, fresh and sweet-smelling clothes!

Even when the war came, I was 11 then, life to me didn't seem much changed, the battle-fields seemed far away – news was scanty and long in reaching us and to me, seemed very remote. I remember vividly seeing the first batch of recruits go in August 1914, many of whom, alas, did not return. Remember too, the shock the news of each casualty gave me. The Spanish Flu epidemic of 1918 troubled us greatly too – so many died in neighbouring villages. Food rationing I don't remember worried us at all, but I guess our parents did.

What lovely peaceful days they were! Unhurried, happy, leisurely days to me a teenager, despite the war years. I know there was much poverty, harder work, especially for Mothers of families, but I am glad I lived then, looking back in this present age of rush, bustle and noise.

Who knows whether in another hundred years (provided that this present generation does its custodial duties well) someone will be able to write with the same degree of pride and affection about their Cawthorne childhood? Cawthorne will, of necessity, have changed but, with luck, will remain a caring, independent, socially well-balanced, village community.

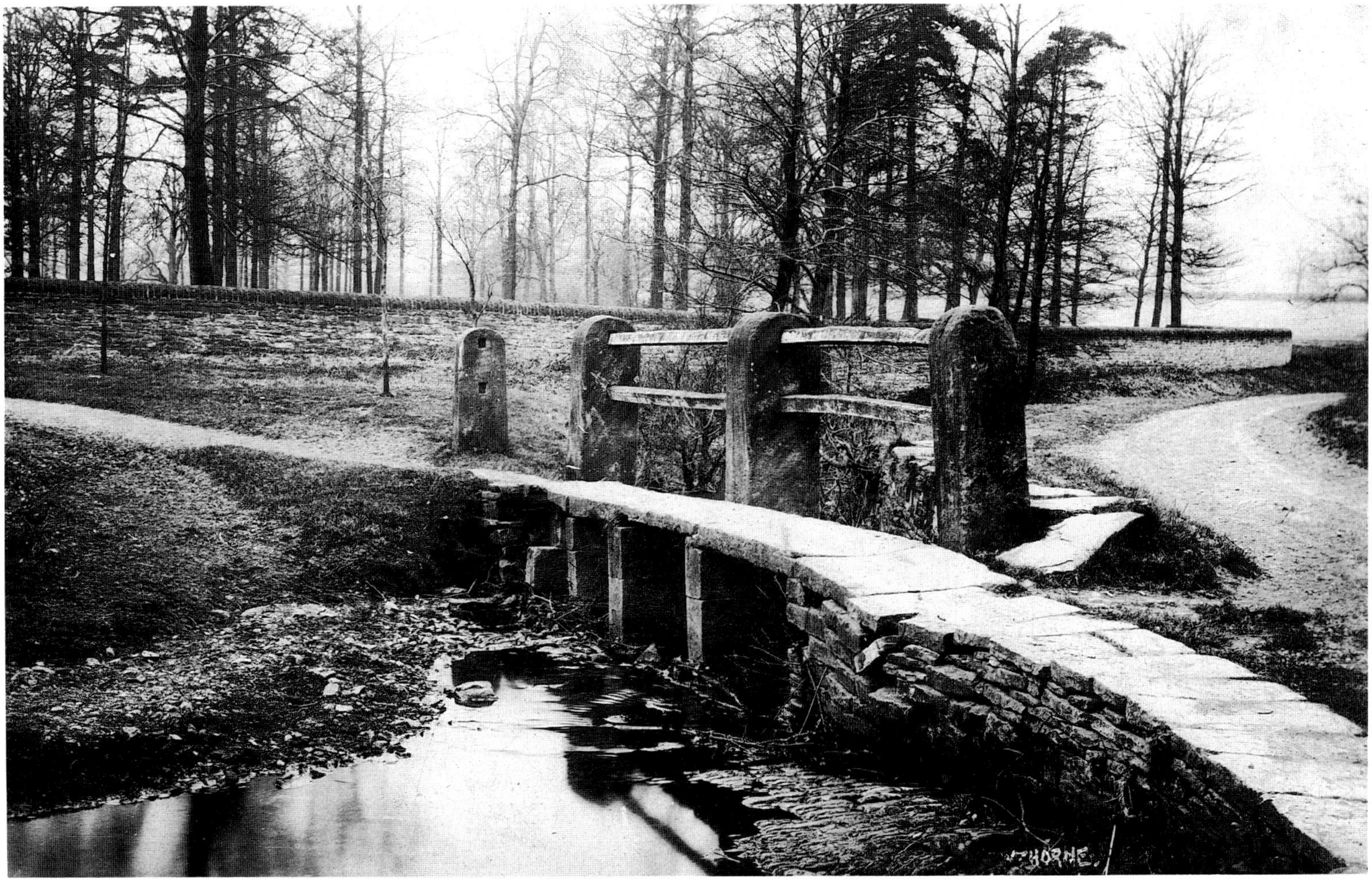
HORNE.

Deffer Hill
Dean Hill Spring
Dean Hill
Tannery
Lodge
Rookery
Upper Spring
Deffer Wood
Summer House
CANNON HALL PARK
Cannon Hall
Deer Shed
Lodge
Jowett House
Susannah Spring
Cascade Bridge
Jowett Mill
Killamarsh
Lodge
Spring House
Daking Brook
Daw Walls
Raw Green
Fryer Royd
Daw Hill
Hollin Royd
Flash House
Clough Green
Heald Head Quarry (Sandstone)
Heald Head
Brick Field
Brick Kiln
Bentcliff Hill Plantation
Shots Hill
Dixon Wood
Hill Top
Rowling House
Kiln House
Pashley Green
Peace Grove
C A W T
C A W T
3707
3707
T A

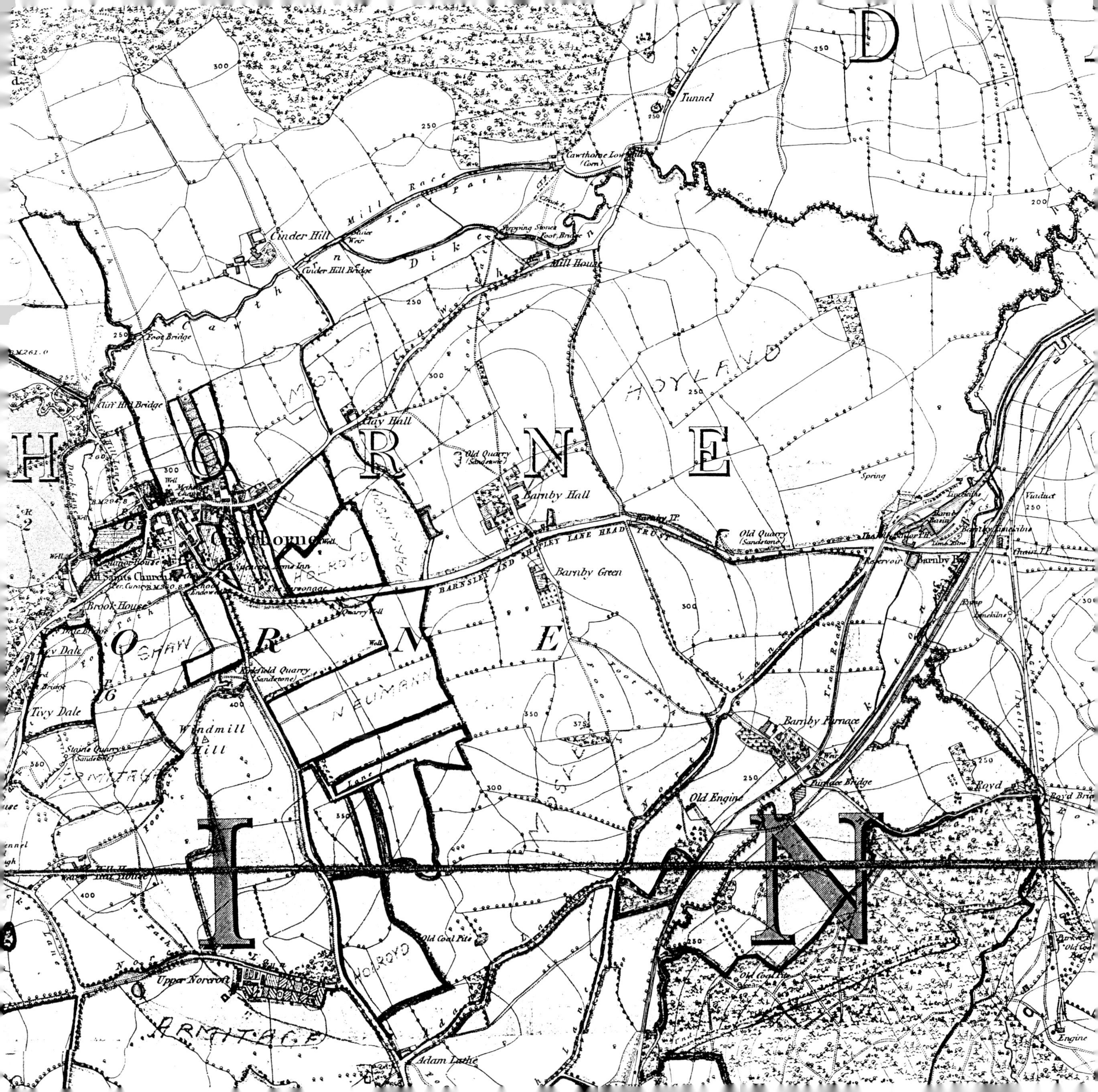

D
Tunnel
Cawthorne Low Mill (Corn)
Mill Race
Foot Path
Cinder Hill
Cinder Hill Bridge
Stepping Stones
Foot Bridge
Mill House
Cawthorne Dike
Foot Bridge
Cliff Hill Bridge
MOXON
HOYLAND
Hay Hall
H O R N E
Old Quarry (Sandstone)
Barnby Hall
PARKINSON
HOLROYD
Cawthorne
Brook House
All Saints Church
Barnsley and Shepley Lane Head Trust
Barnby Green
Old Quarry (Sandstone)
Reservoir
Barnby Basin
Limekilns
Viaduct
Spring
Tivy Dale
O R N E
SHAW
Kirkfield Quarry (Sandstone)
NEUMANN
Windmill Hill
Stains Quarry (Sandstone)
Tram Road
Barnby Furnace
Furnace Bridge
Old Engine
Royd
Royd Bridge
I N
Old Coal Pits
HOLROYD
Upper Norcroft
ARMITAGE
Adam Lathe
Engine

INDEX

All Saints Church, Cawthorne
    Bell-ringers & bells   12
    Cawthorne Musicians   12
    Parish Clerk   12-14
    Pipe organ   12
    Refurbishing in 1870's   14, 41-2, 72
    Sextons   14
    General   9

Bodley and Garner (Architects)
    Refurbishing of All Saints' Church (1875-80)   14

Cannon Hall Estate
    Agents for:
    J.A.G. Lees (present agent)   60, 101
    Hugh Pardoe   39, 60, 167
    Charles Wemyss   28, 60, 118, 133

Cawthorne
    Cawthorne Brass Band   140-143
    Cawthorne Choral Society   140
    Cawthorne "Feast"   57, 127-129
    Cawthorne Methodist Church   45-50
    Cawthorne Parish Council   148-150
    Cawthorne Places named within the text:
      Bank House   77
      Banks Hall   77
      Bark House Wood   40
      Barnby Basin   56
      Barnby Furnace   37, 39, 73
      Bentcliffe Hill   147
      Brook Houses   37
      Cinder Hill   40, 57
      Clay Hall   77, 80
      Collier Fold   37, 77
      Dale House   104
      Dean Hill   40
      Deffer Wood   80
      Fountain House   77
      Hill House   104
      Jowett Sawmill   9, 70
      Killamarsh Windmill   9
      Low Mill   9
      Malt Kiln Row   9, 14, 37, 61
      Norcroft   10
      Norcroft Colliery   10
      Taylor Hill   59, 77

The Red House   61
Woolstocks Lane   10

Cawthorne Public Houses:
The Spencer Arms   56
The Golden Cross   56, 59
The White Hart   56
The Jolly Sailor   56, 65
The Farmers' Arms   56

Cawthorne Residents named in the text
Walter Moxon   37
Joshua Charlesworth   37, 49-50
Joseph Chappell   137
Joshua Kaye   37
Mrs Balme   39
Mrs Eliza Shaw   40
The Wilkinson Family   40
George Wright   40
John Blacker   42-44
Henry Alfred Puddephatt   45
Richard Charlesworth   45-50
William Moxon   51
John Harrison   51, 59-60
John Fretwell   51-52, 118, 122, 123
Mary ("Polly") Fishburn   53
Elizabeth Clegg   53
Edward Lawson   57
J.W. "Mick" Glennon   60
Alice Moxon   60
West Family   61
Joseph Bramah   61
Wilfred Parkinson   69
Noel Moxon   69, 70, 123, 125, 133
Sam Bagshaw   69
Arnold Broadhead   69
Ben Swift   72
Samuel Swift   72, 118
Caleb Moakson   73
Douglas Charlesworth   73, 125, 143
William Moxon   77
James Albert (Jim) Moxon   77
Hannah Hawkshaw   77
Mrs Shaw   77
Mrs Morley   77
Lawrie Morley   77

Dr. Whincup   87
Dr. Rowley   87
Ben Fish   87, 123
Albert Broadhead   107
Mr. Beanland   107
Victor Broadhead   108
William Lockwood   108
William Glover   108
George Swift   118
George Hindle   123
James Balme   123, 139
D. N. Stables   123
Benjamin Harral   123
Tom Parkin   125
Jos Broadhead   130
George Roberts   132
Sam Barraclough   133
Kenneth H. Wood   141
"Billy" Machen   141
Harold Batty   141
George Parkinson   147
Mildred Holroyd   198-9, 217-218

Cawthorne Show
133-139

Cawthorne "Sing"
139

Cawthorne in Wartime:
1914-18
"1st XI" Volunteers   160-161
Belgian refugees   161-162
Douglas Charlesworth's wartime diary & poems   163-172
Zeppelin raid   171
Erection of war memorial   172
Personalities mentioned:
Rev. Cotton   165-166
William Lockwood   169
Dick Crossland   169
Joe Fretwell   169
Frank Moxon   171
Horace Morley   171
George Horton   171
Sam Bagshaw   171-172
The Laycock Brothers   171
Victor Broadhead   172

John Fallas　172
　　　Carl Neumann　172
1939-45
　　　Army in Cannon Hall Park　179
　　　Black-out　174
　　　Cawthorne Home Guard　175-177
　　　Personalities mentioned:
　　　　Sam Bagshaw　177
　　　　Anthony Barker　177
　　　　Pat Blacker　179
　　　　Angus Broadhead　177
　　　　Henry Crossland　177
　　　　Sir Hugh Dundas　173-174
　　　　John C. Dundas　173-174
　　　　Harry Fish　176
　　　　Stuart Fish　177
　　　　Noel Moxon　177
　　　　A.J. Taylor　179
　　　　Philip Walker　176
Education in Cawthorne
　　　101-112
Fraser, Simon W.
　　　192
Friendly Societies
　　　130-133
Heslops of Barnby Hall
　　　14
Industry in Cawthorne:
　　　Coal-mining　63-70
　　　"The Waggon road"　63-64
　　　Barnby Canal basin　64-66
　　　Silkstone Railway　64-66
　　　Acton's Stoneware　70
　　　Naylor Brothers　70
　　　Jowett Saw Mill　70
　　　Swift Family – masons　72
　　　Charcoal Burning　81
Open-cast mining in Cawthorne
　　　193-194
Parish Clerks of Cawthorne:
　　　Richard Moxon (d. 1800)　12
　　　John Livesley　12-14
　　　Joseph Milnes (d. 1868)　14

Pilkington, Ida Mary (1864-1920)
　　　Marriage to John Montague Spencer Stanhope　85
　　　Founding of Victoria Cottage Institute　85-87
Pratt, Rev Charles Tiplady. Curate of Cawthorne (1866-74),
Vicar (1874-1915), author of "The History of Cawthorne" (1882)
　　　Early life and description　33
　　　Other references　106, 107, 109-112, 123, 125
　　　His pronouncements in his "Parish Magazine"
　　　　Village health　39-40
　　　　Temperance　57-59
　　　　Library & Reading Room　100-101
　　　　The school & education　109-112
　　　　Cawthorne Feast　127-129
　　　　Cawthorne Show　133-139
　　　　Cricket　148
　　　　Outbreak of War (1914)　158
　　　　Sundry Subjects　150-156
Ruskin, John
　　　"friend" of Cawthorne Victoria Jubilee Museum　118
Schools (see also Education in Cawthorne):
　　　Village School/Head-masters/mistresses:
　　　　Richard Wigfall (1547)　101
　　　　Peter Deane (1639)　101
　　　　George McWhan　118
　　　　Miss Evans　103
　　　　Arthur Senior　103
　　　　George Warren　102, 103, 106
　　　School Staff
　　　　Mrs Annie Robinson　102
　　　　Mrs Mary Watts　102
Other Educational establishments:
　　　Dame School　101
　　　Mrs Wood's private school　101-102
Sextons of Cawthorne:
　　　Ben Taylor (d. 1879)　14
　　　William Ward (d. 1930)　14
　　　William Machen　14
Spencer, John, the "old squire" of Cawthorne
　　　2-3
Spencer Stanhope
　　　Walter (1750-1821):
　　　　Education　3
　　　　Inherits Cawthorne estates　3

    Marriage in 1783   3
    Friend of William Wilberforce   4
    Courage & Idealism   4
    Attends wedding of Louis XVI   4
    Cawthorne Volunteers   4-9
    Other   72
John (1787-1873)
  35-36, 130
Lady Elizabeth Wilhelmina (1795-1873), daughter of Thomas Coke of Holkham and wife of John Spencer Stanhope
    Lady Elizabeth's Charity   106
Rev. Charles (1795-1874) Non-resident
Vicar of Cawthorne 1822-74   28
Walter Thomas William K.C.B. (1827-1911)
    Refurbishing of All Saints' Church   14
    Patron of Abel Hold   28
    Patron of Museum   122
    Funeral   107
    Other references   36-37, 41, 103, 104
John Roddam (1829-1908), Pre-Raphaelite Artist
Refurbishing of All Saints' Church   14, 41, 42
Cawthorne Museum   118, 120, 122
Other   37
John Montague (1860-1944)   104, 106, 120, 192
Margaret Elizabeth Ida (1891-1964), known to locals as "Miss Betty", "Mrs. Fraser" and "Mrs. Fraser Spencer Stanhope"
  107, 123, 192

Swift, Samuel (sculptor)
    72, 118

Turnpike Road (Barnsley to Shepley Lane Head)
    38

Victoria Cottage Institute
    85-87

Victoria Jubilee Museum
    118-125

Wakefield, Bishops of:
    Dr. Eden   85-87
    Rt. Rev. Colin James   125

Wilberforce, William (1759-1833)
    Anti-slavery movement   3
    Friendship with Walter Spencer Stanhope   4

Woolley Rev. Charles A.L., Vicar of Cawthorne (1921-30):
    Agreement with bell-ringers 1921   12

Sponsors & Subscribers

The publication of this book has been made possible by the kindness of sponsors who backed the idea with money from the early stages and subscribers willing to order and pay for copies in advance of publication. Grateful thanks are due to the following:

Sponsors

Hugh Harrison of B.M.B (Barnsley) Ltd.
Cynthia Walker
Philip O. Walker
Geoffrey Durrans of James Durrans & Sons Ltd.
John R. Puddephatt
Martin Taylor of Dodworth Construction Ltd.

Subscribers

A
Mr. & Mrs. Sam Acton
Rev. & Mrs. T. Peter Arnold
Mrs. L. Arnold
Christine Andrews
George & Margaret Armitage
Philip & Pat Armitage
Mr. Richard A. Airey
Trish Arundel
Diana Asquith
Mr. & Mrs. N. Addy
Raymond & Susan Ashton
Emily Ashton
Louise Ashton
Mr. E. Appleyard
Kay Aylott
Mr. & Mrs. Donald Acton
Mrs. Jean Austin
Peter A. Arnold

B
Joan & Angus Broadhead
Iris & David Broadhead
Paul & Diane Broadhead
Mr. & Mrs. Allan Broadhead
Allan & Hazel Broadhead
Judith Broadhead
Loraine & Fraser Broadhead
Margaret & Peter Broadhead
Bruce & Pauline Broadhead
Robert & Gladys Bagshaw
Brian & Rita Bagshaw
Mr. Ronnie Bagshaw
Vernon & Audrey Bagshaw
John & Alice Butler
Mrs. Annie Boffin
David Boffin
Bob Barr & Margaret Barr
    (née Loukes)
Robert A. Barr
Mrs. W. B. Barlow
Mr. John W. Barlow
Mr. Eric Barlow
Bradford & Ilkley Community
    College
Mrs. Sheila Brown (née Morley)
Julie Bexon
Mr. & Mrs. Arthur Boddy
Mr. & Mrs. J. Roger Barber
Rev. & Mrs. J. E. Baines
Mrs. M. E. Blackwell & David
Mr. A. P. Burkinshaw

Mrs. Muriel Booth
John & Bronnie Beever
Mr. & Mrs. J. R. Beeson
Mr. Malcolm G. Barker
Mrs. J. Bentley
Rev. D. Barraclough
Mrs. M. Baxter
Mr. John Brailsford
Mrs. Doris Brailsford
Mr. D. Broadbent
Mr. & Mrs. A. G. Butters
A. & R. Burton
Banks Hall Residential Home
Mr. & Mrs. H. J. Booth
Mrs. S. E. Butcher
Mr. & Mrs. A. Batty
E. Beardsley
Dorothy Brown
C. N. Booth
Norman Bowers
Mr. & Mrs. D. P. Buckingham
Mr. & Mrs. G. P. Buckingham
Rosemary A. Brain
Mr. & Mrs. Peter Bowden
Mr. P. Beardsall
Mrs. A. C. Bunn (née Soper)
Mr. H. Blayden
Mr. & Mrs. Harry Brown
Mr. Frank Bacon
Mr. & Mrs. A. E. Bates
David & Pat Burkinshaw
Queenie Butterfield (née Maxfield)
Andrew J. Brown
Graham Brooke
Mr. D. Booth
Mrs J. Bailey
Anton & Pauline Buckley
Joanne A. Blakeley
Rita Britton
Stan Bulmer
Richard A. Bagshaw
Janet Birkinshaw

C

Cawthorne Victoria Jubilee Museum
D. S. Cooke & G. M. Cooke
C. D. Cooke
L. E. Cooke
Mr. F. A. Cowling
Mr. S. A. Cowling
Mrs. H. Clarkson
Mrs. Jennifer Colmer
Mr. & Mrs. Martin Charlesworth
Mrs. P. Craven (née Milnes)
Mavis Crossland
Mr. M. Clapham
David Clapham
Mr. & Mrs. D. Chinnock
Mr. D. M. Crossley
Mr. Nigel Casson
Mr. Philip J. Claxton
Erica & Ian Claxton
Anne & Ed Colgan
Mrs. A. Common (née Broadhead)
Mrs. Enid Coldwell
Erica Clarke
David & Deborah Cunliffe
Mr. & Mrs. R. Carbutt
Mr. & Mrs. R. M. S. Cordingley
Eric & Margaret Clegg
Mrs. Elizabeth Cressey (née Lawson)
Betty Crabtree
Mrs. Alice Coates
Mrs. B. M. Crossland
Erica Charlesworth
Joan Clancy
George Crossland
Jill Crossland
C. M. Cane
Mr. & Mrs. Philip Crossland
Kathleen Cater (née Kent)
Mr. W. L. Charlesworth
Cannon Hall Museum

D

Frank & Christine Draper
John Draper
Tim Draper
Sir Hugh Dundas
Alan Dodd
Jim Diver
Rev. Lawrence R. Dalton & Mrs Dalton
Mrs. C. A. Donner
Mr. M. E. Dyson
Mrs. Ruth Davey (née Masters)
M. C. Donaldson
Mary P. Dickinson
Mr. & Mrs. J. Denton
Mrs. Dione Dodson
Mr. & Mrs. G. T. Day
Freda Daniel (née Barlow)
Mr. P. Dickinson
Chris Dempster & Michelle Barry
Annette P. Dancer

E

Rhona & Eric Ellis
Mrs. Margaret Eyre
Anne Earnshaw (née Fish)
John Ellin
R. Edmunds
Mrs. E. Ellis
Mr. & Mrs. H. H. Eyre
Mr. & Mrs. R. J. Errington
Mr. & Mrs. S. A. Eyre

F

Margaret & Stuart Fish
Mr. & Mrs. Stanley Fish
Mrs. Polly Fish
Mr. Barry Fish
Mr. Martin Fish
Kath & Eddie Foster
Gillian M. Fox (née Bagshaw)
Joan & Jack Faulkner
S. W. Fraser

Michael Fitton
Mrs. Judy Foster
Mrs. K. M. Furness
Mrs. Janet K. Fenemore (née Milnes)
Mrs. B. H. Foulds
Mr. & Mrs. I. D. G. Forsyth
Nick Farman
Miss Dora Fish
Richard & Ann Flowerday
Peter Fairholm
Mrs. Beryl Fensome

G

Jane & Mark Greaves
Mrs. Diana Gilfillan
Mr. Ben Goldthorpe
Mrs. O. Gentle
Mr. & Mrs. Robert Gardham
Mr. & Mrs. G. Griffin
Mr. Malcolm Green
Mrs. Grace Glover, late of Keresforth House
C. B. & C. J. Garden
J. B. & E. F. Gribbin
Mr. D. N. Grimes
Mr. J. F. Goodchild
Mr. A. Galvin
Mrs. C. N. Gascoyne
Bob Gibb
Mr. & Mrs. H. Gill
Ian Graham
Sarah Greenwood (née Charlesworth)
Mrs. Valerie Geddes
Mrs. E. Glover
D. & M. C. Gaunt
A. J. & M. H. Goldthorpe

H

Mr. & Mrs. Hugh Harrison
Les Herbert & Mary Herbert (née Hughes)
Stan Hughes
Ralph Hughes

Mr. & Mrs. W. Holroyd
Miss J. Holroyd
Dr. R. J. Holroyd
John & Mary Higgs
Mr. & Mrs. Roy Hilton
Robin & Rachel Harbottle
Mrs. Ivy Hill
Harold Haynes
Mr. & Mrs. John Hales
Miss M. Hopton
Mrs. D. Hirst
Mr. & Mrs. A. F. Hirst
Tony Hindley & Cynthia Hindley (née Milnes)
Mr. A. Wemyss Hindley
Mr. Colum M. Hindley
Miss Everild B. Hindley
Mrs. S. M. Haigh
Eileen C. Haigh (née Morley) & John Haigh
Mr. A. J. Healey
Sybil & Peter Hamer
Mrs. Hammerton
Mr. & Mrs. W. Heeley
Mr. & Mrs. R. Horbury
Michael & Alison Hooson
Mr. G. S. Hunter
Mr. & Mrs. C. Hutchinson
Philip & Elaine Hartley
Mr. & Mrs. J. L. Horsfield
Dr. David Hey
Andrew Hughes
Mrs. E. Horn
Leslie & Mabel Hinchliffe
J. M. & J. P. Holmes
Mrs. Linda M. Heeley
Mr. S. G. Hargreaves
Mrs. Margaret T. Hodgson (née Acton)
Keith & Trudy Hutchinson
Mr. & Mrs. Peter Hillas
Mr. George Happs
Mr. Roy Happs
Pat & Martin Hirst
J. Heaton

Mrs. D. Hook
Emma Hutchings
Kate Hutchings
Miss A. F. Hall
Mrs. Shirley Holland
Mrs. Doris Heigho
Elizabeth Holling
Karen Horton
Mr. D. Hebden
Mrs. C. Hanson
Milly Hodson
Dr. Shirley E. Hoyes
Judith & Brian Howell
Marie Houghton (née Lowe)
Mrs. P. Hunter
Mrs. Mary Hodgson (née Bates)
Mr. & Mrs. F. R. Hill
Mr. David Hinchliffe M. P.
Mr. C. E. Hinchliffe

I
Mrs. K. M. Ingham

J
Joan Jackson
Anne Jackson
Mr. & Mrs. W. T. Jackson
Joan E. Jubb (née Loukes)
Mr. & Mrs. M. P. Jones
Dr. & Mrs. S. Jones
Phil & Nara Jones
Mrs. B. Jones
J. D. & L. M. Jennings
Mr. Charles Jukes
Sylvia James (née Maxfield)
Ted Johnson

K
Ada Mary Kenworthy
Peter & Mary Kilner
Mr. & Mrs. H. Klass
Mary Kilburn
Mrs. J. Kukula
Mrs. Lily Kaye

Alvin Kellett
Mrs. D. Knowles
Mr. & Mrs. W. Kent
Peter Kent
John Kent
Richard Kent
Mr. & Mrs. D. S. Kaye

L
Mrs. Christine Lindley
John Lydon
Mr. & Mrs. L. K. R. Lax
Mr. & Mrs. H. Lofthouse
Anne Lever (née Vollans) & Allan Lever
Mr. & Mrs. H. A. Leigh
Dan Linton
Mrs. P. Lamont
Mr. G. F. Lucas
Mr. & Mrs. George Lowery
Keith and Sylvia Le Breton
Mr. & Mrs. B. M. Liversidge
John & Jo Lees
Mrs. J. D. Lawrence
M. Lisle
J. E. Lockwood
Miss K. M. Leeds
Mrs. Harriet Lynch (née Swift)
Mrs. E Lockwood

M
Mr. & Mrs. J. A. Moxon
Margaret Moxon
Valerie Moxon
Christine M. Moxon
Mrs. Hilda Milnes
Mrs. Dorothy M. Milnes
Mr. & Mrs. Austin Masters
Miss Naomi Masters
Mr. D. Masters
Charles Brian Midgley
Mrs. R. Mellor
Millhouse School
Mr. & Mrs. M. Milinkovic

Mrs. R. Mountford
Mrs. J. Murray
Dr. & Mrs. D. F. McFeely
Dr. & Mrs. P. O. Mann
Norman Moody
Mrs. M. McLaughlin
Brian Murray
Mr. & Mrs. Frank Matthewman
Mr. & Mrs. J. Mellor-Frith
Mr. H. Moisley
Mr. G. Moisley
John Musker
Mrs. M. E. Mosley
Miss A. Mosley
Enid & Geoffrey Mosley
Margaret Mills
Mr. J. Morley
Mrs. Barbara Mosley
David Maxfield
Mr. John McGlynn
Rev. & Mrs. H. E. S. Meanley
Edwin Mills
Julia E. Mason (née Horsfield)
Heather Matthewman
Mrs. Kathleen Machen
Mr. & Mrs. I. R. Morris
Donald Mosley
Dr. P. D. Matthewman
C. A. Matthewman
V. C. A. Matthewman
Elizabeth, Lady Muir (née Dundas)
Denise Marsh (née Lowe)

N
Una & Tony Newton
Richard Newton
Robert Newton
Richard & Kath Northern
Mr. & Mrs. S. T. Nuttall
Anne Naylor
Megan Nel (née Robinson)
Mr. J. D. Nixon
Mr. & Mrs. C. R. Nicholson

Olive Nichols
Graham & Val Noble
F. A. & B. M. Nuttall
S. G. Nuttall

O

Mr. & Mrs. R. G. Oates
Judith Osborne-Cribb

P

Mr. & Mrs. A. H. Park
Mr. & Mrs. C. K. Parker
Mr. & Mrs. B. H. Pugh
J. T. W. Pugh
R. H. Pugh
Tom & Judi Pennock
Maureen & John Parkin
Mrs. Maureen Parkinson
John Parkinson
Richard Parkinson
Miss M. Priest
Mr. P. Priest
Joan Parkin
Mr. & Mrs. Joe Parkinson
Mr. Cyril Parkinson
Mr. & Mrs. Wilfred Parkinson
John & Helen Porteous
Mrs. K. Pearson (née Boffin)
H. B. Puddephatt (U.S.A)
Chas W. Puddephatt (U.S.A.)
Mr. & Mrs. Phillip Padgett
Penistone Grammar School
Mrs. M. Padget
Roger Porter Brown
Mark & Julie Penty
Mrs. J. Pell
Dora Penrose

R

Miss Margaret Rose
Peter & Bella Raper
Stanley Race
Eddie Robinson & Pat Robinson
    (née Blacker)
Howard Robinson

Elaine Robinson
Bev Roberts
Mike & Anne Roberts
Mrs. M. Roberts
Mr. & Mrs. L. Rimmington
John & Janet Roslyn
Chris & Rob Rishworth
E. G. Roberts
Stanley & Joyce M. Robinson
Mr. & Mrs. E. Roe
John & Thelma Rowland
Mrs. Davena Rose (née Gibb)
J. & T. Ritchie
Roggins Local History Group
    Silkstone
Mrs. G. M. Richardson
Jean B. Russell
Julie Round
Mr. & Mrs. S. Rusby
Trevor & Verena Richards
Mr. & Mrs. Trevor Robinson
Cyril Rusby
Mr. & Mrs. H. Rawson
Mr. & Mrs. C. M. Rowlands
Mrs. Winifred Royston
Mr. D. Roberts

S

Douglas N. Stables
Rev. F. B. Swift
Misses J. & M. Swift
Heather Swift
Jean H. Swift
Oliver Swift
Dr. N. & Dr. A. Summerton
Miss M. I. Smith
Mr. & Mrs. D. B. Spanjer
Mr. & Mrs. G. E. Strawbridge
Miss Clarice Senior
Prudence M. Shaw
Mr. H. W. Spooner
Mr. & Mrs. H. Stables
Mr. J. Barry Sutton
Mrs. V. Sandy
Mr. J. C. Stubbins

Miss Sheila K. Stead
George E. Strutt
Mr. & Mrs. H. Sales
Rev. Canon & Mrs. R. T. G. Sharp
Geoffrey R. Senior
Mr. & Mrs. J. Smethurst
Mr. & Mrs. G. S. Shirt
The Spencer Arms Cawthorne
Mr. W. E. Spencer
Mr. & Mrs. B. Stringer
Enid Samuel
Miss P. Shackleton
Mrs. Vera Sykes
Mr. & Mrs. G. Sharp
Katy M. Smart
Mr. & Mrs. I. M. Sunderland
Anne E. Stewart
Alan Smith
Michael & Ruth Shirt
Chris Sergeant
Anne Snodgrass (née Moxon)
Margot Short (née Swift)
George Senior
Mrs. B. Sutton
Mrs. G. Spencer

T

Jack & Joan Turton
Mrs. K. Turton
Mr. & Mrs. Graham Tye
Mr. & Mrs. J. B. Todd
Mr. & Mrs. D. J. Travis
Dr. & Mrs. A. B. Taylor
Mr. D. Tutin
Mr. & Mrs. D. Tipler
Jane Taylor (née Machen)
Mrs. Dorothy Trimby (née
    Clarkson)

V

John & Ruth Vollans
Eric & Grace Vollans

W

Mrs. Cynthia Walker

Mrs. Ruth Walker
John & Susan Walker
John F. Wilkinson
Mr. & Mrs. Duncan Wood
R. M. & S. E. Wicks
Bernice Wright
Wakefield Girls' High School
Sylvia Wright
Jack White
Neville Mosley Wiles
Mr. & Mrs. A. Paul Wiles
Mr. & Mrs. D. J. W. Wheeler
Mr. & Mrs. Sid Wray
Mrs. K. I. M. Walker
Thalia Wild
R. C. Watkinson
S. A. Watkinson
C. R. Watkinson
Mr. & Mrs. Reginald Whitehead
A. Whittaker
Mr. & Mrs. A. C. Wood
J. R. Wilkinson
Mrs. V. Wilkinson
Andrew & Gillian Wilkinson
F. Wheelhouse
Derek Williamson
Mrs. P. E. Winter
Mrs. A. Whittlestone
D. Wilkinson
Mrs. D. Rosalind Wilson (née
    Milnes)
Mr. T. Wadsworth
Mrs. Eileen Willis
Mr. & Mrs. E. T. Watkins
Wakefield Metropolitan District
    Libraries
The Wilkinson Family
The Wood Family
Mrs. C. A. Walker (née
    Lockwood)
Susan Wolff
Mr. & Mrs. R. T. Waddington
Grenville Waddington
Rachel Waddington
Lynne Westhead

E. Wake
E. & M. B. Walton
Mrs. A. L. H. Willis
Mary Woodley

Y
Mrs. E. M. Youel
Mrs. Doris Young (née Hughes)
Mr. & Mrs. J. G. Yaxley

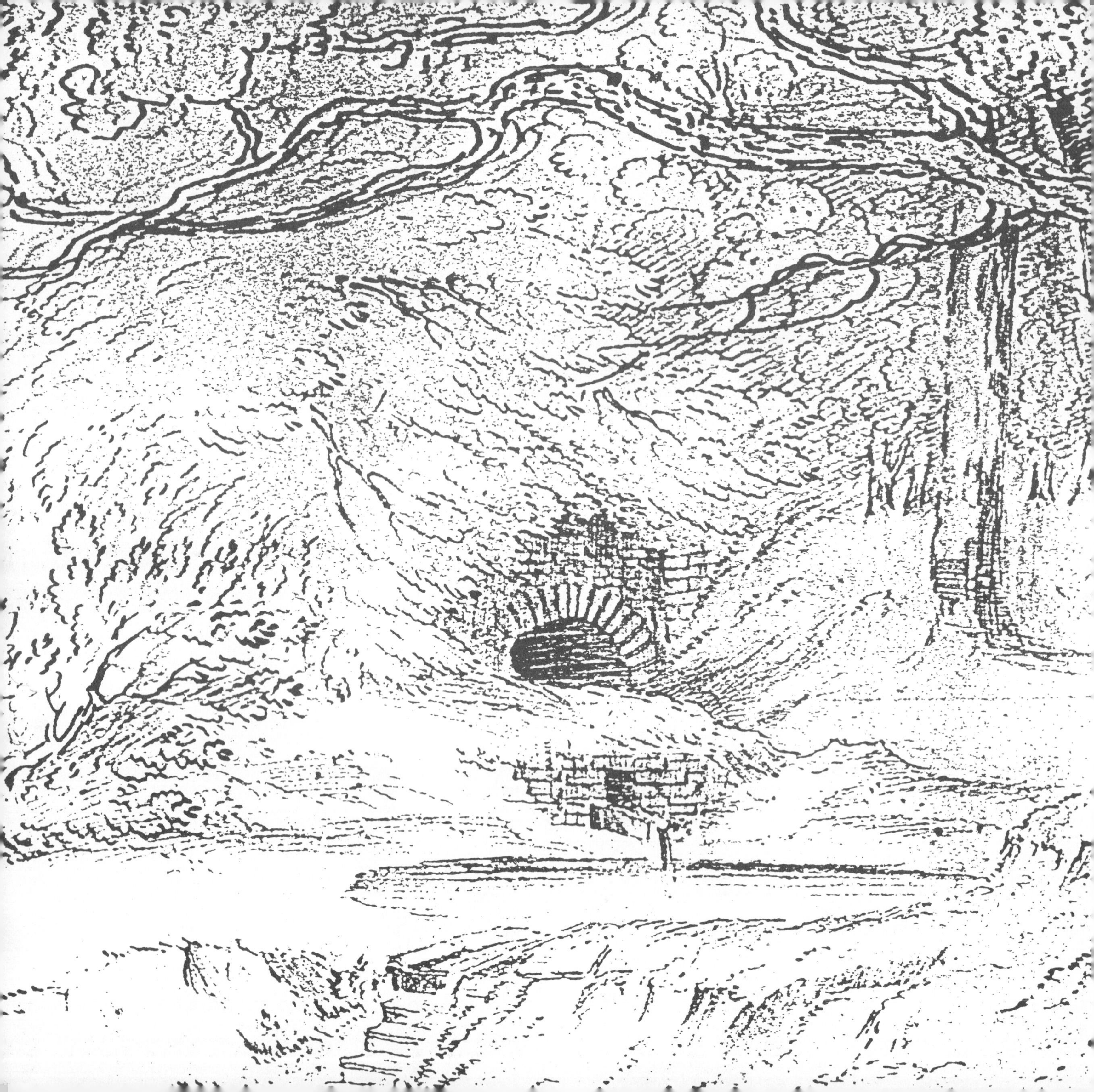